Y0-BVO-351

Social Philosophy Research Institute Book Series
No. 3

FUNDAMENTALS OF CHINESE PHILOSOPHY

Laurence C. Wu

Consulting Editor:
Robert Ginsberg

B
5231
.W84x
West

UNIVERSITY
PRESS OF
AMERICA

LANHAM • NEW YORK • LONDON

Copyright © 1986 by

University Press of America,® Inc.

4720 Boston Way
Lanham, MD 20706

3 Henrietta Street
London WC2E 8LU England

All rights reserved

Printed in the United States of America

Co-published by arrangement with the
North American Society for Social Philosophy

ISBN (Perfect): 0-8191-5571-3
ISBN   (Cloth): 0-8191-5570-5

All University Press of America books are produced on acid-free
paper which exceeds the minimum standards set by the National
Historical Publications and Records Commission.

Acknowledgments

Permission to quote from the following books was kindly given by the publishers:

1. Wing-tsit Chan, _A Source Book in Chinese Philosophy_, Princeton University Press, 1963.

2. H. G. Creel, _Chinese Thought: from Confucius to Mao Tse-tung_, The University of Chicago Press, 1953.

3. Dubs, H. H. (tr.), _The Works of Hsüntze_, London, Probsthain, 1928.

4. Burton Watson (tr.), _Han Fei Tzu: Basic Writings_, Columbia University Press, 1964.

FUNDAMENTALS OF CHINESE PHILOSOPHY

Table of Contents

v

Preface

This book is intended as a guide to the main schools of thought in Chinese philosophy. It introduces the reader to fundamental concepts and problems which Chinese philosophers over a period of three thousand years have found fascinating and have attempted to explicate and clarify. Chinese philosophy plays an important role in the political, social, and economic life of Chinese people. Hence, an understanding and appreciation of Chinese philosophy is helpful to understanding Chinese people and civilization.

This book gives a comprehensive treatment of the valuable insights of the Chinese philosophical heritage. The selection of topics and philosophers is determined mainly by my understanding of the Chinese philosophical classics. While personal viewpoints are often inevitable, I have tried to follow the consensus of Chinese scholars through many centuries of effort. The reader is urged to broaden and deepen his/her understanding by consulting some of the primary source materials listed in the bibliography.

The idea of writing Fundamentals of Chinese Philosophy was formed when I taught a course on Oriental philosophy eight years ago. Several students commented on the difficulty of the Chinese language and the extensive philological and etymological discussions in the textbooks. One common complaint was about the different ways of transliterating Chinese terms and names into English. I sympathized with them. Ideally, students should have some mastery of the Chinese characters. Some textual analysis and philological comment is both necessary and desirable in the teaching of Chinese philosophy. But this can be done without requiring the students to know the Chinese characters. Chinese names and terms should be transliterated consistently and in the most perspicacious manner. We now have two systems of transliteration: the Wade-Giles system and the pin-yin (phonetic) system. For people who do not know the Chinese language, the confusion and inconvenience caused by the different ways of transliteration are an unnecessary but serious obstacle to their learning. Although scholars are still debating the merits of the two systems of transliteration, a good case can be made that overall pin-yin is more parsimonious and accurate than the Wade-Giles system. Since 1979 all major newspapers, magazines, and television stations in the United States have adopted the pin-yin, hence textbooks on China should be written with the pin-yin so that the readers can relate what they read in the books to what they read in other media. I therefore decided to use the pin-yin system of transliteration for Chinese terms and names in this book.

A Chinese glossary at the end of the book concisely explains each word or term. For the purpose of cross reference, each Chinese character is transliterated both with the pin-yin and the Wade-Giles system.

Professor Robert Ginsberg of The Pennsylvania State University read my manuscript and made numerous helpful stylistic suggestions. His encouragement in the revision of my manuscript is deeply appreciated. I thank my wife Geri for her support and encouragement in writing this book. I express my appreciation to Western Maryland College for granting me a sabbatical leave in the Spring of 1983.

A Guide to the Pronunciation of Chinese Words (pin-yin)

Symbol	As in English	Symbol	As in English
a	large	ng	hung
a after y or i	and	o	port
		ou	goal
ai	like	p	pipe
ao	out	q	cheese
b	by	r	row
c	cats		bird
ch	church	s	sour
d	doubt	sh	shoe
e	ago	t	tour
e after y or i	yes	u	true
ei	eight	u	you
f	fate	uo	warm
g	guide	w	wife
h	how	x	sheet
i	machine	y	yard
j	jeep	z	birds
k	kite	zh	joe
l	light		
m	mother		
n	need		
	an		

Chapter 1:   Introduction

The Background and the General Characteristics
of Chinese Philosophy

Since Chinese philosophy has had a history within
the context of Chinese civilization, beginning students
may find a brief overview of Chinese history helpful.
Chinese civilization first developed in the Yellow
River basin around 2500 B.C. The traditional (and
legendary) account of the beginning of Chinese history
offers many cultural heroes to whom many important
inventions are attributed. Even the founder of the
first Chinese dynasty Xia (c. 2205-c. 1766 B.C.) was
probably an idealized mythical figure. However, with
the coming of the Shang dynasty (c. 1766-c. 1122 B.C.)
we have solid historical evidence concerning the
cultural development of the early Chinese. From the
"oracle bones" used in that period, we can infer the
genesis of the Chinese language and the Shang method of
divination.

The Zhou dynasty (c. 1122-249 B.C.) is the golden
age of Chinese philosophy. The Zhou rulers established
a feudal system which at first operated well. But in
time, the political power of the Zhou rulers diminished
and the feudal system disintegrated so that each feudal
lord was a virtual independent ruler of his territory.
The result was confusion, chaos, and the widespread
suffering of the people. In this period systematic
philosophical thought emerged in China and the "hundred
schools" of thought contended with each other. China's
"first teacher," Confucius (Kong Fu Zi, 551-479 B.C.),
can be considered the earliest philosopher in China.

The disintegration of the Zhou feudal system
resulted in the period of the Warring States (403-221
B.C.) which ended with the unification of Qin Shi
Huang-di, the first emperor of the Qin dynasty (221-207

1

B.C.). The Qin rulers employed the legalist philosophers to carry out the legalist way of government, and legalism was adopted as the state philosophy. The Qin, however, was short-lived. The Han dynasty (206 B.C.-220 A.D.) succeeded the Qin and continued the work of unification and territorial expansion. The Han Confucian scholar Dong Zhong-shu was responsible for making Confucianism the state philosophy. Thus, the Han's political unification brought an end to intellectual and cultural pluralism.

Buddhism was introduced into China around 60 A.D. and slowly but steadily gained acceptance among the Chinese. A large portion of the Buddhist scriptures was translated through the joint efforts of the Indian and Chinese monks. The impact of Buddhism on China has been positive and widespread. Not only do Chinese scholars sometimes use Chinese philosophical concepts to understand Buddhist scriptures, but they also incorporate Buddhist ideas into their way of thinking. Chanism (Zen) and Neo-Confucianism are the two results of this creative synthesis. Buddhist influence is not confined to philosophy or religion, for it is felt in sculpture, painting, architecture, and literature. Before the nineteenth century, the Chinese called foreigners barbarians, the only exception being the Indians, because of their Buddhist influence.

Four hundred years of the Period of Disunity followed the collapse of the Han dynasty. Then China was unified again under the Sui dynasty (590-618) which, like the Qin, was short-lived. The civil service examination was first formally introduced in Sui dynasty and became an important institution of the Tang dynasty (618-906).[1] The adoption of this system greatly improved the quality of China's bureaucrats. Candidates were examined for their knowledge of the Chinese classics, especially the Confucian classics. This may not be the best way to select administrators, yet the system served the Chinese remarkably well for fifteen hundred years. The civil service examination system is central to traditional Chinese society. Because virtually all males, without any restriction on class background, were eligible to take the examination, the dream of every family was one day one of its members would succeed in the examination. As H. G. Creel points out, "When the results of the examination were posted, the interest in them was like that in the outcome of a crucial football match, Derby day, and a national election combined in one."[2]

Under the Tang, China regained her unity and political strength. Buddhism reached its golden age in China, and Chinese culture flowered and expanded to her neighboring countries. The Tang capital of Chang-An became a cosmopolitan city, thanks to foreigners who came to trade or study.

The Song dynasty (960-1279) followed the Tang. The Song was militarily and politically the weakest among the Chinese dynasties. However, its cultural achievement was no less brilliant than the Tang's. Many productive philosophers lived in that period, among them the great synthesizer Zhu Xi. After Zhu Xi, the dominant philosophy in China has been Neo-Confucianism. The term Neo-Confucianism is a newly coined Western equivalent for Dao Xüe (the study of Dao). Neo-Confucianism is a synthesis of Confucianism, Daoism, and Buddhism, with Confucianism the dominant feature.

The Mongols conquered the Song and established the Yüan dynasty (1280-1368). The Mongol warriors were not interested in cultural activities. The Ming dynasty (1368-1643) drove the Mongols out of China and is well-known for its naval expeditions to Southeast Asia, the Persian Gulf, and Africa. The monumental work, Yong-lo Encyclopedia was sponsored by the Ming emperor Yong-lo. In terms of original intellectual achievements, the Ming dynasty is not distinguished. Probably the only original thinker of the time was Wang Shou-ren (also known as Wang Yang-ming, 1472-1529). His brand of Neo-Confucianism is known as the school of universal mind.

The Manchus came into China in 1644 and established the Qing dynasty (1644-1911). The first half of the Qing dynasty was one of the most prosperous periods of Chinese history. Unfortunately, the Manchu power decayed quickly after its mid-term. After the Opium War (1839), it was the familiar story of defeats and humiliations at the hands of the Western Powers and Japan. In 1911, Dr. Sun Yat-sen finally succeeded in overthrowing the Manchus and founded the Republic of China. Dr. Sun then faced a host of political, social, and economic problems which were not susceptible of any solutions. Decades after the founding of the Republic of China, political chaos was accompanied by cultural disorder. The situation was aggravated by the encroachments of the outside powers. Western ideas as well as Western machines found easy acceptance by many Chinese. One of the Western ideas that attracted the attention of many Chinese intellectuals was Marxism-Leninism. Mao Ze-dong, though not an intellectual, was one of those young Chinese who decided to work for the cause of communism, probably because he saw communism as the only effective means whereby China could regain her political and economic independence.

In 1949, Mao defeated Jiang Kai-shek who then retreated to the island of Taiwan. Today the island of Taiwan (Nationalist China) prospers economically and enjoys a sense of self-confidence while the communists have made mainland China a truly sovereign and independent country. After Mao died in 1976, Maoism was de-emphasized and the value of Confucianism and other philosophical schools has been recognized. Chinese communist scholars use Marxist concepts and theories to interpret Chinese classics. The fashion is to say that Chinese philosophical heritage is not only compatible with Marxism but the two complement each other. Feng You-lan (1895-   ) is generally considered to be the most influential Chinese philosopher today. Feng espouses the communist ideology, but his philosophy is of the rationalistic Confucianism which will be discussed in Chapter 10.

It is often said that during the period of the Warring States (403-221 B.C.) there were a "hundred schools" of thought. This is an overstatement. In Si-ma Qian's Historical Records, we find six major schools of thought. They are:

1. The Yin-Yang school (Yin-Yang Jia):

   This school expounds the working of the Yin-Yang (negative-positive, female-male) forces in the universe.

2. Confucianism:

   The Chinese name for this school is Ru Jia (school of literati). It is primarily a system of ethics based on the teachings of Confucius.

3. Mohism (Mo Jia):

   Based on the teachings of Mo Zi (fl. 479-438 B.C.), the main themes of this philosophy are universal love, utilitarianism, and non-aggression.

4. The Legalist school (Fa Jia):

   Fa means law or pattern. This school emphasizes the importance of law in an efficient government and an orderly society.

5. The School of Names (Ming Jia):

The followers of this school were interested in the technical aspects of argument and debate, just as the Greek Sophists were.

6. Daoism (Dao De Jia):

The philosophy of the Way and its Power is associated with the teachings of Lao Zi (6th or 4th century B.C.) and Zhuang Zi (fl. 399-295 B.C.). Daosim emphasizes spontaneity and the cultivation of inner strength.

According to Liu Xin (46 B.C.-23 A.D.), a prominent historian, there were ten schools of thought. In addition to the six schools mentioned above, he listed the Diplomatist School, the Ecclectic School, the Agricultural School, and the School of Story Tellers. However, these four schools are unimportant from a philosophical point of view. Consequently, we will study only the six major schools of thought classified in the Historical Records.

Chinese philosophy is humanistic through and through. "Humanism" is the one word that characterizes Chinese philosophy. In all philosophical schools of China, the central concern is human relations. Humanism is usually understood as the attitude of mind which seeks to assert the intrinsic value of human life here on earth. Chinese humanism can be construed in this broad sense. However, it should be distinguished from the Renaissance humanism in Europe. Renaissance humanism emphasized a human being as a free, independent individual; but Chinese humanism emphasizes a human being's relationship with other human beings. In Renaissance humanism, the greatness of human potentialities belongs to the individuals, whereas in Chinese humanism, human potentialities can be realized only through society. In other words, a person's relationship to other persons is more important than

6

the person as an individual. Furthermore, the Chinese conceive of a person as essentially a moral being. All his activities should result in moral good. The classical Chinese philosophers neglected the study of the physical universe because they believed that such study was unrelated to the production of moral good, just as many theologians in medieval Europe believed that no knowledge was worthy unless it contributed to the salvation of the soul. Thus, Chinese humanism is quite different from Renaissance humanism.

Philosophy has played a greater role in the history of the Chinese civilization than in any other. It has been so woven into the broad fabric of Chinese family and society that it is felt in every aspect of life, most notably in government. Because philosophy permeated all aspects of life in China, a special word for it did not exist until the nineteenth century.

The Chinese term for the word "philosophy" is zhe-xüe (哲学 , pronounced tetsugaku in Japanese). This is the term coined by Dr. Nishi Amane (西周 , 1829-1897) of Japan, when he was working for the center for the Investigation of Barbarian Books (Bansho Shirabe-sho 蕃書調所). After Dr. Nishi published his Hyakuichi Shinron (A New Theory on the Hundred and One Doctrine 百一新論), the term zhe-xüe (哲学) was adopted in East Asia. Zhe-xüe means the study of wisdom. Thus, its meaning is close to "the love of wisdom" by which the ancient Greeks understood the term "philosophy." Significantly, the Chinese character Zhe (哲 , wisdom) contains the pictographs of hand and mouth, thus denoting the combination of word and action, or theory and practice. Herein lies one basic characteristic of Chinese philosophy, namely, the inseparability of theory and practice. The task of the philosopher is not to expound his philosophy but to live it. Philosophy is not divorced from real life. The aim of studying philosophy is to enable one to become a better and happier person. "Wisdom" for the

Chinese means "practical wisdom." Practical wisdom is more than intelligence. It requires intelligence, but it also includes the ability to make the right decision on particular occasions. The Chinese would agree with Aristotle that moral virtue must be combined with practical wisdom (phronesis). The test of a philosophy is its ability to transform its advocates into morally worthy persons.

The second basic characteristic of Chinese philosophy is the strong affinity between philosophy and religion. Confucianism has performed the functions of religion in China for many centuries. The Chinese quite often do not make a distinction between moral and spiritual values. In the traditional Chinese mind, the terms "true" (是 , shi) and "false" (非 , fei) almost always have moral and spiritual connotations. All the traditional schools of philosophy in China maintain that truth is a moral and spiritual notion. The traditional Chinese do not hold the "correspondence theory" of truth. For them, truth resides within a person and has the power of transforming him into a morally and spiritually more worthy human being. The Chinese concept of truth is similar to what Søren Kierkegaard says about "how one becomes a Christian" in Concluding Unscientific Postscript. Kierkegaard says that truth is subjective, it is not something that has independent existence to be studied or analyzed. The Chinese will agree with the Bible that "you shall know the truth, and the truth shall make you free" (John, 8: 32). The spiritual aspect of truth is particularly strong in Chinese Buddhism where truth is conceived as "true principle" (zhen li). Meditation, as a way of understanding and incorporating the truth, becomes philosophically significant.

The synthetic method of Chinese philosophy is another important characteristic. Chinese philosophers are inclined to look for truth in the synthesis of partially true views. For them, the search for truth is the search for the most comprehensive way of accounting for the continuously expanding human experience. Chinese philosophers rarely think in terms of "either-or" but rather in terms of the complementariness of different views and practices. Thus, they do not choose between theory and practice, but choose both theory and practice; for theory and practice complement each other, thereby constituting a whole. This synthetic method naturally leads to tolerance and appreciation for theories and views of others that are different from one's own. A good example is Buddhism. Philosophically, Buddhism does not have much in common with any of the major schools of Chinese thought. Yet, the Chinese embrace Buddhist philosophy with open arms, although few Chinese would claim to be Buddhists.

Few Chinese today are strictly Confucianists, or Daoists, or Legalists, etc. Many Confucianists today are really Neo-Confucianists. Most Chinese refuse to accept any labels. Lin Yütang[3] once remarked with humor that every Chinese is a Confucianist when he succeeds and a Daoist when he fails. Confucianism represents the Yang of Chinese philosophy whereas Daoism represents its Yin. Philosophy, just as a living person, has its Yin and Yang.

On the whole, Chinese philosophy is a rural philosophy. Western philosophy, on the other hand, is urban. Chinese philosophy embodies the kind of outlook on the world that we expect to have been developed by country folks. Human affairs and natural phenomena are viewed as cyclical. The idea of the cycle is probably derived from the homely experience of observing seasonal changes. A farmer observes that a plant grows and matures from a seed to a seedling, then it flowers and drops its seeds to start the process again. Nature is full of regular recurrent patterns of events. Since a farmer's work depends so much on the climate, he cannot fail to notice the regular movements of the sun and the moon and the succession of the four seasons. When the moon has become full, it wanes; then it waxes again. Indeed, Lao Zi's proposition that "reversal is the movement of Dao,"[4] has been accepted by all the schools of Chinese philosophy. The Chinese call this the "Returning," and believe that "in Returning we see the mind of Heaven and Earth."[5] This belief has contributed to the resilience and patience of the Chinese people.

Two attitudes are associated with this rural philosophy. One is the propensity on the part of Chinese philosophers to view the world not mechanically but ecologically. When a Chinese philosopher needs an example for discussion, he typically chooses flowers, animals, mountains, clouds, rivers, etc., rather than artifacts such as clocks, ships, or buildings. This suggests that for a Chinese philosopher, the country is dearer to his heart than the city. The second is the adherence to the doctrine of the golden mean. "Never too much" and "To go too far is just as bad as to fall short" are the two familiar Chinese maxims. Having too much or overdoing something carries with it the risk of getting the opposite of what one hopes for. The adherence to the doctrine of the golden mean explains the absence of asceticism in China.

To Western students of Chinese philosophy, the Chinese language presents special problems. The Chinese language is non-phonetic. It does not have an alphabet, and its visual form is more important than its pronunciation. Its pictorial visibility provides a suggestiveness far surpassing the Indo-European languages. However, its grammar is simple and crude as compared with English. Comparatively speaking, the Chinese language is not logically articulated, but it builds up complex ideas by suggestion and imagery. This is particularily true in classical Chinese in which Chinese philosophical treatises were written until the twentieth century. Classical Chinese

language is an excellent tool for poetry but not for
s y s t e m a t i c philosophical or scientific thought.
Generally, Chinese philosophers operate in an intuitive
manner.   They often say what they intuitively feel is
the case without argument to support it.   In
consequence, one finds in Chinese philosophical
writings profound insights, brilliant aphorisms,
interesting metaphors, but few elaborate arguments.
Many passages appear disjointed.   In the works of Xún
Zi, Mencius, Mo Zi, and Zhu Xi, one finds some
analytical reasoning and arguments.   But by the
standard of Western philosophic sophistication, they
are not articulate enough.

Classical Chinese language has creative ambiguity.
Lao Zi's Dao De Jing is a good example.   Because of the
elliptical nature of the language, even Chinese
scholars disagree, sometimes sharply, on the exact
meaning of a passage of Dao De Jing.   Yet, regardless
of their interpretations, they all agree on the
profundity and richness of the book.   Linguistic
ambiguity of some passages does not diminish the
philosophical value of the book.   To appreciate a
philosophical work such as Lao Zi's, one needs to have
imagination and sensitivity.   It would be a grave
mistake to infer from the apparent disjointedness and
ambiguity of Chinese philosophical prose to the
conclusion that Chinese philosophers are confused in
thought.   Cross-cultural understanding calls for
sympathy and imagination.   Understanding Chinese
philosophy is no exception.

By and large, Western philosophy aspires to
clarity and certainty.   Some Western philosophers
today abandon prose for the clear and unambiguous
symbolic notations of mathematical logic.
Consequently, their writings are comprehensible only to
the professionals in their field.   While the rigor and
precision of such a philosophic style is admirable, its
subject-matter is sadly narrow.   The dominance of such

a style could lead to the impoverishment of philosophy. Borrowing the Yin-Yang terminology again, the Yang of Western philosophy needs the Yin of Chinese philosophy.

Having been brought up in a traditional Chinese family in Taiwan and received graduate education in the United States, I have had occasions to compare the strengths and weaknesses of the two cultures. Experience as an assistant professor of philosophy in several American universities and colleges confirms my belief that much of the Chinese way of looking at the world may be of value to Westerners in the twentieth century. I hope this book will be of help to the reader in this way.

Notes

Chapter 1

1. During the Han dynasty many government posts were filled with people recommended by local officials on the basis of their general reputation. Sometimes these candidates were required to take a written examination before actual appointment. If we include the Han practice, the civil service examination system will be in existence for over two thousand years.

2. Chinese Thought from Confucius to Mao Tze-tung, p. 10.

3. Author of Wisdom of Confucius, My Country and My People, The Importance of Living, and several other books on China. He was instrumental in popularizing Chinese thought in the United States.

4. Dao De Jing, chapter 40.

5. Yi Jing (The Book of Changes), Appendix I.

Chapter 2

Confucianism: The Social Humanism

a. Confucius and His Central Teachings.

The name "Confucius" has been associated with Chinese culture for more than two thousand years. "Confucius" is the Latinized word for the Chinese name Kong Fu Zi, or Master Kong. This is the name of the man the Chinese have reverently spoken of as "The First Teacher," that is, the greatest teacher in Chinese history.

Confucius's family name was Kong, his personal name was Qiu. He was born in 551 B.C. in the state of Lu, located in the present Shandong province in eastern China. The state of Lu was known for its cultural refinement for centuries before Confucius was born. As a child, Confucius was unusually inquisitive and showed a strong interest in rituals and learning. In his early twenties, he held several minor government posts, married, and established himself as a tutor. His reputation as a wise and learned man spread rapidly, attracting an increasing number of students. Like other educated men of his time, Confucius had political ambitions. He believed that his ideas of good life and good society would not take hold unless he applied them to the people's everyday life through his administration. However, his political career was a failure. For thirteen years, he travelled from one state to another, hoping to find the right prince who would give him an opportunity to try his social and political reform. In this quest, he was destined to be disappointed. All the rulers he met were interested in the strength of their army or the wealth of their state. Yet Confucius talked only about virtues, peace, and harmony! During these years of travel, Confucius endured many hardships and dangers. Once he almost starved to death.   At the town of Kuang, Confucius and his accompanying disciples were physically attacked by the people of Kuang who mistook Confucius for a hated local politician.   Five years before Confucius's death, the administration changed in his native state of Lu. Confucius was invited to return home.   He accepted the invitation, but having realized that he was too old to hold any political office, he devoted all his time to teaching and editing the classics.

What did Confucius teach to have exercised such a strong influence over so many people for such a long time?   Over the centuries, so many words and deeds have been attributed to him that it is difficult to tell the man from the myth.   Our best source of information comes from the book Lun-yü or The Analects which was compiled by his students shortly after Confucius's death.   It is an edition of the conversations Confucius had with his disciples.   Because The Analects is a collection of conversations held in different times and places with different people, the book lacks structure or formal design.   Knowledge of the social contexts of the conversations is essential in understanding what Confucius says.

Human-heartedness (ren, 仁)

The most important concept in Confucianism is probably ren. Ren is the most fundamental virtue which a person is to cultivate.   Ren has often been translated as "love," or "benevolence," or "human-heartedness." The Chinese character for ren contains the pictograph of a person and the ideograph of two, thus signifying the ideal relationship between two persons.   Because the Chinese character lun (倫) which is often translated as "ethic," is derived from the symbol for "person," and the character for "morality" (德) is derived from the symbol for the human heart, I prefer to translate ren as "human-heartedness," although it is correct that the ideal

16

relationship between two persons is love. Confucius said: "Human-heartedness consists in loving others."[1] The role of the concept of ren in Confucianism is comparable to that of charity in Christianity.

Ren is more a virtue of action than a personality trait. Ren has its seat in the human heart, but it is there only as a potentiality. It can be actualized in interactions of a person with others. The manifestations of ren can take many forms. In The Analects, Confucius was asked time and again by his students to explain the meaning of ren. He gave different answers to different questioners under different circumstances. This is the hallmark of Confucius's individual instruction. Here are some of the answers:

> When Fan Qi asked about ren, the Master said: "love people."[2]

> When Yen Yüan asked about ren, the Master said: "If you can control your selfish desires and subject them to the rules of propriety and if you can do this for a single day, it is the beginning of ren for the entire world. Ren is self-sufficient and comes from your inner self; it requires no outside help." Yen Yüan asked for more details. The Master said: "Don't see the improper, don't hear the improper, don't talk about the improper, and don't act improperly."

> When Zhong Gong asked about ren, the Master said: "When you meet a person outside of your house, greet him as if he were a great noble. If, as a government official, you have to

17

draft people for labor, you should
approach your task with the same
seriousness that you would use in
performing a religious ritual. Don't
do to others what you yourself do not
desire."[3]

Righteousness (Yi, 義)

Confucius spoke constantly about yi. Yi is
translated as righteousness. The Chinese word yi lacks
the sense of smug self-righteousness the English word
may connote. Yi means the "rightness" or "oughtness"
of a situation. In certain situations, one must do
things because they are right to do. These things must
be done for their own sake, without any non-moral
considerations such as profit or benefit. "The
superior man comprehends yi, the small man comprehends
li (profit)."[4] The person who really loves others is
one able to perform his duties in society. Thus, the
Confucianists speak often of "doing for nothing," a
notion similar to the Hindu karma yoga.

For Confucius, motives of an action are more
important than the results. He would agree with
Immanuel Kant that in moral matters the pure intention
is already the deed. Intentions have intrinsic values.
If a person forms an intention to do something morally
blameworthy, but is prevented by external circumstances
from translating his intention into overt action, we
still regard him as blameworthy. On the other hand, if
someone has a good intention to do something
praiseworthy but is prevented by external circumstances
from doing it, we nonetheless consider him
praiseworthy. Perhaps only one outcome of action is of
moral relevance, namely, the effect on the character of
the person who does his duty or evades it. Yi is the
reason Confucius travelled for thirteen years to many
states, seeking an administrative position, despite its
low likelihood. In response to the ridicule that

Confucius was "one who knows he cannot succeed, yet keeps on trying to do it,"[5] Confucius's disciples said: "The reason why the superior man tries to go into politics is because he holds this to be right, even though he is well aware that his principle cannot prevail."[6] So long as one keeps on trying, one is not defeated. From a moral point of view, if one does one's duty, the duty through one's very act is morally done, regardless of the external success or failure of one's action. Therefore, "the wise are free from doubt, the virtuous from anxiety, the brave from fear."[7]

Zhong (conscientiousness, 忠) and Shu (altruism, 恕)

The superior man exhibits the virtues of zhong and shu, which are the two ways of practicing ren. Confucius pointed out positive and negative ways of practicing ren: do to others what you wish yourself, and do not do to others what you would not others do to you. The Analects XII, 2, quoted above in discussing human-heartedness, is a negative formulation. The following is a positive formulation:

> The Master told Zi-gong, "The man who possesses ren, wishing to be established himself, seeks also to enlarge others, and wishing to be prominent himself, also helps others to be prominent. To be able to judge others by what is near to ourselves may be called the method of realizing ren."[8]

Chūn-zi (gentleman, superior man, 君子)

The literal meaning of chūn-zi is "princeling," and up to Confucius's time, the term chūn-zi almost invariably denoted a man of good birth and high social position. Confucius, however, used the term to denote a gentleman, or a morally superior man who is not necessarily of aristocratic background. Men are capable of achieving excellence in many forms: intellectual, physical, or moral. Confucius regarded moral excellence as the highest form of human achievement. A gentleman is in harmony with all things and a sense of peace and fulfillment is in him. The opposite of chün-zi is xiao-ren, the petty, small man who worries constantly about gains and losses.[9]

Since Confucius conceived of no sharp distinction between ethics and politics, chün-zi is also a key concept in his political philosophy. Only if every person is transformed into a chün-zi can we have a good government and a happy social order. A well-ordered, happy society is based on the virtues of each individual member. One of the clearest and most comprehensive statements on ethics in Confucian classics reads as follows:

> The ancients who wished to preserve the fresh or clear character of the people of the world would first set about ordering their national life. Those who wished to order their national life would first set about regulating their family life. Those who wished to regulate their family life would set about cultivating their personal life. Those who wished to cultivate their personal life would first set about setting their hearts right. Those who wished to set their hearts right would first set about making their wills sincere. Those who wished to make their wills sincere would first set about achieving true knowledge. The achieving of true knowledge depended upon the investigation of things.

When things are investigated, then
true knowledge is achieved; when true
knowledge is achieved, then the will
becomes sincere; when the will is
sincere, then the heart is set right;
when the heart is set right, then the
personal life is cultivated; when the
personal life is cultivated, then the
family life is regulated; when the
family life is regulated, then the
national life is orderly; and when
the national life is orderly, then
there is peace in the world.[10]

Thus, politics to Confucius was merely the extension of
personal ethics to the larger society.

Li (propriety, 礼)

The Confucian ideal of a chün-zi or a cultivated
gentleman centers around the idea of li (propriety).
In The Analects, li is mentioned frequently. It should
be clearly distinguished from another word which
happens to be transliterated in the same way, namely,
profit (li). Li is a complex concept which includes the
notions of propriety, ceremony, rite, social
sensitivity, and etiquette. If we take yi
(righteousness, performance of duty) as providing the
content of Confucian moral life, then li may be taken
as providing the form of moral life. Li is often the
rule of conduct that reflects a person's good will
which may or may not result in materially benefiting
other people.

Before Confucius's time, li was primarily a
religious notion denoting the correct manner of
performing religious rites. Confucius shifted the
focus from Heaven to Earth by using the word li to
refer to a civilized code of social behavior. Knowing
li is knowing how to comport oneself with grace and

urbanity in all social situations. "Manner maketh man," said the wise medieval theologian William of Ockham. Li is probably the most important component in the making of the Chinese character. Li is quite peculiar to the Chinese culture and because of its complex nature has induced problems of interpretation and emphasis for later Confucianists. In the everyday life of oriental people, li is often reflected as "face." Oriental people seek earnestly to "save face" in their social interactions.

Xiao (filial piety)

Confucius shifted emphasis from ancester worship to filial piety (xiao). Confucius did not deny that the spirits of the dead ancestors still exist, but he maintained that the best way to honor our ancestors is to honor and respect our parents, and by extension, our other blood relatives. Confucius made it clear that xiao means more than just giving one's parents physical care and comfort. Xiao is an attitude of reverence toward one's parents which includes genuine concern for the parents' emotional and spiritual welfare. After the death of one's parents, one should do one's best to bring about their unfulfilled aims. This is more significant than offering sacrifice to the spirits of the deceased parents.

We owe our parents the gift of life. Moreover, our parents nurtured and educated us until we became independent. Therefore, we must protect our body from harm, for that body is from our parents. Beyond protecting and respecting our body, we should honor our parents by doing well in our work and thus making their name known and respected. Although xiao originates in the family, it is more than just a family virtue. It is the stem out of which grows all moral teachings. To be a good man, one must first be a good son, learning how to respect and serve one's parents.

Confucius's Common Sense Philosophy.

The above discussion of the key concepts of Confucius's philosophy indicates clearly that Confucius's philosophy is a fine blend of common sense and practical wisdom. It contains no deep metaphysical speculations such as utterances on the origin or the ultimate nature of the universe, nor does it tackle such basic epistemological questions as: "What is the relationship between language and reality?" or "How do we justify our knowledge claims?" On the contrary, it contains a collection of moral maxims and homey anecdotes which are didactic. A cursory reader of the Confucian classics may understandably find them commonplace and unexciting. How then can we explain the undeniable and ineradicable Confucian influence in China and East Asia?

One should never underestimate the validity and power of common sense as a hardcore of human beliefs. But the answer to the question lies in the historical background of Confucius's life, his personality, and his style of teaching. In pre-Confucian China, custom and tradition provided sufficient cohesion to keep Chinese society reasonably peaceful and prosperous. By Confucius's time, however, the political power of the Zhou dynasty had deteriorated to the point of impotence, with stability and prosperity replaced by turmoil and poverty. Social mores no longer had the binding power on the people's behavior. The almost continuous warfare between the feudal lords became increasingly vicious. Weapons were more deadly, and military tactics and strategies were diligently studied and applied by the specialists to make killing more efficient. In a time like this, Confucius did not choose to become a recluse, but sought to restore social order through education. He believed that education was the most effective way to change human behavior. People must be taught to want to do the right thing and not be forced to do what is expected of them. He taught the concrete and practical method of moral education. Moral education is to begin at home. Children are taught through their interactions with other family members that they are moral beings and that it is their nature to want to do the right thing, regardless of reward or punishment.

Confucius argued that a good society needs more than the long arm of the government to make it good. Force is uncivilized and external. No state can constrain its people all the time, not even most of its people most of the time. Positive faith on the part of the people is needed to have a civilized society. Hence Confucius said that a ruler should rule the people by his virtuous example and not by force.

> To govern is to keep straight. If you, sir [the Baron of Lu], lead the people straight, which of your subjects will venture to fall out of line?[11]

When Qi Kang Zi asked Confucius whether the lawless and the wicked should be executed, Confucius answered:

> In your government what is the need of killing? If you desire what is good, the people will be good. The character of a ruler is like wind and that of the people is like grass. In whatever direction the wind blows, the grass always bends.[12]

On the other hand, Confucius was no romantic utopian. He did not believe that love alone, without proper social structures and arrangements, can be the answer to the social ills. Although Confucius talked a great deal about ren (human-heartedness), he also emphasized the different social situations to which ren generates a proper response. <u>Ren</u> is not a single emotion but a potentiality that manifests itself differently in different social situations. Thus, one should not love a stranger in the same way or as much as one loves one's parents. When asked "Should one love one's enemy, those who do us harm?" Confucius replied: "By no means. Answer hatred with justice and love with benevolence. Otherwise you would waste your benevolence."[13] The Confucian doctrines of <u>zhong</u> (conscientiousness to others) and <u>shu</u> (altruism) imply conscientious effort to practice <u>ren</u>, but not repaying good for evil.

Confucius and his seventy students probably formed the first private institution of higher learning in China. A spirit of intellectual democracy existed in this institution. Confucius accepted all those who were serious about learning regardless of their class background. He believed that any man can become a chün-zi (gentleman) if he has a proper education. Concerning his admission policy, he said: "I have never refused to teach anyone, even though he came to me on foot, with nothing more to offer as tuition than a package of dried meat."[14] He praised one of his students for being able, "though wearing a tettered hempquilted gown, to stand beside those wearing costly furs without the slightest embarrassment."[15] Confucius had high expectation for all his students. Perhaps that is why he was strict in his requirements as to their intellectual development. Confucius made no claim to the possession of the ultimate truth. He wanted his students to think for themselves. He claimed to be only a transmitter of knowledge, not an originator. He considered his function as a teacher to be transmitting to his students the ancient cultural heritage. However, in interpreting the classics, Confucius did contribute many original ideas. Confucius did not only teach humility, he practiced it. He was confident and ready to admit that he might be wrong. "Among any three men walking in the street, there is one who could be my teacher," Confucius declared, "I shall follow their good traits, while correcting my own weaknesses which I have also found in them."[16] For Confucius, teaching was not only a profession, it was his way of life, his lifetime's dedication. Near the end of his life, he described himself as follows: "He is this sort of man: so intent upon enlightening those eager for knowledge, that he forgets to eat, and so happy in doing so that he forgets his sorrows, and does not realize that old age is creeping up on him."[17]

Confucius used simple, gentle language in his conversations with students. Students were drawn to him by his sincerity, humility, and immense erudition. He disliked ornate language, and we have no record of his delivering a public lecture. Yet he was a very effective teacher when speaking to a small group. Confucius never tried to be popular; "A man with clever words and an ingratiating appearance is seldom a man of ren (humanity)."[18] When his student Zi Gong asked: "What would you say of the man who is liked by all his fellow townsmen?" Confucius said: "That is not sufficient. What is better is that the good among his fellow townsmen like him, and the bad hate him."[19]

Confucius encouraged people to adhere to the doctrine of the mean. He did not advise his students to do the extraordinary or the impossible. There was always a touch of common sense and humanness in Confucius's words and deeds. Once Confucius heard of the following story:

> A man was short of ginger and went to Wei-sheng Kao to borrow some. Instead of telling the man that he himself did not have any, Wei-sheng Kao went out of his back door without his friend's knowledge and borrowed some from his neighbor in order to

lend it to his friend who had come to borrow.

Confucius remarked that Wei-sheng Kao did not do the right thing. The right thing to do in such situations is to tell his friend the truth. When the skeptic Cai Wo tested Confucius with the question: "If someone said there is a man in the well, the altruist, I suppose, would go after him," Confucius pointed out that even an altruist would first make sure there was a man down in the well! When Confucius's favorite student Yen Yüan died, Confucius was overwhelmed with grief. The Analects tell us what happened:

> When Yen Yüan died, the Master
> bewailed him exceedingly, and the
> disciples who were with him said,
> "Master, isn't your grief excessive?"
> "Is it excessive? If I am not to
> mourn bitterly for this man, for whom
> should I mourn?"
> The disciples wished to give Yen Yüan
> a great funeral, and the Master said:
> "You may not do so."[20]

Confucius's reason for disapproving an expensive funeral was that neither Yen Yüan's family nor Confucius's disciples could afford it. When Yen Yüan's father suggested that Confucius sell his chariot to raise money for the funeral, Confucius refused, saying that he had not sold his chariot for his own son's funeral and that he needed the chariot for travelling.

Confucius was reticent about the supernatural, although he had religious convictions. When asked about serving the spirits of the dead he replied: "If we are not yet able to serve men, how can we serve spiritual beings?"[21] When Zi-lu asked about death, Confucius said: "If we do not yet know about life, how can we know about death?"[22] The above dialogue shows much about Confucius's humanism. Confucius did not ridicule talks of spirits or afterlife, but pointedly drew our attention back to human beings. Confucius's empirical approach to human knowledge prevented him from talking about the spirits or the occult, except on rare occasions. "Yu, shall I teach you the way to acquire knowledge? To say you know when you do know and say that you do not know when you do not know--that is the way to acquire knowledge."[23] "Hear much and put aside what is doubtful while you speak cautiously of the rest. See much and put aside what seems perilous while you are cautious in carrying the rest into practice."[24] Confucius wanted to ground human happiness and freedom on rational behavior rather than dubious speculations on the supernatural. True happiness is possible when one spontaneously desires to do what is right. This Confucius achieved. "At seventy I could follow the desires of my mind without overstepping the boundaries of what is right."[25]

Confucius's emphasis on filial piety has generated considerable discussions and controversies in Chinese history. In The Analects , XIII, 18, we read:

> The Duke of She addressed Master Kong (Confucius) saying, "In my country there was a man called Upright Gong. His father appropriated a sheep and Gong bore witness against him." Master Kong said: "In my country the upright men are of quite another sort. A father will screen his son, and a son his father which incidentally does involve a sort of uprightness."

Confucius's remarks here can be taken as a retort to the Duke of She by ridiculing his view of Gong's action. In effect, Confucius is saying in this case of conflict between filial piety and duty to the state, filiality is to have the priority. The Legalists, who came on the Chinese intellectual scene about two hundred years later, criticized Confucius for holding the priority of filial piety over legal justice. We will have a more detailed discussion of this controversy in Chapter 5. However, The Analects, XIII, 18, requires a few more comments here. The context of the passage does not suggest that Confucius is offering a fixed rule of action concerning such conflict of obligations. In view of Confucius's emphasis on virtue rather than legal compliance, it is plausible to interpret Confucius as saying that in general our obligation toward our parents cannot be disregarded in favor of legal justice. In special cases such as murder or treason, we may decide otherwise. The case of a father stealing a sheep does not constitute a special case. Being a son, one has a special obligation toward one's father. The law can take care of itself without depending on the son's serving as witness against his father for rendering a just and impartial decision. On the other hand, bearing witness against one's father's misconduct will destroy the family harmony, and one will no longer function within the family and perhaps the larger clan. Therefore, the son should not bear witness against his father.

Unfortunately, Confucianism deviated from Confucius's original teachings in later centuries and became rigid and dogmatic. The study of Confucianism sometimes meant nothing more than the compilation of mountains of words, and a number of Confucianists were pedantic and unreasonable. Moreover, Confucianism has been used to justify nepotism and apotheosis of political power. But these are perversions for which Confucius should not be held responsible. Even as a code of behavior, Confucianism has been abused. For example, filial piety was hailed as the first virtue of the nation, but some people carried it to such an extent that it seemed either a farce or an illness. Chinese children used to read The Twenty-four Examples of Filial Piety. Some of the filial piety described in this book would appear to Americans today as idiotic or insane. The book describes a man cutting off a piece of flesh from his arm and boiling it in the medicine pot for his father. The man believes that the soup would cure his father's illness. According to Francis L. K. Hsu, some Chinese imitate this kind of filial behavior.

> In the district histories and geneological records to be found in every part of the country are many individual biographies of local notables. After a cursory reading of about fifty of them, I obtained at least five instances in which men and women were said to have sliced flesh from their arms to be boiled in the medicine pot of one or another of their parents. One man did this twice during one of his father's illnesses. Because the elder's condition remained serious, the filial son decided to take a more drastic course of action. He cut out a piece of what he thought was his "liver" instead. Both he and his father died shortly afterward.[26]

In the old China, some fathers believed they had the right to put their daughters to death to save the family honor if, for example, they were found to be pregnant before marriage. How alien this kind of behavior is to Confucius's common sense philosophy! Yet things of this nature have been taught in Confucius's name. In view of Confucius's profound influence on Chinese people for such a long time, we should not be surprised by instances of the abuse of his teachings.

As we have seen, Confucius was both a realist and an idealist. His approach to morality is at once pragmatic and principled. He attempted to achieve harmony between the ideal and the real, between men and society, and between man and Heaven. The perennial appeal of Confucius's teaching attests to its enduring value. Some Chinese communists maintain today, justifiably, that Confucius was a champion of the rights of the common people. Even Mao Ze-dong conceded that Confucius, along with Marx, Engels, and Lenin, deserves our careful study. The most remarkable aspect of Confucius's teaching is that its realism manages to be continually inspiring to the Chinese people. Confucius's ethic is a rational approach to human happiness and good society without any supernatural grounding. Confucius taught the Chinese that happiness and virtue are correlatives which are complementary to each other. Happiness, the Chinese learned, depends not on external circumstances but on one's own virtue. Virtue is not only its own reward, it gives us happiness. The Chinese are well known for their cheerfulness and contentment. This spirit of happiness can be readily found among the Chinese regardless of their educational level, social or financial status. This is Confucius's contribution. It is the noblest of human achievements.

b. Mencius: The Energetic Disciple and His Theory of
          Human Nature

"Mencius" is the Latinized form of the name Meng Zi, or Master Meng. His family name was Meng, his personal name was Ke. He was probably born in 371 B.C. in the present Shandong province. Mencius's mother is said to have moved her residence three times in order to provide Mencius with a proper neighborhood and educational environment. Mencius studied with the disciples of Confucius's grandson Zi-si and took upon himself the mission of defending Confucianism against the other competing schools of thought. For this contribution to, and defense of, Confucianism, he has been honored by the Chinese as "the second sage," second only to Confucius.

Mencius travelled from state to state, seeking as did Confucius a high level government position to put his philosophical ideas into practice. Like Confucius, he never obtained any position of real authority. However, the social and intellectual climate of Mencius's time was quite different from that of Confucius's time. Distinct positions in thought other than Confucianism had emerged, and debates between thinkers had become familiar activity both at courts and in the marketplace. The rulers of the "Warring States" competed to attract the best brains. A great public interest existed in the ideas of the prominent scholars and their appearance at the rulers' courts. In general, these teacher-scholars were well treated by the rulers. They stayed in the special guest palaces, wined and dined by their hosts. The custom of the time demanded that the rulers speak to them in humble language and honor them with rich gifts. Thus, Mencius was able to "travel about, followed by several dozen carriages and several hundred men, living off one of the feudal lords after another."[27] In his travels, Mencius had many heated debates with other thinkers and some unpleasant moments with the rulers, but he never experienced physical hardship or danger, as Confucius did. The fashion of the time enabled Mencius to chastise reigning feudal lords like school children for their "evil" ways of governing their people. These feudal lords listened to him politely but were glad to see him off.

The book Mencius was probably edited by Mencius's disciples under his close supervision. The book is fairly lengthy but has a better organization than The Analects. From Mencius, we can infer that Mencius was forceful, energetic, eloquent, and uncompromising. Whereas Confucius was the only eminent philosopher in

32

his time, Mencius had to compete with other acknowledged thinkers to get the attention and favors of the rulers. Confucius admitted on several occasions that he was wrong; Mencius argued arduously and deviously to avoid having to admit he was wrong. The difference in styles between Confucius and Mencius was probably due to personality differences as well as differences in circumstances. The following is an example:

The government of the northern state of Yen was in considerable confusion, with the result that there was much suffering and disaffection among its people. At this point Mencius was asked by a minister of the state of Qi whether Qi ought to attack Yen. Accounts differ as to what Mencius said; in any case he did not oppose the invasion. Such intervention could have been justified both on political and humanitarian grounds, but, after Qi's troops controlled Yen, the invaders treated those they had liberated badly, so that the people of Yen revolted. At this point Mencius was taxed with having advised Qi to undertake the invasion. He could probably have defended himself on perfectly valid ground, but he sought refuge in a quibble.

Mencius said that he had only been asked, by Qi's minister whether Yen might properly be attacked. Since the government of Yen was not conducting itself properly, he had answered, "it may." If Qi's minister had gone on to ask him <u>who</u> might properly attack it, Mencius would then, he explained, have said that only a righteous ruler appointed by Heaven for the task might attack it. But, unfortunately, the government of Qi had not asked him this question but had merely gone on to make the attack. Under these circumstances, Mencius asked, how could he possibly be accused of having advised Qi to attack Yen?[28]

Mencius's manner of reasoning comes dangerously close to casuistry. Compare the story of Croesus, the king of Lydia, and the Oracle at Delphi. Croesus was about to attack Persia. Being a prudent man, he consulted Delphi on the matter and was given the oracle that "If Croesus went to war with Cyrus (the king of Persia), he would destroy a mighty kingdom." Believing that the Oracle assured him of his victory, Croesus went to war with Cyrus but was quickly defeated and captured by Cyrus. After Cyrus spared Croesus's life, Croesus wrote to the priests of Delphi to complain about the Oracle's prediction. The priests replied that the Oracle had been right. In going to war Croesus had destroyed a mighty kingdom: his own! It was an unfortunate omission on the part of Croesus not to have asked which mighty kingdom would be destroyed.

Yet, a couple of instances do not establish a general pattern. On the whole, Mencius conducted himself with dignity, honesty, and courage in the company of the rulers and the court officials. He never stooped to curry favor from them. On several occasions, Mencius confronted the rulers with their wrongdoing and asserted that they deserved to be punished.

Mencius asked the king of Liang: "Is there any difference between killing a man with a club and with a blade?"

"There is none," the king replied.
"Is there any difference between doing it with a blade and with one's manner of governing?"
"No," the king said.
"Well, then, since the king's manner of governing is causing some of his people to starve to death, the king is in fact a murderer!" Mencius told the king.[29]

In his conversations with the king of Qi, Mencius told him that the ministers should remonstrate against the king if he erred. If, after the ministers' remonstrance, the king does not mend his ways, the ministers should dethrone him, or, if necesary, kill him. The king's face "changed color" when he heard this. Mencius argued repeatedly that government is for the people, not for the ruler. He declared that scholar-officials should work under a ruler for the good of the people but not for a ruler personally.

Mencius's Moral Psychology: The Original Goodness of Human Nature

Confucius emphasized li and regarded ren, yi, zhong, shu, and xiao as necessary virtues for a good life. He implied that human nature is good, but never explicitly said so. It remained for Mencius to elaborate this idea and to present supporting arguments. Mencius was interested in psychology and was perceptive in observation of man's character. He said: "No part of a man's body is more excellent than the pupil of his eye. It cannot conceal wickedness. If all within his breast is correct, the pupil is bright, if not, it is dull. Listen to his words and observe the pupil of his eye. How can a man hide his character?"[30] In his effort to find a psychological basis for the principles of ren and yi, Mencius arrived at the doctrine that human nature is innately good.

35

This is his greatest contribution to Chinese thought.

Kao Zi, a contemporary thinker of Mencius, argued that human nature is neither good nor evil but has the potentiality to become good or evil, depending on the circumstances. He said:

> Human nature is like water current. If it is led to the east, it flows eastward; if it is led to the west, it flows westward. Like water which can be led to either of the two directions, human nature is neither good nor evil. It depends upon the direction towards which it is led.[31]

Mencius replied:

> Water is indeed indifferent to the east and west, but is it indifferent to high and low? Man's nature is naturally good just as water naturally flows downward. There is no man without this good nature; neither is there water that does not flow downward. Now, you can splash water and cause it to splash upward over your forehead; and by damming and leading it, you can force it uphill. Is this the nature of water? It is the forced circumstance that makes it do so. Man can be made to do evil, for his nature can be treated in the same way.[32]

Mencius was good at arguing by analogy. Kao Zi did not know about gravitational force, for he did not counter that water flows downward because it is pulled by gravity. Mencius suggests that man is born with some good elements in his nature which will unfold themselves as a man matures, unless hindered by bad environment. Admittedly, man has other elements in his psyche such as the drives for sex and food. If not duly controlled, these drives can lead a man to do evil things. But in and of themselves, they are morally neutral, that is, they are neither good nor evil. These are the elements man has in common with other animals. To support his view, Mencius used the example of the sense of sympathy in men. Any man who sees a small child about to fall in a well, will immediately rush to save the child. Any man, Mencius says, will do this without stopping to think about who the child is or whether he will gain the gratitude and favor of the child's parents. According to Mencius, every man is born with the four incipient beginnings or "buds" of human-heartedness (ren), righteousness (yi), respect or propriety (li), and the knowing capacity to distinguish good from bad (zhi).

> The feeling of commiseration is the beginning of human-heartedness. The feeling of shame and dislike is the beginning of righteousness. The sense of modesty and yielding is the beginning of propriety. The sense of right and wrong is the beginning of wisdom. Man has these four beginnings, just as he has four limbs.[33]

Moreover, Mencius points out that men's mouths, ears, and eyes are made alike. These organs have similar likes and dislikes. Therefore, he says, all men should approve similar moral principles.

Such is Mencius's view of human nature. Human history does not seem to support Mencius's view. The Christian doctrine of original sin also makes people inclined to disagree with Mencius. The controversy on the question whether human nature is good or evil may be an interminable one, like many other philosophical issues. In book VI of <u>Mencius</u>, Kao Zi and Mencius had a long discussion on this question without settling the dispute. In a sense, Mencius's proposition that human nature is good is tautological, since by "good" he means that which is most fully congruent with human nature. He may be aware of this in his debate with Kao Zi when he said: "When you say that what is inborn is called nature, is that like saying white is white?"[34] This is not to say that as a moral first principle, "human nature is good" is meaningless or insignificant. In any case, assuming that human nature is good, the following propositions are its logical consequences:

1. Men have the innate ability to distinguish good from evil.

2. Men have the innate ability to do good.

3. The purpose of learning is to recover the original goodness of mind.

4. Men must let these innate moral capabilities develop to their fullest extent through moral actions.

5. Evil is the result of man's own failure.

Mencius's Social and Political Philosophy.

The most radical idea of Mencius's political philosophy is that people have the moral right of revolution if the ruler loses his "mandate of Heaven" by behaving immorally. The state is a moral institution and the head of the state ought to be a moral leader. When a ruler fails to be a moral leader, he forfeits his right to rule, and the people will have the right to resist him, and, if necessary, kill him in the course of the rebellion. In such cases, we have tyrannicide, not regicide. When the king of Qi asked: "May a subject then put his sovereign to death?" Mencius replied:

> One who outrages the human virtues is called a brigand; one who transgresses against righteousness is called a ruffian; One who is a brigand and a ruffian is called a mere fellow. I have heard that the fellow called Zhou was put to death, but I have not heard this was killing a sovereign.[35]

Mencius did not challenge the hereditary right of monarchs to rule, but he insisted they should rule for the benefit of their subjects. He said that the people are the most important element in a state and the ruler the least important. He went so far as to suggest that the Mandate of Heaven which gave the ruler his position was tantamount to the expression of the people's will. "Heaven hears as the people hear, Heaven sees as the people see."[36] This statement effectively makes the people the standard for judging the government and the standard for Heaven itself. Mencius was extremely sensitive to the people's suffering because of disorder and violence. He urged the rulers to practice benevolent government or "the policy of benevolence" (ren zheng). Ren zheng consists of humanizing the penal code, reducing taxation, promoting agriculture and increasing production, teaching the people the virtues of filial piety, humility, loyalty, and faith. The key to political success is in practicing benevolent government, not in possessing a strong army. Better for a ruler to have the loyalty and confidence of his subjects than to have a strong army. Mencius, having seen so much war-induced sufferings, was strongly opposed to war. He maintained that those who delight in war and conquest and are skillful in military tactics are big criminals and ought to be

39

punished. However, he did not oppose what he called "righteous wars." He did not elaborate on what is a "righteous war." Presumably, a war of conquest is not righteous, but fighting to defend one's country against an aggressor is a righteous war. Mencius's advice to invade the state of Yen to restore order there could be defended on humanitarian grounds and thus could be considered a righteous war.

Mencius appreciated the importance of satisfying people's basic economic needs. He told the rulers that only when people were economically sufficient could they be expected to conduct a virtuous life.

> An enlightened monarch should see to it that people should produce enough to support their parents and their wives and children. In good years they should have enough to eat, and in bad years they should not have to be starved to death. If so, it would be easy to lead them to a virtuous life as they would be happy to follow. Nowadays people do not have the means to support either their parents or their wives and children. They suffer even in good years and cannot escape death in bad years. When they are confronted by possible death everyday, how can you expect them to have time to engage in rites and righteousness.[37]

A state must be built on a strong economic basis. The ruler should survey his lands and study the most productive way of using them. Mencius advocated diversified farming, conservation of fisheries and forests. Mencius believed that the equal distribution of land was the foundation of an agrarian economy. He may have originated the idea of the "well-field system." According to this system, each square <u>li</u> (about 1/3 mile) of land is to be divided into nine squares, each consisting of one hundred Chinese acres. The arrangement of the nine squares resembles in form the Chinese character for "well" (井), whence the name of the system. The central square is the "public field," the eight surrounding squares are the private land of the eight farmer families who work on the "well-field." All the eight families are to cultivate the central square collectively, and their own field individually. The produce of the public field goes to the government and constitutes the farmers' taxes. The eight families work together in certain times of the year and naturally form a community which provides social life, friendship, and mutual aid. Each "well-field system" would be both an economic and administrative unit.

Economic self-sufficiency is only the beginning of "the way of a true king" (<u>wang dao</u>). The king must also educate his subjects. Mencius proposed the establishment of a system of public schools for teaching the people higher culture, especially the proper human relationship. Mencius believed that the division of labor is necessary and desirable. He said that since some people are brainy, while others are brawny, they should not do the same kind of work. In his debate with Xü Xing, a philosopher of the "agricultural school," Mencius said it is unreasonable to expect every man to manufacture all the things one needs. He pointed out that even Xü Xing did not make his own cloth or cooking pots. Each type of people can contribute a special talent to the society. When each ruler practices benevolent government and every man understands proper human relationship and cultivates his personal virtues, then peace and goodwill shall triumph over violence and injustice.

Mencius's Philosophical Mysticism.

Although Mencius's primary concern is good society, he also talks about cultivating the great qi (breath, vital spirit). When asked about what qi is, he said it is mysterious and hard to explain. It is some kind of vital spirit or energy that pervades man and the universe. Cultivation of this great qi may result in the realization of the oneness of the individual self and the universe. "When I cultivate this great qi within me, all things are then complete within me."[38] The essence of man is the same as that of all things. Therefore, "he who completely knows his own nature, knows Heaven."[39] By Heaven, Mencius means nature or the cosmic order which is a moral one. For Mencius, the moral principles of man are also the metaphysical principles of the universe. If a man knows Heaven, he is not only a citizen of society but also a "citizen of Heaven." This is an important part of Mencius's teaching, for the good life of man depends on his virtues, and virtues depend on the spiritual understanding of man's nature or Heaven.

The method of cultivating the great qi has two aspects. One is the spiritual understanding of Dao (the truth, or the way). The other is the practice of yi, or the fulfillment of duty. Thus Mencius's cultivation of the great qi looks like the combination of Hindu jnana yoga (the discipline of spiritual understanding) and karma yoga (the discipline of action, or work). Mencius cautioned that this type of cultivation must be allowed to come to fruition naturally and cannot be rushed or forced.

> We should not be like the man of Song. There was a man of Song who was grieved that his grain did not grow fast enough. So he pulled it up. Then he returned to his home with great innocence, and said to his

people: "I am tired today, for I have
been helping the grain to grow." His
son ran out to look at it, and found
all the grain withered.[40]

c. Xün Zi: Realism and Philosophy of Culture.

About one hundred years after Mencius, the
Confucian scholar Xün Zi maintained that human nature
is evil. Whatever goodness a man has, he acquired it
through training. Xün Zi represents the realistic wing
of Confucianism. Although Xün Zi was a first-rate
scholar, he is not well known in the West, and
therefore his name has not been Latinized. Xün Zi's
personal name is Kuang, but is better known as Xün
Qing, a more respectful way of referring to him. He
was born in the northern state of Zhao around 300 B.C.
He had the misfortune to teach two bright men who later
repudiated Confucianism to become leading Legalist
philosophers. For this reason, and for his tough-
minded realism, Xün Zi has been mistakenly called a
Legalist.

Xün Zi paid careful attention to clarity and
precision in the meanings of terms and the logical
relationships of concepts and categories. The book
that bears his name is clearly written as a systematic
philosophical essay rather than a collection of
conversations such as The Analects or Mencius. The
best known chapter of the book is probably the one with
the title "Human Nature is Evil." The first half of
the chapter reads as follows:

> The nature of man is evil;
> whatever is good in him is the result
> of acquired training. Men are born
> with the love of gain; if this
> natural tendency is followed they are
> contentious and greedy, utterly
> lacking in courtesy and consideration

for others. They are filled from birth with envy and hatred of others; if these passions are given rein they are violent and villainous, wholly devoid of integrity and good faith. At birth man is endowed with the desires of the ear and eye, the love of sound and color; if he acts as they dictate he is licentious and disorderly, and has no regard for <u>li</u> or justice or moderation.

Clearly, then, to accord with man's original nature and act as instinct dictates must lead to contention, rapacity, and disorder, and cause humanity to revert to a state of violence. For this reason it is essential that men be transformed by teachers and laws, and guided by <u>li</u> and justice; only then will they be courteous and cooperative, only then is good order possible. In the light of these facts it is clear that man's original nature is evil, and that he becomes good only through acquired training.

Crooked wood must be steamed and forced to conform to a straight edge, in order to be made straight. A dull blade must be ground and whetted, to make it sharp. Similarly human nature, being evil, must be acted upon by teachers and laws to be made upright, and must have <u>li</u> and justice added to it before men can be orderly. Without teachers and laws, men are selfish, malicious, and unrighteous. Lacking <u>li</u> and justice they are unruly, rebellious, and disorderly.

Anciently the sage-kings, knowing this, instituted li and justice and promulgated laws and regulations to force and beautify men's natural tendencies, and make them upright. They made them docile and civilized them, in order that they might readily be guided. Then for the first time there was good government, and accord with the right way (dao). At present, men who are transformed by teachers and laws, who accumulate learning, and who act in accord with li and justice, are gentlemen. But those who give free play to their natural tendencies, taking satisfaction in doing just what they please without regard for li and justice, are small-minded men. In the light of these facts it is clear that man's original nature is evil, and that he becomes good only through acquired training.

Mencius says that the fact that men can learn proves that their original nature is good. But this is not the case. Mencius has not properly understood what human nature is, nor adequately distinguished betweeen the original nature and acquired character. Man's nature is what he is endowed with at birth by Heaven; it cannot be learned or worked for. Li and justice were originated by the sages. Men can learn of li and justice by study, and incorporate them into their characters by effort. What cannot be acquired by study or effort, but is innate in man, is his nature. But everything that can be learned and worked for is acquired character. This is the difference between nature and acquired character.

It is given, as part of man's original nature, that the eye can see and the ear can hear; these powers are not things apart from the eye and ear themselves. Nor can the powers of sight and hearing be learned. Mencius says that all men are by nature good, and become evil only because they lose and destroy their original nature. In this, however, he is mistaken. For if this were true it would then be the case (since, in fact, men are not born good) that as soon as a person were born he would already have lost what is supposed to be his original nature. In light of these facts it is clear that man's original nature is evil, and that he becomes good only through acquired training.

The idea that man's original nature is good must mean that his character, without any change from its most primitive state, is admirable and good. If this were true, then the qualities of being admirable and good would be as indissolubly linked to a man's character and mind as the powers of seeing and hearing are bound up with his eyes and ears. In fact, however, man's nature is such that when he is hungry he wants to gorge himself, when he is cold he desires warmth, and when he works he wants to rest. Nevertheless we see hungry men who, in the presence of food, restrain themselves and yield precedence to their elders. We see those who toil without resting, because they are working for the sake of their elders. These later actions are contrary to human nature, and they violate men's instinctive desires, but they accord with the way of a filial son and with the principles of li and justice. Thus, if one accords with his natural tendencies he does not yield precedence to others; if he yields precedence to others he violates his natural tendencies. In light of these facts it is clear that man's original nature is evil, and that he becomes good only through acquired training.[41]

In many ways the ideas of Xün Zi are antithetical to those of Mencius. With regard to the question whether man's original nature is good or evil, Xün Zi's general thesis is that man's basic nature is slothful, avaricious, and animal, and that everything that is good or valuable is the product of human effort. The function of education is to shape the human being in the mold of morality. Mencius, on the other hand, says that nurture means simply to free man for his innate moral growth. Xün Zi's theory of the original evilness of human nature may remind a Westerner of the Christian doctrine of original sin. A Westerner may also associate Xün Zi with Thomas Hobbes, and Mencius with Jean-Jacques Rousseau. Yet Xün Zi (and Mencius) believed in the perfectibility of man. For Xün Zi, man can be perfected through moral education without any providential grace. Xün Zi's writing shows that he does not believe in God or ghosts. He says that ghosts are imagined by confused people. Beating a drum to cure rheumatism will wear out the drum, but will not cure the rheumatism. If you pray for rain and it rains, that proves nothing, for it would have rained anyway, even if nobody prayed for it.

Ethics for Xün Zi is a set of highly normative and objective standards of behavior. These standards are to be inculcated by intensive education and enforced by social control. For this reason, Xün Zi expects a government to be strong and authoritarian. Human civilization is regarded by Xün Zi as man's triumph over himself. Man is man because he has the intelligence and ability to overcome his baser instincts. To be civilized is to replace what is natural with what man has made. The vocation of man is to utilize what is given by Heaven and Earth to create his own culture. A Westerner may be reminded of Sigmund Freud's Civilization and Its Discontents. Freud says that the price we pay for having civilization is to countervail some of our instincts through sublimation, suppression, repression, etc. Xün Zi says that we must have li to set reasonable limits to the satisfaction of our desires. Furthermore, li in its broad sense also guides our desires into the proper channels. Xün Zi emphasizes in his book directing our desires toward spiritual rather than material things.

That human beings have developed a high culture is proof for Xün Zi of man's capacity to triumph over his nature. Despite the original evilness of his nature, man's intelligence enables him to know what good is and to become good. Because men are intelligent, they know that in order to live well they need social organizations and cooperative actions. Men need cooperative actions to hunt physically stronger animals. Moreover, good life requires the support of many other members of the society. In a passage reminiscent of Mencius, Xün Zi says: "A single individual needs the support of the accomplishments of hundreds of workmen. Yet an able man cannot be skilled in more than one line of work, and one man cannot hold two offices simultaneously. If people all live alone and do not serve one another, there will be poverty."[42] To have a good social organization where people live harmoniously and productively together, we must have rules of conduct. Thus, the intelligent men created li. Once we have li, morality follows, for he who acts in accordance with li acts morally. In short, whereas Mencius says that any man can become a Yao or Shun (two legendary sages) because he is originally good, Xün Zi argues that any man can become a sage because he is endowed with intelligence.

Xün Zi is remarkably modern in his philosophy of language. Xün Zi is interested in the human mind's capability to organize and classify sense data. He writes: "The mind gives meaning to impressions [received by the senses]. It gives meaning to impressions, and only then, by means of the ear, can sound be known; by means of the eye, can forms be known. . . . When the five senses note something but cannot classify it, and the mind tries to identify it but fails to give it meaning, then one can only say that there is no knowledge."[43] He asks questions about the relationship between words and objects and attempts to answer them. One fundamental question about language is: "Why do things have names and how do we apply these names?" The first part of the question is easy to answer. Xün Zi says things have names because they are convenient labels for talking about them. We need names to group similar things together and to distinguish things that are different. The second part of the question is more involved. The word "horse," for example, is used to refer to horses of different sizes, colors, and characteristics. According to Xün Zi, after a man has seen horses of different sizes and colors, he forms a "concept" (which is designated by a name) of horse. After the formation of a concept, if a man sees a horse again, he will use a reasoning process that may be called "analogical projection" to correctly identify it as a horse. The horse that he sees now may be of a different color or size from the ones he saw, but enough resembling characteristics enable him to extend the name "horse" to the animal. Xün Zi says that "the testimony of the senses" is the basis of naming. In the case of "horse," there does not seem to be any characteristics that all horses have in common and that no other creatures have. Instead, similar characteristics are shared. None of the horses is characterized by all these characteristics, but every horse is characterized by some of them. They are what Ludwig Wittgenstein calls "family resemblances." Members of a family are recognizable as members not because they all share an identical set of characteristics but because of the overlapping of several sets of characteristics. In the case of other concepts such as "circle" or "square", an exact set of properties is evident. One can then compare the sense impressions with the "mental image" that one has formed to represent such kind of things. The correct application of the names in these cases is easier.

Xün Zi used his theory of language to defend Confucianism against other contending schools of thought. His theory of language was developed from the Confucian doctrine of "the rectification of names," which Confucius and Mencius used in their political discourses. Xün Zi improved the doctrine and applied it to epistemological as well as political discussions. Although he advocated authoritarian government, Xün Zi was faithful to the Confucian concepts of a moral universe and of government for the benefit of the governed. His thesis that li is the core of human culture shows his Confucian orientation. Hence, one may properly consider Xün Zi to be a Confucianist rather than a Legalist or a Dialectician.

Chapter 2

1. The Analects, XII, 22.

2. Ibid., VI, 2.

3. Ibid., XII, 2.

4. Ibid., IV, 16.

5. Ibid., XIV, 41.

6. Ibid., XVIII, 7.

7. Ibid., IX, 28.

8. Ibid., VI, 28.

9. Confucius is not talking about women because he lived in a patriarchal, male-dominated society. Obviously, any man or woman whose conduct is noble, unselfish, just, and kind, is a "gentleman." The other philosophers we will be discussing as part of the Chinese tradition are all men and part of that continuing male-dominated society. They too will be talking about human beings as men, but this need not inhibit our applying their thoughts to women and men.

10. Da Xüe (The Great Learning, 大学), I, 4, 6. The Great Learning is one of the four Confucian classics and is believed to have been edited by Confucius's grandson Zi Si(子思).

11. The Analects, XII, 17.

12. Ibid., XII, 19. Qi Kang Zi was a powerful lord of

the state of Qi.

13. Ibid., XIV, 36.

14. Ibid., VII, 7.

15. Ibid., IX, 26.

16. Ibid., VII, 21.

17. Ibid., VII, 18.

18. Ibid., I, 3.

19. Ibid., XIII, 24.

20. Ibid., XI, 9-10.

21. Ibid., XI, 11.

22. Ibid.

23. Ibid., II, 17.

24. Ibid., II, 18.

25. Ibid., II, 4.

26. Francis Hsu, Americans and Chinese (3rd ed.), Honolulu, The University of Hawaii Press, 1981, p. 82.

27. Mencius, III, 2, 4.

28. H. G. Creel, Chinese Thought, p. 67.

29. Mencius, I, I, 4.

30. Ibid., IV, 1, 15.

31. *Ibid.*, VI, 1, 6.

32. *Ibid.*

33. *Ibid.*, II, 1 6.

34. *Ibid.*, VI, 1, 6.

35. *Ibid.*, I, 2, 8.

36. *Ibid.*, VII, B, 17.

37. *Ibid.*, I, 1, 7, 21.

38. *Ibid.*, II, A, 2

39. *Ibid.*, VII, A, 1, 1.

40. *Ibid.*, II, A, 2.

41. *Xùn Zi*, ch. 23.

42. *Ibid.*, ch. 10.

43. *Ibid.*, ch. 22, "On the Rectification of Names."

Chapter 3

Daoism: The Philosophy of
Spontaneity and Creativity

Introductory Remarks.

In terms of influence over the life and thought of
the Chinese people, Daoism is second only to
Confucianism. In many respects, Daoism is the opposite
of Confucianism, and with Buddhism, serves to balance
the Chinese mind. Daoism rose as an intellectual and
spiritual response to the deplorable social conditions
of the East Zhou dynasty. In the times of Confucius
and Mencius, some Chinese chose to live as recluses,
deep in the mountains and close to nature, to escape
the troubles of the world. Some of these men felt the
need to justify their action and so they wrote about
their philosophy of life. Yang Zhu, who is believed to
have lived in the fourth century B.C., may be
considered one of the earliest Daoists. Yang Zhu
advocated the pursuit of freedom, the preservation of
personal integrity and peace of mind, and the avoidance
of ensnarement by material things.[1] Chinese tradition,
however, credits Lao Zi with having founded Daoism.
That Lao Zi existed is beyond doubt, although scholars
have not ascertained whether he lived in the sixth or
the fourth century B.C. Lao Zi is also credited with
the authorship of the Daoist canon Dao De Jing (The Way
and Its Virtue). Some Chinese scholars believe that
Dao De Jing is the work of several persons in different
times rather than of one person. Besides Dao De Jing,
the other important work in Daoism is the book of
Zhuang Zi, written by Zhuang Zhou (also referred to as
Zhuang Zi, or Master Zhuang), who lived between 399 and
295 B.C. Zhuang Zi is a more substantial and better
organized philosophical work than Dao De Jing,
consisting of thirty-three brilliantly composed essays.

In terms of brilliance of mind, power of imagination, subtlety, and wit, no other Chinese writer surpasses Zhuang Zhou.

The ideas of Yang Zhu, Lao Zi, and Zhuang Zi represent three phases of early Daoism. While Yang Zhu's primary concern is prudence, Lao Zi offered his original speculation on the ways of the universe and of human life. Zhuang Zi developed Lao Zi's ideas and carried his speculation to a new height. Later, in the period of Disunity (220-590 A.D.), Daoist commentators such as Wang Bi (226-249 A.D.), and Guo Xiang (d. 312 A.D.), incorporated some Confucian and even some Buddhist ideas in their interpretations of Dao De Jing and Zhuang Zi. This brand of Daoism is called Neo-Daoism, or Xuan Xue (Mysterious Learning), as the Chinese call it.

a. Lao Zi and Dao De Jing.

"Lao Zi" in Chinese means "old boy" or "old Master." Obviously, Lao Zi is not the real name of the founder of Daoism, but rather a title of endearment and respect. The name "Lao Zi" may have been associated with the fantastic legend about his birth: that he was carried in his mother's womb for 82 years, and born a wise old man with white hair. Lao Zi's family name is Li, and his personal name is Er. He is also known by his posthumous name Li Dan. According to Si-ma Qian, the great Han dynasty historian, Lao Zi was born in the state of Qu in the sixth century B.C. He served as an archivist in the court of Zhou and was reported to have received and conversed with Confucius when the latter was a young man. Impressed by the profundity of Lao Zi's wisdom Confucius said after the interview:

> Of birds, I know they have wings to
> fly with, of fish that they have fins
> to swim with, of wild beasts that
> they have feet to run with. For feet

there are traps, for fins nets, for
wings arrows. But who knows how
dragons surmount wind and cloud into
Heaven. This day I have seen Lao Zi.
Today I have seen a dragon.[2]

According to Zhuang Zi, Confucius was enlightened by
Lao Zi about the meaning of Dao.

When Confucius, not yet having
achieved Dao, went south to see Lao
Zi, he was asked: "I have heard that
you are the wise man from the north.
Have you also received the Dao?"
"Not yet." Confucius replied. Lao
Zi went on, "How have you sought it?"
Confucius said: "I sought it in
rituals and rules, and after five
years I have not yet achieved it."
"And how then did you seek it?"
Confucius said: "I sought it in the
principles of Yin-Yang, but after
five years I had not yet found it."
Lao Zi then explained: "The reason
why the Dao cannot be transmitted is
none other than this: if there is
not a presiding center within, it
will not remain there." Lao Zi
continued: "It is unfortunate that
you have not met a ruler fit to rule
the world. The Six Classics which
you mentioned are but the worn-out
footprints of the sages of the past.
The footprints were made by shoes,
but they are not the shoes
themselves. Hawks stare at one
another and without moving their eyes
their young are conceived. There is
a male insect which chirps with the
wind while the female chirps against

it, and their young are thereby produced. There are hermaphroditic animals which produce their own young independently." Confucius reflected on these remarks for a period of three months and then returned to Lao Zi and said: "Magpies and their kind hatch out their young from eggs. Fish reproduce their kind by the impregnation of their own milt. The wasp gives rise to itself by the process of metamorphosis. When the younger brother is born, the older brother cries." Pleased with this answer, Lao Zi told Confucius, "It is well indeed! You have grasped <u>Dao</u>."[3]

The condescending tone of Lao Zi in this dialogue with Confucius is typical of Daoist writings about Confucius. It also suggests the story is fabricated by the Daoists to make a point or to enhance Daoism. Many scholars today doubt that Confucius and Lao Zi ever met. The seemingly illogical and nonsensical dialogue about the reproduction of hawks, insects, and animals is designed by Zhuang Zi to break our logical mental habit in order to reach a higher state of mind. This kind of illogical conversation is also typical of <u>Zen</u> dialogues and shows the Daoist influence in <u>Zen</u>. We shall say more about this in Chapter 8.

In his old age, Lao Zi became convinced that the decline of the Zhou dynasty was irreversible and decided to leave his post. He is said to have climbed on the back of a water buffalo[4] and travelled westward toward Tibet. According to Si-ma Qian, Lao Zi was recognized by a gatekeeper at the Hankao Pass. The gatekeeper having failed to persuade Lao Zi to turn back, begged him to leave some words of wisdom to benefit the civilization he was deserting. Lao Zi consented and spent three days at the gatekeeper's house to write down 5,000 Chinese characters. He titled his little book Dao De Jing and gave it to the gatekeeper. Si-ma Qian concludes his biography of Lao Zi by saying: "He [Lao Zi] then went away, and nobody knew what had become of him."

Dao De Jing is sometimes known as Lao Zi. It consists of eighty-one short chapters, each a poem-like arrangement of sentences. The book is divided into two parts: the first deals with Dao, the second with De. The Jing means canonical work or revered books such as scripture. Dao De Jing, with its 5,000 Chinese characters,[5] has cast a spell on Chinese culture and those who study it, inducing learned scholars to read commentaries on it and then commentaries on commentaries. The book can be read in an hour, or, as many Chinese choose to, in a lifetime. Often Chinese scholars commit the 5,000 characters to memory and recite them from time to time as the spirit moves them. Rereading and recitation of Dao De Jing is a joy and consolation known to many Chinese. The book contains aphorisms on metaphysics, ethics, epistemology, and politics. On the whole, it stresses simplicity and naturalness in lifestyle and in thought for the sake of harmony with the world. The book has three levels of meaning: at the commonsensical level, it gives advice on self-preservation and the art of being happy; at the philosophical level, it teaches the relativity of truth and of all values; at the mystical level, it intimates the union of individual consciousness with the single unifying first principle of Dao. Dao is the pivotal concept of Dao De Jing.

b. The meaning of Dao (道).

Dao (道) means "road," or "way," or "path." Etymologically, it is derived from an ancient character which contains three elements: a road, a human head, and a human foot. The meaning of Dao as "the way," "the path," is still indicated in the present form of the character where " 〒 " signifies the headdress of a leader, and "辶" signifies the path walked by a leader. The leader's path is the right path. De is an elusive concept, sometimes translated as "power" or "virtue." The character for De (德,) contains the element of heart (心), thus signifying the heart's adherence to the principle of Dao. Metaphorically, De is related to another word also pronounced de (得) but which means "to obtain," "that which obtains," or "the effects of that which obtains." We may understand De as the manifestation of Dao in concrete situations. In the Dao De Jing, Dao is used to refer to the way of the ultimate reality, the way of the universe, and the way of human existence.

As the way of the ultimate reality, Dao cannot be perceived by the senses, nor described or expressed in words. It cannot be comprehended by ordinary thought or imagination. The first chapter of Dao De Jing declares:

> The Dao (way) that can be told of is
> not the eternal Dao;
> The name that can be named is not the
> eternal name.
> The Nameless is the origin of Heaven
> and Earth;
> The Named is the mother of all
> things.
> Therefore let there always be non-
> being so we may see their subtlety,
> And let there always be being so we
> may see their outcome.
> The two are the same,
> But after they are produced, they
> have different names.
> They both may be called deep and
> profound.
> Profound mystery, the mystery of all
> mysteries,

The entrance into all mysteries.

So the ultimate Dao is transcendent and ineffable. It is the ground of all existence, the source (der Ursprung) from which all life springs and to which all returns. In the mystical union with Dao, we may have the experience with the nameless. But this Dao-experience is ineffable: it cannot be expressed in words. Therefore, "he who knows does not speak, he who speaks does not know."[6] The Dao-experience at best can only be described in negative terms. No vision or hearing of the voice of God is in it. For this reason, Daoist mysticism may be called nature mysticism. One must be emptied of all passions, detached from all sensory perceptions and intellectual activities. One becomes "like an empty cup," and then what was once emptiness becomes pure-being.

Dao as the way of the universe is both transcendent and immanent. Since Dao supports all things in its natural state, the function of Dao is manifested in the workings of nature. What individual things possess of Dao is the De, or function of Dao. Dao in this sense is like the lex aeterna, the eternal law of nature in accord with which the universe operates, or Heraclitus's logos which gives order and intelligibility to the world. Though things are ever changeable and changing, laws govern the changing process of things.

> The all-embracing quality of the
> great virtue (De) follows alone from
> Dao.
> The thing that is called Dao is
> eluding and vague.
> Vague and eluding, in it is the form.
> Eluding and vague, in it are things.
> Deep and obscure, in it is the
> essence.
> The essence is very real; in it are

evidences.
From the time of old until now, its
name (manifestation) ever remains.
By which we may see the beginning of
all things.
How do I know that the beginnings of
all things are so?
Through this [Dao].[7]

"Dao" is the hidden and nameless, yet it is Dao that
skillfully provides for all and brings them to
perfection."[8] Among the laws that govern the changes,
the most fundamental is that "reversing is the movement
of Dao."[9] This is Lao Zi's metaphysical law that when
a thing reaches one extreme, it reverts from it.

The principles of Yin and Yang were known to the
Chinese prior to the time of Lao Zi. They were
regarded as opposites, and all things were considered
to be the results of the interaction between Yin and
Yang. But Yin and Yang, opposed as they are, cannot
produce themselves or interact with each other.
Something else is required for the Yin-Yang
interaction. Lao Zi's insight in this connection is
the suggestion that Dao functions as the basis for the
interaction of Yin and Yang.

Dao produced the One.
The One produced the two.
The two produced the three.
And the three produced the ten
thousand things.
The ten thousand things carry the Yin
and embrace the Yang, and through the
blending of the material force (qi)
they achieve harmony.[10]

Dao as the way of human existence refers to the
way of life that is most harmonious with the operation
of natural laws. When a person understands the

structure of nature and his essential relations to it, all his actions will be cooperations with the natural laws. This is the concept of wu-wei (無 為). Wu-wei is often translated as "non-action" or "having no activity." However, it does not mean complete lack of activity or doing nothing at all. It means a creative way of acting with efficiency and simplicity, without artificiality or waste of energy. The way to do is simply to be, that is, let nature take its course, do nothing unnatural or artificial to interfere with nature's operation. As Lao Zi says: "Dao invariably does nothing and yet there is nothing that is not done."[11] The way water supports objects and carries them effortlessly on its tide is a symbol of wu-wei. Following the principle of wu-wei, "one may move so well that a footprint never shows, speak so well that the tongue never slips, reckon so well that no counter is needed."[12] Those who truly understand wu-wei act without strain, "work without working," and succeed without trying. The opposite of wu-wei is overdoing. The Daoist expression for overdoing is "painting feet on the snake,"--the Daoist equivalent of "gilding the lily"--which is unnatural and artificial. Overdoing is not only unnecessary, but also destructive--painting feet on the snake ruins an otherwise perfect painting of a snake.

Applying the principle of wu-wei to politics, Lao Zi says that the best government is the least government because it governs without interference. Lao Zi believes that a sage should be the head of a state. Being a sage, he realizes that the troubles of the world come from too many people trying to do too much. The sage-ruler guides the state with the principle of unobtrusive facilitation--he lets things happen of their own accord but never forces them. Therefore Lao Zi says: "I act not and the people of themselves are transformed. I love quiescence and the people of themselves go straight. I concern myself with nothing, and the people of themselves are prosperous. I am without desire, and the people of themselves are simple."[13] "A leader is best, when people barely know that he exists. . . . Of a good leader, who talks little, when his work is done, his aim fulfilled, they will say 'We did this ourselves.'"[14] On the other hand, a ruler's doing too much or maintaining too many social and political institutions will bring about the opposite effect.

> The more restrictions and prohibitions in the world, the poorer the people will be. The more sharp weapons the people have, the more troubled will be the country. The more cunning craftsmen are, the more pernicious contrivances will appear. The more laws are promulgated, the more thieves and bandits there will be.[15]

A simple, primitive society is preferable to a complicated, advanced one where "luxury breeds envy and envy brings strife," and no one is really happy. An ideal society is economically self-sufficient and produces nothing other than necessities to satisfy the basic needs of the people. No one envies another, as no one has more than the other. As envy ends, so would rivalry and strife.

"He who assists the ruler with Dao does not dominate the world with force. The use of force usually brings requital."[16] Man should avoid being strident or aggressive not only toward other men but also toward nature. The Daoist attitude toward nature is the opposite of the modern Western attitude which has it roots in the Judeo-Christian tradition. The Westerners tend to contrast nature with man and regard nature as an antagonist to be controlled or conquered. The Daoists regard nature as a source of energy and inspiration. Identification or harmony with nature, rather than conquest of nature, is the Daoist goal. In Chinese landscape paintings, we often find the delicate and intimate feelings of the artists. The theme of harmony with nature is usually present in a Chinese landscape painting. In such paintings, man accommodates himself to nature and does not change it. Human figures are hardly noticeable and blend in harmoniously with mountains, water, trees. A Chinese landscape painter, before taking up brush and silk, would go out to nature. From the mountaintops the painter surveys the world with a calm expansion of the spirit until he feels one with nature.

When Mount Everest was scaled by climbers (with the help of oxygen tanks, and other tools and gadgets), newspapers in the West headlined it "the conquest of Everest." To a Daoist, nothing could be more inappropriate than the word "conquest" for such an event. The efforts involved in the climb were tremendous, but to climb the peak of Everest, stay there a few minutes, then scurry down to lower levels is hardly to "conquer" Mount Everest. A Daoist would say that the climbers visited or "befriended" Everest. From a Daoist point of view, to say that one wins a friend when speaking of friendship or that one conquers a woman (or man) when speaking of sexual love is also inappropriate.

> Those who would take over the earth
> And shape it to their will
> Never, I notice, succeed.
> The earth is like a vessel so sacred
> That at the mere approach of the
> profane
> It is marred
> And when they reach out their fingers
> it is gone.[17]

65

Lao Zi on Self-knowledge and Happiness.

One cannot discuss Dao De Jing without mentioning Lao Zi's insights on self-knowledge and happiness.

> He who knows others is intelligent;
> He who knows himself is enlightened.
> He who conquers others has power.
> He who conquers himself has strength.
> He who is contented is rich.
> He who acts with vigor has will.
> He who does not lose his place [with Dao] will endure.
> He who dies but does not really perish enjoys a long life.[18]

Self-knowledge is the key to personal happiness. To gain self-knowledge, one must attain the clarity of mind which is possible only when one is detached from external distractions.

> The five colors can blind,
> The five tones deafen,
> The five tastes cloy.
> The race, the hunt, can drive men mad
> And their booty leave them no peace.
> Therefore a sensible man
> Prefers the inner to the outer eye.[19]

What matters is not how much we have, but how much we enjoy what we have. Lao Zi wants us to simplify our life and limit our desires. Advertisers in America have been telling the American public that happiness, or "quality of life," to use a fashionable phraseology, depends on the satisfaction of our ever-increasing desires. This advertisers' way--the Dao of the advertisers--is the opposite of Lao Zi's way.

With self-knowledge comes humility and contentment. But,

Surrounded with treasure
You lie ill at ease,
Proud beyond measure
You come to your knees;
Do enough, without vying,
Be living, not dying.[20]

Standing tiptoe a man loses balance,
Admiring himself, he does so alone.
...[21]

At no time in the world will a man
who is sane
Over-reach himself,
Over-spend himself,
Over-rate himself.[22]

c.   Zhuang Zi and Zhuang Zi.

   Zhuang Zi (c. 369-c. 286), Master Zhuang, is
considered by many scholars the greatest of Daoists.
His personal name was Zhou and he calls himself Zhuang
Zhou in his writings. He was born in the state of Meng
in middle eastern China. He had a brilliant mind and
preferred to live as a hermit, though he had the
reputation of a wise man. Zhuang Zi had a quick wit;
his essays are full of fantasy and humor. Some of his
essays are so subtle that sometimes even his critics
mistake Zhuang Zi's blame for praise. The book bearing
his name Zhuang Zi is a collection of thirty-three
essays, some of which may have been written by later
Daoists and included by the great commentator Guo Xiang
(c. 312) who edited the book. Zhuang Zi develops Lao
Zi's insights in Dao De Jing and presents them in
excellent philosophical essays. Zhuang Zi contains
many interesting and profound metaphors. How to
interpret these metaphors is a problem every reader of
the book faces. In reading Dao De Jing, linguistic
ambiguity is the main problem.

Relativism.

On the practical level, Zhuang Zi teaches the way to be free and happy. On the theoretical level, Zhuang Zi advocates relativism and skepticism in epistemology and ethics. Everything except Dao itself is relative. Human happiness, freedom, goodness, and truth are, so long as we recognize them as relative, nevertheless valuable.

One feature of Zhuang Zi's philosophy which many people find intriguing is his anthropocentrism. After Zhuang Zi dreamed that he was a butterfly, he did not take it for granted that it was he, Zhuang Zi, who dreamed of being a butterfly but asked the question: "Was it Zhuang Zi dreaming that he was a butterfly or the butterfly dreaming it was Zhuang Zi?" Again, Zhuang Zi says: "Men eat vegetables and flesh, and deer eat tender grass. Centipedes enjoy snakes, and owls and crows like mice. Which of the four know the right taste?"[23] Those who say that man is the measure of all things are sadly narrow-minded. Zhuang Zi's disregard for human social conventions is both entertaining and inspiring. When he was old and about to die, his students planned to buy the best coffin in town for their venerated teacher. "Why should you buy any coffin for me at all, not to mention a good coffin? I prefer to use the whole universe as my coffin," Zhuang Zi protested. His students replied: "We are afraid that your body would be eaten up by hungry vultures." Zhuang Zi sighed and said: "It is true that without a coffin my body will be eaten up by vultures. But do you realize that with a coffin my body will be eaten up by ants? Now you are proposing to take my body away from the vultures and give it to the ants. Is that fair to the vultures? Why should you favor the ants and discriminate against the vultures?"[24]

This anti-anthropocentricism is helpful in understanding Zhuang Zi's views on knowing the world. A thing may appear differently to different people if their perspectives are different. The same thing may appear differently to you if you change your perspective. But if our sense organs were different, we would perceive things differently. For example, a butterfly's eyes have no retinas. Instead, they have hundreds of optic receptor cells. Consequently, a butterfly's visual perspectives are different from humans'. Human visual perception involves forming an image on the retinas whereas butterflies have mosaic vision. A butterfly "sees" in the same way a computer represents a picture. When a butterfly sees a flower, it sees more colors than we do because, among other things, it can see infrared. (The color perception of butterflies can be simulated by special cameras.) Butterflies also have a visual field of 260 degrees-- much wider than humans'. When a butterfly approaches a flower, what it sees is in a real sense the result of what it does. Butterflies' way of seeing is a good way. It enables them to find food, mates, and hiding places.

Observation and description of the world involve not only sense organs but also the conceptual-linguistic framework of mind. The mind does not create the world. To know features of the world, we need not only the phenomena to be observed but also concepts and theories to describe the phenomena and a linguistic system to represent these concepts and theories. In the terminology of today's scientific philosophers, observations are "theory-laden" because the concepts used in the observations are "embedded" in theories. Theories are more properly said to be constructed than discovered. Thus, Newton's theory of universal gravitation is a result of Newton's imaginative construction rather than the discovery of new phenomena. There is no a priori reason why we should use a certain conceptual-linguistic framework in knowing the world.

Some people (let's call them realists) say that a scientific theory which has been accepted by the scientific community does hold of nature, that is, it tells us something about the way the world really is. Zhuang Zi would say that this way of treating scientific knowledge is too simplistic. He recommends that we give up detailed theoretical description of nature and fall back on the properties of things observed in their actual use. He says:

> It was separation (fen) that led to completion (cheng); and from completion ensued dissolution (hui). But all things, without regard to their completion and dissolution, return again into the Unity of Nature. Only the far-reaching in thought can know how to comprehend them in this Unity. This being so, let us give up devotion to our own preconceived views, and follow the common and ordinary views, which are grounded on the use of things. The study of that use leads to comprehension, and that secures success. That success gained, we are near to the object of our search and there we have to stop. When we stop, and yet do not "know" how it is so, we have what is called Dao.[25]

Although Zhuang Zi does not use the terms "laws" or "theories," he may be referring to them when he uses the terms "separation," "completion," and "dissolution." When study of the use of things yields success, we should stop, that is, stop using our ordinary perceptual-cognitive scheme and let nature take its course. At this point we should, Zhuang Zi says, "Forget the passage of time and forget the distinction of right and wrong. Relax in the realm of the infinite and thus abide in the realm of the infinite."[26] This is what Feng You-lan calls "the knowledge of no knowledge." This is the knowledge of Dao (the way of the ultimate reality). Because Zhuang Zi may sometimes disparage human knowledge and because "knowledge of no knowledge" is an awkward expression, some writers call this knowledge of Dao, "Dao-experience," or "Dao-attitude."

The realists are too serious about their knowledge claims. For Zhuang Zi, "ordinary knowledge depends on something to be correct, but what it depends on is uncertain and changeable. How do we know that what I call nature is not really artificial and what I call artificial is not really nature?"[27] The point is that the world and the language users are inter-involved. Language is used to communicate with nature as well as with other people. We use our language to organize and articulate our experiences with the world. But language users are parts of the world. Thus, they cannot get out of the world and contemplate it from outside.

In Chapter 14 of Zhuang Zi we find Zhuang Zi asking: "Is the sky revolving around? Is the earth remaining still? Are the sun and moon persuing each? . . . Is there perhaps some mechanical arrangement so that they cannot help moving? Or is it perhaps that they keep revolving and cannot help themselves?" Zhuang Zi does not tell us whether the sun revolves around the earth or the earth revolves around the sun. A realist would claim it is right to say that the earth revolves around the sun but wrong to say the sun revolves around the earth. For a realist, the heliocentric theory concerning the movement of the sun and earth is true and the geocentric theory is false. Zhuang Zi would reply that the heliocentric theory is more convenient and parsimonious. But he would not say that the geocentric theory is false in the sense that it does not help us deal effectively with the world. After all, the geocentric theory and the heliocentric theory have equal explanatory and predictive power, and to say that the sun moves around the earth may be appropriate to situations. Moreover, the prevailing astrophysical theory claims the sun does move, just as the whole galaxy moves. When the realists discriminate between two functionally equivalent descriptions, they commit the sin of what Zhuang Zi calls "three in the morning."

> Those who wear out their intelligence to try to make things one without knowing that they are really the same may be called "three in the morning." What is meant by "three in the morning?" A monkeykeeper was once giving out nuts and said "three in the morning and four in the evening." All the monkeys became angry. He said, "If that is the case, there will be four in the morning and three in the evening." All the monkeys were glad. Neither the name nor the actuality had been reduced but the monkeys reacted with joy and anger differently. The keeper also let things take their own course. Therefore the sage harmonizes the right and wrong and rests in natural equalization. This is called following two courses at the same time.[28]

Some people will say: "But there is a difference between three in the morning, four in the evening, and four in the morning, three in the evening." But there is not much point in making the distinction. For Zhuang Zi, the realists are not so much wrong as being too serious and narrow in their view. J. P. Sartre called people who are too serious "stinkers," the word Zhuang Zi would have used. Zhuang Zi's view is that the so-called "reality" is as dynamic and ever-changing as human life. He is concerned that human beings often violate Dao with their minds. To know Dao and live in accordance with Dao, we must realize the capability and limitations of our minds. Here we have Lao Zi's advice: "To know that you do not know is best. To pretend to know when you do not know is a disease. Only when one recognizes this disease as a disease can one be free from the disease."[29]

To know the world we need not only look at it but also understand the functions of our language. Indeed, to dissociate our language from our knowledge of the world is impossible. The use of language is a human action that often produces knowledge. Zhuang Zi says: "A road becomes so when people walk on it, and things become so-and-so to people because people call them so-and-so. How have they become so? They have become so because people say they are so. How have they become not so? They have become not so because people say they have become not so."[30] Zhuang Zi is trying to get us to attend to our way of relating to things as responsible, in part, for the way things are to us. We may become so accustomed to our way of relating to things that we "forget"[31] that this is just one of the many means to an end. Forgetting this, we also forget how to "follow two courses at the same time."

To follow two courses at the same time, we need to transcend the limitation of our language. Concepts and theories are human mental constructs. They are useful tools for dealing with the world. The use of these tools generates distinctions and separations and at the same time limits our view of the world. So long as we use concepts and theories to view the world, our world is inevitably categorized and limited by our mental constructs. To peer at the world as it is, we need to apprehend it directly and without any preconceived ideas. Thus, only the mystic see the world as it presents itself to the mystic vision. Zhuang Zi uses the metaphor of a mirror to illustrate this mystic vision: "The mind of a perfect man is like a mirror. It does not lean forward or backward in its response to things. It responds to things but conceals nothing on its own. Therefore, it is able to deal with things without injury to their reality."[32] Ordinary people see the world through the spectacles of our conceptual-linguistic framework. This conceptual-linguistic framework is like the grid on a surface. It is used to study the world. It is something we impose on the real world in the process of trying to understand it. But it is not the real world. The right course of action is not to enrich our language or improve it, or purify it, but to transcend our language and "forget"[33] it. This is so because beyond a stage of understanding, language no longer serves its purpose but stands in the way of comprehending the world as a unifying whole in which all the separations and distinctions (including the opposition between the self and the world) are overcome. Speaking of Dao and human intellect, Zhuang Zi says: "The fish nets serve to catch fish; let us take the fish and forget the nets. . . . Words exist because of meaning; once you've gotten the meaning, you can forget the words. Where can I find a man who has forgotten words so I can have a word with him?"[34] These words are intended as paradoxical. As noted earlier, in order to avoid contradiction, we should construe "forget" in the sense of ceasing to care and not in the sense of losing memory or the ability to do something. Zhuang Zi's remarks here are his ingenious "words" which can stimulate the production of philosophical insights but which we must "forget" in order to get at the very thing itself.

Zhuang Zi's Philosophy of Life.

According to Zhuang Zi, free and full exercise of

one's natural ability is happiness. The secret of relative happiness is to live in harmony with nature and follow what is natural in oneself. This Daoist lifestyle will enable one to gain a realistic perspective about things in the world and thus achieve peace of mind and release from bondage. Human misery and suffering are the "penalty of violating the principle of nature." The pain inflicted on man by his own mind is the result of the lack of understanding. For example, a child who is prevented from going out to play because of rain may become angry or sad. A sensible adult in the same situation will not suffer anger or sadness because he understands things better than the child. So, the greater the understanding of things, the less we will suffer from them. Consequently, we enjoy greater happiness.

Fear of death or anxiety about it is one major source of human unhappiness. But this need not be the case. Zhuang Zi says that if we understand the principle of relativity, then we will understand that life and death are relative phases of the process of Dao. When Zhuang Zi's wife died, Hui Zi, a dialectician, went to convey his condolences but was surprised and disgusted to find Zhuang Zi drumming upon an inverted rice bowl and singing a song. Hui Zi said: "She lived with you, brought up your children, and grew old. That you should not mourn her is bad enough, but pounding on a bowl and singing--this is going too far, isn't it?"[35] Zhuang Zi said:

> You misjudge me. When she died I was
> in despair, as any man well might be.
> But soon, pondering on what had
> happened, I told myself that in death
> no strange new fate befalls us. . . .
> If someone is tired and has gone to
> lie down we do not pursue him with
> hooting and bawling. She whom I have
> lost has lain down to sleep for

awhile in the Great Inner Room. To
break in upon her rest with noise of
lamentation would but show that I
know nothing of nature's Sovereign
Law. That is why I ceased to
mourn.[36]

Death is but one phase of the process of <u>Dao</u>. It is
rest and peace. "How do I know that loving life is not
a delusion? How do I know that in hating death I am
not like a man who having left home in his youth, has
forgotten the way back?"[37] Zhuang Zi is using his
understanding of natural laws to disperse his despair.
He still has emotions, but he manages not to be
disturbed by them. What Spinoza calls "the peace of
the soul" is what Zhuang Zi experiences here. Spinoza
says:

The ignorant man is not only agitated
by external causes in many ways, and
never enjoys true peace of the soul,
but lives also ignorant, as it were,
both of God and of things, and as
soon as he ceases to suffer, ceases
also to be. On the other hand, the
wise man, insofar as he is considered
as such, is scarcely moved in his
mind, but, being conscious by a
certain external necessity of
himself, of God, and things, never
ceases to be, and always enjoys the
peace of the soul.[38]

Zhuang Zi believes that man is a spiritual being who
can, through an understanding of nature, attain a state
of freedom which annuls all bondage. Spinoza's
"intellectual love of God" (<u>amor</u> <u>Dei</u> <u>intellectualis</u>) is
an act of understanding and love which brings us inner
freedom and independence. But, for Spinoza, God is
Nature. Hence, Zhuang Zi and Spinoza are making the

same point.

Zhuang Zi suggests in chapter one ("Free and Easy Wandering") of Zhuang Zi that the way to obtain absolute happiness is to identify oneself with Dao. Do not set your individual consciousness aside from the rest of the universe. Drop the shackles of human convention, put away your anxious thought, and wander alone with Dao in the kingdom of the Great Void! Happy is the man who transcends not only the ordinary distinctions of things but also the distinction between the self and the world, the "me" and the "not-me."

Since everything except Dao is relative, to take worldly things seriously is silly. Indeed, to strive with fanatical zeal to achieve success or wealth is ridiculous. A man who is intent on success at all costs is like a patient suffering from a high fever. Zhuang Zi repeatedly counsels us to value our internal freedom, not the external position or wealth. Zhuang Zi has a profound disinterest in the things the world prizes. The following two stories of Zhuang Zi bring out this point and also serve as examples of Zhuang Zi's sardonic wit:

> Once, when Zhuang Zi was fishing in the Pu River, the king of Qu sent two officials to announce to him: "I would like to trouble you with the administration of my realm." Zhuang Zi held on to the fishing pole and, without turning his head, said, "I have heard that there is a sacred tortoise in Qu that has been dead for three thousand years. The king keeps it wrapped in cloth and boxed, and stores it in the ancestral temple. Now would this tortoise rather be dead and have its bones left behind and honored? Or would it rather be

alive and dragging its tail in the mud?" "It would rather be alive and dragging its tail in the mud," said the two officials. Zhuang Zi said, "Go away, I'll drag my tail in the mud."[39]

When Hui Zi was prime minister of Liang, Zhuang Zi set off to visit him. Someone said to Hui Zi, "Zhuang Zi is coming because he wishes to replace you as prime minister!" With this Hui Zi was filled with alarm and searched all over the state for three days and three nights trying to find Zhuang Zi. Zhuang Zi then came to see him and said, "In the south there is a bird called the Yüan Qu--I wonder if you have ever heard of it? The Yüan Qu rises up from the South Sea and flies to the North Sea, and it will rest on nothing but the Wu-tong tree, eat nothing save the fruit of the Lian (Persian lilac), and drink only from springs of sweet water. Once there was an owl who had gotten hold of a half-rotten old rat, and as the Yüan Qu passed by, it raised its head, looked up at the Yüan Qu, and said, 'Shoo!' Now that you have this Liang state of yours, are you trying to shoo me?"[40]

Zhuang Zi elaborates Lao Zi's concept of wu-wei and uses the examples of a butcher and an archer to illustrate the meaning of wu-wei. There was a butcher whose knife did not get dull for nineteen years. He was so skillful in butchering oxen that it was said that even after an ox had been cut up into pieces, the ox still did not know that he was dead. His secret was to seek out the empty space between the bones or ligaments and pass his knife through it. This is the way he worked:

> I go at it by spirit and don't look with my eyes. Perception and understanding have come to a stop and spirit moves where it wants. I go along with the natural makeup, strike in the big hollows, guide the knife through the big openings, and follow things as they are. So I never touch the smallest ligament or tendon, much less a main joint. A good butcher changes his knife once a year because he cuts. A mediocre butcher changes his knife once a month because he hacks. I've had this knife of mine for nineteen years and I've cut up thousands of oxen with it, and yet the blade is as good as though it had just come from the grindstone.[41]

An archer who is shooting for fun may shoot accurately. But offer him a prize of gold if he hits the mark, he will become tense, thinking about how important it is to hit the mark, and he will miss the mark!

Zhuang Zi aims at smashing the conventional values, particularly Confucian morality. He ridicules the sober Confucianists for not understanding the relativity of good and bad, right and wrong, truth and falsity, beauty and ugliness. Take thievery, for example. Those who stole nations became kings and dukes, and those who stole such small items as "fishing hooks" were condemned as thiefs and punished accordingly. Who are the worse thieves, the kings and dukes who killed thousands of innocent people to steal a nation or the small man who was forced by hunger to steal a fishing hook? The bigger the crime, the more do people glory in it. Zhuang Zi argues that the Confucianists, by glorifying the bigger crimes and condemning the smaller ones, committed a hypocritical act. Moreover, the kings and dukes who they glorify might not have the virtues as may be possessed by a common thief. Zhuang Zi attempts to correct what he considers to be Confucian rigidity and hypocrisy by inventing stories about Confucius and his followers. In one of the stories, Confucius tries to persuade the notorious robber Chi to give up his "evil ways." But the robber Chi scolds him:

> Topped with a cap like a branching tree, wearing a girdle made from the ribs of a dead cow, you pour out your flood of words, your fallacious theories. You eat without ever plowing, clothe yourself without ever weaving. Wagging your lips, clacking your tongue, you invent any kind of "right" or "wrong" that suits you, leading astray the rulers of the world, keeping the scholars of the world from returning to the Source, capriciously setting up ideals of "filial piety" and "brotherliness." All the time hoping to worm your way into favor with the lords of the fiefs or the rich and eminent! Your crimes are huge, your offenses grave, You had better run home as fast as you can, because if you don't, I will take your liver and add it to this afternoon's menu.[42]

Trembling all over, Confucius tries to talk about the virtues of bravery, righteousness, wisdom, and justice. But robber Chi claims to possess these virtues himself. Chi says: "Qiu (Confucius's personal name), come forward! Those who can be swayed with offer of gain or reformed by a babble of words are mere idiots, simpletons, the commonest of men. . . . To know where the valuables are hidden indicates high intelligence. To enter into a house first shows bravery. To leave it last is an act of righteousness. To know whether to enter a house or not is wisdom, and to divide spoils according to merits is justice. It is impossible to become a great robber without possessing all of these five virtues."[43]

One of the best known passages in <u>Zhuang Zi</u> is the following:

> Zhuang Zi and Hui Zi were strolling along the dam of the Hao River when Zhuang Zi said: "See how the minnows come out and dart around where they please! That's what fish really enjoy!" Hui Zi said: "You're not a fish--how do you know what fish enjoy?" Zhuang Zi said: "You are not I, so how do you know I don't know what fish enjoy." Hui Zi said: "I am not you, so I certainly don't know what you know. On the other hand, you are certainly not a fish-- so that still proves you don't know what fish enjoy!" Zhuang Zi said: "Let's go back to your original question, please. You ask me <u>how</u> I know what fish enjoy--so you already knew I knew it when you asked the question. I know it by standing here beside the Hao."[44]

My reaction to the passage when I first read it was: "That is a piece of Zhuang Zi's sophistry! Surely Hui Zi's question 'How do you know what fish enjoy?' does not imply that Zhuang Zi knew it. Hui Zi was asking for an explanation or justification of Zhuang Zi's claim that he knew it." However, repeated readings of Zhuang Zi yielded a deeper meaning of the passage. Zhuang Zi's comment on what fish really enjoy reveals his way of relating to that situation. When standing beside the river Hao and seeing the fish dart around, Zhuang Zi chose not to discriminate between himself and the minnows or between himself and the beautiful riverside scenery. Hui Zi's question arises when we choose to emphasize the difference between Zhuang Zi and the fishes. But if so, Zhuang Zi would then emphasize the difference between Zhuang Zi and Hui Zi and say, "How do you know that I don't know?" Zhuang Zi would also entrap Hui Zi by the logic of his own use of the word "how." Zhuang Zi's point is that by asking "How do you know?" Hui Zi has committed the sin of "three in the morning" mentioned earlier in the story of the monkeys and the monkeykeeper. Hui Zi, like the monkeys, insists on the difference, and so errs. Zhuang Zi adds: "Let them if they want to. The wise unite what is and what is not. . . . This is called walking two roads."[45] "The sage embraces things. Ordinary people discriminate among them and parade their discrimination before others."[46]

Zhuang Zi did not believe that arguments prove anything, although he was good at argument and enjoyed the sport.

> Suppose you and I argue. If you beat
> me instead of my beating you, are you
> really right and am I really wrong?
> If I beat you instead of your beating
> me, am I really right and are you
> really wrong? Or are we both partly
> right and partly wrong? Or are we
> both wholly right and wholly wrong?
> Since between us neither you nor I
> know which is right, others are
> naturally in the dark. Whom shall we
> ask to arbitrate? If we ask someone

who agrees with you, since he has already agreed with you, how can he arbitrate? If we ask someone who agrees with me, since he has already agreed with me, how can he arbitrate? If we ask someone who disagrees with both you and me to arbitrate, since he has already disagreed with you and me, how can he arbitrate? If we ask someone who agrees with both you and me, since he has already agreed with you and me, how can he arbitrate? Thus among you, me, and others, none knows which is right. Shall we wait for still others?[47]

d. Daoist Philosophy and Daoist Magic.

Most books on Daoism caution the readers not to confuse philosophical Daoism with religious Daoism. Philosophical Daoism is the corpus of the philosophical ideas and theses presented by Lao Zi and Zhuang Zi, whereas religious Daoism is a hodgepodge of necromancy, alchemy, sorcery, and other magical prescriptions and practices. I prefer to contrast Daoist philosophy with Daoist magic rather than contrasting philosophical Daoism with religious Daoism, for it is difficult to distinguish philosophy from religion, especially in China.

Many Daoists have sought to gain physical immortality and supernatural power by necromancy, alchemy, meditation, and hygienic practices. Given Lao Zi's and Zhuang Zi's view of death as one phase of the transformation of natural process, the quest for physical immortality is contradictory to Daoist philosophy. Perhaps the philosophical ideas of Lao Zi and Zhuang Zi are too subtle and profound for ordinary people to grasp. When the literal-minded people read Zhuang Zi, they often misunderstand the metaphors

Zhuang Zi uses and miss points. They take Zhuang Zi's talk about nurturing the vital energy (qi) to mean the possibility of physical immortality, while Zhuang Zi's mystical knowledge (knowledge of the unifying Dao) becomes supernatural power for them. When Zhuang Zi talks about fast, meditation, nurturing vital energy, he is interested only in mental clarity, not in achieving physical feats that ordinary people are incapable of. In fact, he ridicules the people who try to achieve immortality or other unnatural ends by breath control or stretching and pulling their body in all sorts of ways. But the language of Zhuang Zi's ridicule is so subtle that the literal-minded people could read Zhuang Zi and take it as supporting their practices. One interesting technique which the Daoist magicians claim can enable a practitioner to achieve longevity (and even immortality) is the "embryonic breath." That is to try to breathe in the way the Daoist magicians imagine an infant in the womb would breathe. They counsel a practitioner to lie in bed all day, eat and drink little, hold the breath for a hundred counts and gradually extend to a thousand counts. The assumption is that the person's vital energy (qi) is a limited constant. By breathing slowly one would use up this precious vital energy slowly and thus live longer. This is a "biological clock" theory. The counting of breath suggests that they believe that a person's lifespan can be determined in a mathematically precise manner. One who works hard-- "burns the candle at both ends"-- would live half as long as one who works half as hard.

Daoist magicians formed quasi-religious organizations and had been active in the funeral business. They generated a massive literature of superstitious writings. Some Daoist magicians were embroiled in politics and sponsored violent revolutionary groups. The "boxers" of the Boxers' Rebellion (1898-1900 A.D.) fame were the latest in Chinese history.

In a positive way, Daoism has been associated with the popular Chinese slow motion exercise called "Tai Ji Qŭan" (supreme ultimate exercise). A thirteenth-century Daoist priest named Zhang San-feng (d. 1283 A.D.) is said to have systematized this exercise. It is a graceful, rhythmic exercise, consisting of a sequence of choreographed movements which is executed slowly with breath control and mental concentration. It has been aptly described as "meditation in motion." One can learn to execute the whole sequence of 108 movements so smoothly and effortlessly that one experiences wu-wei. Inasmuch as Chinese philosophy emphasizes practice and experience, perhaps the practice of Tai Ji Qŭan has philosophical relevance. In Psychological Reflections, Carl G. Jung says of Indian philosophy that one cannot understand it without practicing yoga. The same can be said of Daoism and Tai Ji Qŭan.

Notes

Chapter 3

1. Cf. Huai Nan Zi, 13.7a, and Lieh Zi, 7.1b-2a.

2. "The Biography of Lao Zi" in Si-ma Qian, Historical Records.

3. Zhuang Zi, ch. 14.

4. Lao Zi on the back of a water buffalo is a favorite subject of Chinese painters.

5. English translation of the text comes to about 10,000 words.

6. Dao De Jing, ch. 56.

7. Dao De Jing, ch. 21.

8. Ibid., ch. 41.

9. Ibid., ch. 25.

10. Ibid., ch. 42.

11. Ibid., ch. 37.

12. Ibid., ch. 27.

13. Ibid., ch. 57.

14. Ibid., ch. 17.

15. Ibid., ch. 57.

16. Ibid., ch. 30.

17. *Ibid.*, ch. 29.

18. *Ibid.*, ch. 33.   "He who dies but does not really perish enjoys long life" may be taken as meaning immortality of virtue or influence.

19. *Ibid.*, ch. 12.

20. *Ibid.*, ch. 9.

21. *Ibid.*, ch. 24.

22. *Ibid.*, ch. 29.

23. *Zhuang Zi*, ch. 2.

24. This is the story Zhuang Zi invented about himself. Cf. end of ch. 32, *Zhuang Zi*.

25. *Ibid.*, ch. 2.

26. *Ibid.*

27. *Ibid.*, ch. 6.

28. *Ibid.*, ch. 2.

29. *Dao De Jing*, ch. 71.

30. *Zhuang Zi*, ch. 2.

31. The word "forget" here is used in the sense of losing memory or ability to do something.

32. *Ibid.*, ch. 7.

33. The word "forget" here is used in the sense of ceasing to care.

34. Ibid., ch. 26.

35. Ibid., ch. 18. "Perfect Happiness."

36. Ibid.

37. Ibid., ch. 2.

38. Spinoza, Ethics, part 5, proposition XLII.

39. Zhuang Zi, ch.17. "Autumn Flood."

40. Ibid.

41. Ibid., ch. 3.

42. Ibid., ch. 29. "Robber Chi."

43. Ibid.

44. Ibid., ch. 17.

45. Ibid., ch. 2.

46. Ibid.

47. Ibid.

Chapter 4

Mohism: The Religious Utilitarianism

a. Mo Zi: The Founder and His Social Background

Mohism is the philosophy founded by Mo Zi (c. 479-438 B.C.). We add the silent letter "h" to disyllabize the words "Mohism" and "Mohist." By adding the letter "h" we avoid having to spell them "Moist," and "Moism." Mo Zi was born shortly after the death of Confucius, in central northern China, probably in the state of Song. His family name is Mo which has a host of meanings in the Chinese language. His given name is Di. He was probably an unemployed military specialist or engineer. He was strict, authoritarian, and dogmatic both in his philosophy and in his personal conduct. As we will see, some of Mo Zi's ideas strike many people as very un-Chinese in that they are uncongenial to the tone and flavor of Chinese life. Mohism is the only philosophy in China that requires the existence of God and spirits to ensure the world's moral order. Yet one hundred years after the death of Confucius, Mohists became vocal critics of Confucianism and were competing with Confucian scholars for the mind of the Chinese. Confucianists won out. But Mencius felt so threatened by the Mohists that he had to criticize them rhetorically and repeatedly.

Si-ma Qian's Historical Records mentions Mo Zi's name but does not provide any biographical information. Consequently, many conjectures exist regarding Mo Zi's family origin and social background. "Mo" in Chinese means "black, lampblack, ink, the dark mark of a brand or a tatoo." Some scholars conjectured that "Mo" is not a surname but rather an adjective or a title ("the black one," "the dark one,") designating a social class (slaves), a trade (craftsman-builder, black-smith), or people who have been punished by branding on the forehead. Because of Mo Zi's un-Chinese ideas and some linguistic oddities contained in Mo Zi, some suggest that he was an Indian who had a dark complexion. Whatever Mo Zi was, he had a humble background. The book of Mo Zi contains 53 chapters. It is believed to have originally contained 71 chapters, but 18 have been lost. The main themes of the book are jian-ai (universal love, all-embracing love), utilitarianism, and the existence of God and the spirits. Chapters 40-45 of the book are sometimes collectively referred to as the "Mohist Canons," which deals with technical subjects of logic, mathematics, and theory of knowledge. Although the purpose of the "Mohist Canons" is to defend the Mohist doctrines and to refute the arguments of other schools, the "Mohist Canons" does have an intrinsic value and is of special interest to logicians and epistemologists. The 53 chapters of Mo Zi are the work of several authors rather than of Mo Zi alone. Because of the respect for authority and tradition, Chinese authors often attributed their works to some authority figure who was well known by the people.

Recent studies suggest that Mo Zi and his followers came from the class of xia or yu-xia (knights-errant). They were military specialists who in the late Zhou dynasty lost their relatively high social status and titles and became unemployed because of the disintegration of Zhou's feudal system. Mo Zi organized them into a strictly disciplined group capable of military operations. Si-ma Qian says of them that "Their words were always sincere and trustworthy, and their actions always quick and decisive. They were always true to what they promised, and without regard to their own persons, they would rush into dangers threatening others."[1] This organized group of soldiers and engineers pledged no loyalty to any sovereign or state but only to the principles as interpreted by Mo Zi. To the members of this group, Mo Zi's rules prevailed regardless of the laws of the state. Their professional ethic was that they would engage in defensive actions only, never in offensive actions, and that within their group, they would "enjoy equally and suffer equally." Mo Zi and his followers had a solid background in military strategy and engineering which are conducive to analytical thinking; hence the analytical nature of the Mohist Canons. Mo Zi extended the dictum "enjoy equally and suffer equally" to the doctrine that everyone should love everyone else in the world equally and without discrimination. He gave the name "jian-ai" (universal love) to this doctrine. Being warriors, the Mohists lived in constant contact with death. This probably has some bearing on their belief in God and the spirits.

Mo Zi was the first Chü Zi (the supreme head, the supreme leader) of the Mohist organization. New recruits of this organization were subjected to strict discipline, eating only a bowl of vegetable soup a day. Membership in this organization was permanent. The Chü Zi had the authority of life or death over the members of the group throughout their lifetime. We know that Mo Zi once recalled a disciple who was an official in the state of Qi because he participated in a war of aggression waged by Qi. Although this organization became extinct in China, for a period of about two hundred years around the time of Mencius, this organization flourished in many parts of China and formed "states within states" of late Zhou dynasty.

Mo Zi believed that warfare, which has its root in hatred, is the greatest cause of human suffering, for it is the most wasteful of human life and treasure. He proposed that we replace hatred with love. Yet he was no pacifist. He advocated non-aggression, not nonviolence. All the wars he and his group engaged in were defenses against attackers. Being a practical man, he did not believe in "turning the other cheek." His view of universal love does not entail nonviolence.

91

Violence is indeed deplorable, nevertheless sometimes one has to use it to prevent further or greater violence because persuasion is often ineffective and slow in yielding results. This is consistent with Mo Zi's utilitarianism. In a time of frequent wars among the states, Mo Zi spoke for the poor and the downtrodden who suffered the most. He recruited his followers from what we would call the lower and the middle class people. For the common people in Mo Zi's time, such things as dance, music, and rituals were luxuries that were out of their reach and, so far as they were concerned, wasteful and utterly useless. Nor could they afford elaborate and expensive funerals and long mourning periods advocated by the Confucianists. Although Confucius himself insisted on three years' mourning period for the death of one's parents, he did not advocate elaborate or expensive funerals. Mo Zi studied Confucianism for awhile, but rejected it on the grounds that Confucian humanistic study for general liberal arts purposes is a luxury for the aristocrats and that Confucianism's emphases on rites, filial piety, and family loyalty exacerbate the troubles of the society. In Mo Zi's mind, an ideal society is a welfare state of material sufficiency where the basic material needs of the people are satisfied rather than a moral commonwealth with emphasis on intangible values.

b. Controversies with the Confucianists.

In chapter 39 of Mo Zi, entitled "Anti-Confucianism," Mo Zi says:

> Even those with long life cannot exhaust the learning required for their [Confucianist] studies. Even people with the vigor of youth cannot perform all the ceremonial duties. And even those who have amassed wealth cannot afford music. They

> [the Confucianists] enhance the
> beauty of wicked arts and lead their
> sovereign astray. Their doctrine
> cannot meet the needs of the age, nor
> can their learning educate the
> people.

Elsewhere Mo Zi says: "The Confucianists insist on elaborate funerals and the practice of three years of mourning on the death of a parent so that the wealth and energy of the people are thereby wasted."[2] In Mo Zi's opinion, customs and conventions that require the expenditure of much wealth and energy but with no real increase of material well-being should not be condoned but should be abolished. Borrowing to pay for a funeral when one has not enough to eat is senseless. To favor the dead at the expense of the living is illogical. But "at the death of a feudal lord the treasury of the state would be emptied to surround his body with gold, jade, and pearls, and fill his grave with bundles of silk and carts and horses."[3] This kind of waste filled Mo Zi's heart with horror. Three years' mourning required that the individual resign from his work and spend three years in a mourning hut, eating little and doing no work but remembering and honoring the deceased. This also implies that the individual must observe the rule of chastity for at least three years. Mo Zi says that all these practices of burial and mourning interfere with the normal working of the government and economic production, reduce the population, and impoverish the state. Mo Zi recommends that coffins be thin and inexpensive and the mourning period brief (three days for the death of a parent, less for the death of other relatives). The individual should return to his work and be productive again. Mourning for the dead is pointless and silly anyway, for no amount of wail would bring back the deceased. Observing the rules of chastity for three years often destroys the sexual relations between husband and wife, Mo Zi says. Mo Zi has a good point

93

in the following passage which caricatures the Confucianists but is not too far from the truth.

> For if elaborate funerals and extended mourning are adopted as the rule, then upon the death of a ruler there will be three years' mourning; upon the death of a parent there will be three years' mourning; upon the death of a wife or eldest son there will be three years' mourning. There will be three years' mourning for all five relatives. Besides, there will be one year for uncles, brothers and other sons; five months for the near relatives; and also several months for aunts, sisters, nephews, and uncles on the mother's side. Further, there are set rules to make oneself emaciated. The face and eyes are to look sunken, and the complexion to appear dark. Eyes and ears are to become dull, and hands and feet are to become weak and useless.[4]

Mo Zi points out that the Confucianists are inconsistent in stressing the funeral and sacrificial rituals while not believing in the existence of spirits. "To hold that there are no spirits, and yet to learn sacrificial ceremonies, is like learning the ceremonies of hospitality when there are no guests, or throwing fish nets when there are no fish."[5]

The Confucianists' reply to the charge of inconsistency is that the performance of funeral or sacrificial rituals serves the purpose of releasing one's emotions and expressing one's respect and love toward the departed. Although originally the belief in the existence of the departed spirits motivated the people to perform these rituals, this is no longer the case with civilized Confucianists. For them, the significance of the rituals is poetic, not religious. The Confucianists then turn the argument around and charge the Mohists of inconsistency in claiming to believe in the existence of the spirits and yet opposing the performance of rituals for the spirits. However, from a utilitarian point of view, no conflict exists. Mo Zi argued for the existence of God and the spirits to induce the people to practice the doctrine of universal love, for God and the spirits invariably reward those who practice the doctrine in their life and punish those who do not. In short, the belief in God and the spirits has utility. So has the abolition of rituals for God and the spirits. Hence, a Mohist can say no inconsistency exists after all.

Mo Zi accuses the Confucianists of having preached fatalism which destroys the value of free will and the foundation of morality.

> Finally, they [the Confucianists] suppose there is a fate, and that poverty or wealth, old age or untimely death, order or chaos, security or danger, all are predetermined and cannot be altered. Applying this belief, those in authority of course will not attend to work. This is sufficient to ruin the world.[6]

Reiterating his objection to the belief in fate in a special chapter devoted to this purpose, Mo Zi says:

> [If people believe in fatalism] they would not be filial to their parents at home and respectful to the elders in the village and in the district. They would not observe propriety in

95

conduct, moderation in going out and coming in, or decency between men and women. And if they were made to look after the court they would steal, if they were made to defend a city they would rebel. . . . The unnatural adherence to this doctrine [fatalism] is responsible for pernicious ideas and is the way of the wicked.[7]

Mo Zi wants to say that people are responsible for their actions. If people work hard and produce more, they will be rewarded; but if people are lazy and wasteful, they will be punished. The future outcome depends on what we do now. Fatalism contradicts all these propositions. Therefore Mo Zi goes to great length to refute it. He presents his three tests of the value of any doctrine, including fatalism, as follows:

Some standard of judgment must be established. To expound a doctrine without regard to the standard is similar to determining the directions of sunrise and sunset on a revolving potter's wheel. By this means the distinction of right and wrong, benefit and harm, can be known. Therefore there must be tests. What are the three tests? Mo Zi says: its basis, its verifiability, and its applicability. On what is it to be based? It is to be based on the deeds of the ancient sage kings. How is it to be verified? It is to be verified on the senses of hearing and sight of the common people. How is it to be applied? It is to be applied by adopting it in government and observing its benefits to the

country and to the people. This is
what is meant by the three tests of
any doctrine.[8]

Mo Zi then applies these three tests to the doctrine of
fatalism and criticizes it on the following grounds
(which correspond to the three tests):

(1) Fatalism is not in accordance with the will
of Heaven or the teachings of the ancient sage kings.
This is proved by quoting profusely from the classics
which record the teachings of the ancient sage kings.
These quotations also imply that Heaven punishes
severely those who believe in fatalism and rewards
those who do not believe in fatalism. Since our first
duty is to obey the will of Heaven, we must reject
fatalism.

(2) The real existence of fate cannot be proved
by any means. It cannot be proved empirically by the
senses of hearing and sight, for no one from the
beginning of time to the present could testify that he
ever saw or heard _directly_ from such a thing as fate.
Moreover, it cannot be proved morally, because all
moral arguments require the nonexistence of fate.

(3) Fatalism is the creation of tyrants who want
to enslave the people by making them believe in fate,
thereby blaming their miseries on fate rather than the
tyrants. Fatalism is used by bandits and other evil-
doers to justify their actions and to escape from
responsibility. Lazy people welcome fatalism and use
it as an excuse for their non-productivity. When we
see how fatalism works in the world, we know that we
must reject it.

In arguing against fatalism, Mo Zi does not offer
any positive argument for human free will. So far as
Mo Zi is concerned, common sense tells us that one
reaps what one sowed, and this is good enough for him.

A positive argument that will prove we have free will still remains to be made by philosophers. Mo Zi also uses the three tests to support his claim that God (Heaven) and spirits exist. But his argument is considerably weaker than his argument against fatalism.

Let us assume that Mo Zi's refutation of fatalism is successful. Does it follow that Confucianism has been refuted or that Confucianism has been legitimately criticized? Not at all. In attacking fatalism Mo Zi is attacking a strawman, for the Confucianists do not believe in the predetermined fate attacked by Mo Zi. Confucius and Confucianists did often speak of <u>Ming</u> (命). <u>Ming</u> may mean fate, destiny , or decree. To the Confucianists, it means the Decree of Heaven or forces of the whole universe. Confucius says: "At fifty I knew the Decree of Heaven"[9] and "He who does not know <u>Ming</u> cannot be a superior man."[10] By "knowing <u>Ming</u>," Confucius means "knowing the working of the forces of the universe." Success or failure may depend on the existence of these existent conditions or forces of the universe. But a person's moral worth does not depend on success or failure. Some things in life are undeniably beyond our control. However, it does not follow that whatever we do makes no difference to the future outcome. We should do our best concerning the things that we know we should do, without caring for the chances of success or failure. This attitude confers upon us a spirit of equanimity. If one knows that one has done everything one can, one will be able to face the future calmly. To characterize this attitude as fatalistic in the sense Mo Zi describes is mistaken. Therefore Mo Zi's argument against fatalism, if taken as a criticism of Confucianism, commits the fallacy of <u>ignoratio elenchi</u> (irrelevant conclusion, or missing the point).

Mo Zi's argument against music is similar to his argument against rituals. The making of musical instruments requires people's time and natural resources. The training of singers and instrument players also requires considerable labor. Yet the performance of music produces nothing tangible, Mo Zi says. "What is it that causes rulers to neglect government and common men to neglect their work? Music. Therefore, Mo Zi says, 'It is wrong to play music.'"[11] For the Mohists, there should be no singing in life and no mourning in death. But the Confucianists appreciate the high value of music. To the Confucianists, music produces pleasure, purifies emotions, and ennobles human nature. Apparently, Mo Zi not only condemns all pleasure but also wants to eliminate all emotion. He says: "Joy and anger, pleasure and sorrow, love and hate, are to be got rid of."[12]

Since the controversy between the Mohists and the Confucianists over the nature of love has acquired notoriety and philosophical significance, let us examine this controversy in greater detail.

The controversy arises from Mo Zi's interpretation of the central Confucian concepts of ren (love, human-heartedness) and yi (righteousness). For Mo Zi, ren and yi signify an all-embracing love. The practice of ren and yi entails that we love all people equally, just as Heaven loves all people equally. However, as the Confucianists conceive it, love emanates from a person's inner self and extends outward toward the world in different degrees according to the closeness of the receiving persons. Thus, we should love our parents more than a stranger in the street. Since the closest human relationship is between parents and children, the Confucianists emphasize the priority of filial piety. Though Mo Zi does not criticize the notion of filial piety per se, he points out that to think only of one's family is clannish and selfish and that family welfare was often advanced by the Confucianists at the expense of the welfare of the whole society. The welfare of the whole society, Mo Zi insists, should be our first concern. The aim of morality is "the greatest happiness of the greatest number," happiness being defined narrowly in material terms. This is utilitarian morality. A thing is good if it demonstrably results in material benefits to all people equally.

The text most often used in the discussion of this controversy reads as follows:

> Wu Ma-zi said to Mo Zi: "I differ from you, I cannot love universally. . . . I love the people of Zou better than the people of Qu, the people of Lu better than the people of Zou, the people of my district better than the people of Lu, the members of my family better than the people of my district, my parents better than others. This is because of their nearness to me. When I am beaten, I feel pain. When they are beaten, the pain does not extend to me. Why should I resist what does not give me pain and not resist what does give me pain? Therefore I would rather have them killed to benefit me than to have me killed to benefit them." Mo Zi said: "Is this view of yours to be kept secret or to be told to others?" Wu Ma-zi replied: "Why should I keep my opinion to myself? Of course I should tell it to others." Mo Zi said: "Then if one person is pleased with your doctrine, there will be one person who will desire to kill you in order to benefit himself. If ten persons are pleased with your doctrine, there will be ten persons who will desire

to kill you in order to benefit themselves. If the people of the whole world are pleased with your doctrine, the whole world will desire to kill you to benefit themselves. On the other hand, if one person is not pleased with you, there will be one person who will desire to kill you as the propagator of an evil doctrine. If ten persons are not pleased with you, there will be ten persons who will desire to kill you as the propagator of an evil doctrine. If the people of the whole world are not pleased with you, the whole world will desire to kill you as the propagator of an evil doctrine. So then those who are pleased with you desire to kill you and those who are not pleased with you also desire to kill you. This is to say what passes out from your mouth is what kills your body!" Mo Zi continued: "Then, where, after all, does the benefit of your doctrine lie?"[13]

Insofar as Wu Ma-zi says that he loves all people, only some people more than others, he is on safe ground. However, he goes too far in stating that he would rather kill other people to benefit himself. Mo Zi seizes the opportunity to trap Wu Ma-zi in a dilemma. A dilemma is a common form of argument. It has the structure of a valid argument. Whether it is sound depends on the premises of the argument. Either people are pleased with your doctrine or they are not. In either case, your doctrine works against you. Nevertheless, Mo Zi has not answered the main objection to his doctrine of universal love, namely, that to love all people equally is unnatural and unreasonable. For this reason, Mo Zi is criticized by Mencius as having taught an absolutely equal love toward one's parents and toward strangers in the street. Mencius continues rhetorically that to treat our parents as strangers in the street is to behave like beasts. "To love all equally which does not acknowledge the peculiar affection due to a father . . . is to be in the state of beasts."[14]

In fairness to Mo Zi, I must say that nowhere in the 53 chapters of Mo Zi can one find a single instance in which Mo Zi teaches people to consider their father as a stranger in the street. Mencius may have gotten his information about Mo Zi's teachings from a disciple of Mo Zi who pushed his master's teaching to an extreme. In his competition with the Mohists for followers and for the attention of the feudal lords, Mencius might have chosen to dispose of Mo Zi's doctrine rhetorically rather than trying to understand it. Even if we interpret Mo Zi's doctrine of universal love as saying that we should love strangers in the street as we love our parents, this is quite different from saying that we should love our parents as strangers in the street! Mo Zi wants us to extend our love for our parents to "strangers in the street"--our fellow human beings, and not to treat our parents as strangers. Moreover, we should extend the love of our family to other people's families, and we should extend the love of our country to other people's countries as well. This is what Mo Zi calls universal love, and hence Mo Zi advocates the equalization of love when he says we must love all people equally. Mo Zi apparently feels that the Confucianists overemphasized the love of one's parents and family at the cost of neglecting the duty of loving our fellow human beings. He says that even a thief loves his family which he supports by stealing from other families. To rectify the imbalance of love, Mo Zi proposes his doctrine of universal love. No point emphasizing what is already overemphasized. But not emphasizing family and personal love does not necessarily indicate opposition to them. Mo Zi urges us to love all people equally inasmuch as they are members of the human race. But Mo Zi never suggests that we treat all people in the same way. Heaven loves all people equally, yet Heaven rewards the just and punishes the unjust. We have different relationships with different people, and different relationships may require different behavior on our part. Yet this does not diminish the value of the general principle of universal love. One of Mo Zi's disciples puts it very well: "To me, it seems that we are to love all without difference of degree; but the manifestation of love must begin with our parents and relatives."[15] But if all the sons in the world treat all old men as their fathers, a son will not need to show particular love and attention to his own father. "Suppose that everyone in the world practiced universal love, so that everyone loved every person as much as he loves himself. Would anyone be lacking in filial piety?"[16] That Mo Zi recommends a three days' mourning period for the death of one's parent but none for strangers is enough to show that Mo Zi does not neglect the special affection between parents and children.

Another aspect of the controversy is the question whether love entails benefit. Mo Zi says yes, but the Confucianists would not talk about benefit. Basically, the difference is between Mohist utilitarianism and Confucian moralism. The motive of benefits (utilities) is behind all Mohist doctrines. Confucianists on the other hand, have criticized benefits (li) as motive throughout Chinese history. The Confucianists maintain that the motive for an action should be righteousness (yi). For the Confucianists, one important difference between a gentleman (chün zi) and an inferior man (xiao ren) is that the former's actions are motivated by yi, whereas the latter's actions are driven by li (profit). The Confucianists are not against li per se, but they insist that li should be the result of good deeds, not the motive for an action. Mo Zi also talks much about righteousness, but to him righteousness is to be understood in terms of benefits (to all people).

> The Confucianists say that wise men
> insist on loving people but they do
> not care to benefit them. This is an
> erroneous statement. What Mo Zi
> would say is that there is no love
> without benefit.[17]

For Mo Zi, love implies benefit, at least in intention. To love someone is to intend to benefit someone. To exclude the idea of benefit from the definition of love is to destroy the very concept of love. Hence, Mo Zi's doctrine should be called the doctrine of universal love and mutual benefit. Mo Zi is not satisfied in merely telling us, "love thy neighbor as thyself," but he goes further to state that we must love other people's fathers as we love our own; we must love other people's nations as we love our own; we must love other people's property as we love our own. To practice universal love is to exercise a virtue, but since a virtue permits degrees of perfection, so the virtue of universal love is not equal in each individual. Our duty is to reach the perfection of this virtue as best we can. Mo Zi states that the standard of such a perfection is the universal love of Heaven itself. Heaven is the standard of all virtues.

> The love of Heaven toward human
> beings is more universal than the
> love of a wise man toward his
> fellowmen. But the wise men love the
> common people more universally than
> the common people would love the wise
> men. And also the wise men will
> benefit the common people more
> promptly than the common people would
> benefit the wise men.[18]

The way to imitate the universal love of Heaven is to use one's most sincere and undisturbed reason to direct one's act of loving. The more one is sincere and the more one is able to keep one's reason undisturbed by the passions, then so much better is one able to reach a higher degree of perfection in morality. The source of the so-called partial and discriminated love is human passion, namely, the passion of selfishness, which always threatens to disturb the reason, even to dominate it completely. Hence, a calm mind with a clear understanding of the doctrine of universal love is the foundation of moral virtues.

Mo Zi uses utilitarian arguments to support his doctrine of universal love. Mo Zi says that those who practice "love with discrimination" believe that it is unreasonable for them to care for friends as much as they would for themselves, or to look after other people's parents as they would their own parents. Consequently, they do not do much for other people. But those who practice universal love believe that they should care for their friends as much as they would for themselves, and for other people's parents as they would their own parents. In consequence, they do everything they can for other people, and the whole world benefited as a result. Now, is there any question which principle is right? Mo Zi uses a similar argument on the following occasion:

> Wu Ma-zi said to Mo Zi: "Though you love universally, the world cannot be said to be benefited; though I do not love universally, the world cannot be said to be injured. Since neither of us has accomplished anything, what makes you then praise yourself and blame me?" Mo Zi answered: "Suppose a conflagration occurs; one person is fetching water to extinguish it, and another is holding some fuel to

reinforce it; neither of them has yet accomplished anything, but which one do you value?" Wu Ma-zi said that he approved the intention of the person who fetched water and disapproved the intention of the person who holds fuel. Mo Zi said: "In the same manner do I approve of my intention and disapprove of yours."[19]

Mo Zi here takes into consideration the intention or attitude of people in the production of benefit or harm. Every reasonable person believes that good intention or positive attitude normally causes beneficial result while bad intention or negative attitude normally causes harmful result. Mo Zi's point is that to determine which principle is right, we do not have to wait until benefit or harm is produced.

Strange as it may seem, the Confucianists such as Mencius who criticized Mo Zi's doctrine of universal love so severely, taught an almost identical doctrine. With respect to love, the difference between the Confucianists and the Mohists is more temperamental than philosophical. All the central Confucian concepts of ren, yi, zhong, shu, have to do with loving other people. Confucius urged all people under Heaven to live together peacefully and harmoniously. And this requires love. Zhuang Zi reported that Confucius taught the doctrine of universal love.[20] When Mencius came along, he paid more attention to man's inner acts and qualities of mind than did Confucius. Mencius emphasized our natural goodness, our will to do good to others. Mencius came so close to the doctrine of universal love that one wonders how Mencius could have criticized Mo Zi's teaching as dangerous. He was almost quoting Mo Zi when he said: "The man of propriety shows respect to others. . . . He who loves others is constantly loved by others."[21] On another occasion, Mencius said:

> Treat with reverence due to age the
> elders in your own family, so that
> the elders in the families of others
> shall be similarly treated; treat
> with kindness due to youth the young
> ones in your own family, so that the
> young ones in the families of others
> will be similarly treated.[22]

How close this is to Mo Zi's extension of love from
ourselves to others!

c. Logical Analysis and Empirical Methodology.

The Mohists are anti-skeptics. They believe that
intellectual certainty is both attainable and
expressible. "The Mohist Canons" was written
intentionally as an aid in ascertaining the truth. It
contains valuable logical and epistemological theories
to defend common sense against skepticism. The
analysis of knowledge and its components is as follows:
"Knowledge is that in which the knowing faculty meets
the object and is able to apprehend its form and
shape."[23] Empirical knowledge means meeting, in which
the knowing faculty meets an object and registers an
impression, as, for example, the moon. Thus, a knowing
experience contains the following elements: sense
perception, reasoning (understanding), and the object
known. Mo Zi uses the term "knowing faculty" to
include sense organs and the mind. A sense organ is
"that by which one knows but which itself does not
necessarily know."[24] The mind is "that by means of
which one understands the object of knowledge."[25] "The
Mohist Canons" also provides several logical
classifications of knowledge in accordance with
different criteria. One classification of knowledge is
as follows:

1.   Names: "A name is that with which one speaks

107

about a thing"[26] Names are to be further subdivided according to type.

2. Actualities: "An actuality is that about which one speaks."[27] Actualities are things referred to by the names.

3. Correspondence: knowledge of how names and actualities pair up to constitute further knowledge.

4. Action: knowledge about how to do things. This involves will and bodily movement.

In modern logical terms, the first corresponds to the logic of terms, the second to the logic of classes, the third to the logic of function or predication. The fourth is not a logical category, but the art of doing things.

Speaking of "the Mohist Canons," one must give credit to the Mohists for having discussed the notions of necessary and sufficient conditions, which are useful in methodological inquiries and general debate. A necessary condition may be defined as a circumstance in whose absence a specified event cannot occur. For example, oxygen is a necessary condition of combustion because without oxygen combustion is impossible; but in the presence of oxygen we may or may not have combustion. A sufficient condition may be defined as a circumstance in whose presence a specified event must occur. For example, friction is a sufficient condition of heat, because whenever we have friction we also have heat, but friction is not the only way of producing heat. A cause is defined by the Mohists as "that with which something becomes," and is classified into two kinds, the major and the minor. "A minor cause (xiao gu) is one with which something may not necessarily be so, but without which it will never be so."[28] In other words, a minor cause is what we now call a necessary condition (<u>conditio</u> <u>sine</u> <u>qua</u> <u>non</u>). "A major cause (<u>da</u> <u>gu</u>) is one with which something will necessarily be so, and without which it will never be so."[29] A major cause is what we now call a "necessary and sufficient condition." The Mohists apparently did not distinguish a "necessary and sufficient condition" from a sufficient condition. We know that on one occasion Mo Zi used the notions of necessary and sufficient conditions to explain his illness. When Mo Zi was once ill, his critic, Dieh Bi, came to him and inquired:

> Sir, you hold that the spirits are intelligent and control calamities and blessings. They reward the good and punish the evil. Now you are a sage. How then can you be ill? Is it that your teaching is not entirely correct or that the spirits are after all not intelligent?[30]

Mo Zi replied:

> Though I am ill, why should the spirits be unintelligent? There are many ways by which a man can contract diseases. Some are contracted from cold or heat, some from fatigue. If there are a hundred doors and only one be closed, will there not be ways by which robbers enter?[31]

In modern logical terminology, Mo Zi is saying that punishment by the spirits is a sufficient condition for the disease of a man, but not its necessary condition. Because punishment by the spirits is not a necessary condition of having a disease, one cannot infer from Mo Zi's illness that either Mo Zi's teaching is incorrect or the spirits are unintelligent.

For Mo Zi, all knowledge must have a solid

empirical basis. Inference means extending from that which is directly acquired through our senses to that which cannot be directly perceived. The Mohists use the word "dialectic" to designate the study of logical inference.

> Dialectic serves to make clear the distinction between right and wrong, to discriminate between order and disorder, to make evident points of similarity and difference, to examine the principles of names and actualities, to differentiate what is beneficial and what is harmful, and to remove doubts and uncertainties. It observes the happenings of all things, and investigates the order and relation between the various judgments. It uses names to designate actualities, propositions to express ideas, statements to set forth causes, and taking and giving according to classes.[32]

"The Mohist Canons" discusses seven methods of dialectic. The method of imitation and the method of extension, which roughly correspond to deduction and induction, are clearly explained. The method of imitation consists of taking a model. "What is imitated is what is taken as a model. If the cause is in agreement with the imitation, it is correct. If it is not in agreement with the imitation, it is not correct."[33] An example will make it clearer. Suppose we want to find out whether potassium cyanide is poisonous to dogs. The "model" that we take here is the general proposition that potassium cyanide is poisonous to dogs. We then conduct experiments by feeding dogs potassium cyanide. The death of each dog will be taken as a confirming instance of the model. If dogs do not die after being fed potassium cyanide, then we will reject the model. To make an experiment with a model is to "imitate" a model. Hence this method is called the method of imitation. The method of extension consists in "attributing the same to what is not known as to what is known."[34] It is also defined as the "taking and giving according to classes." Another example is helpful. Suppose someone asks us, "How do you know that potassium cyanide is poisonous to <u>all</u> dogs?" Even though many kinds of dogs exist and most of them we have not observed, through previous studies we <u>know</u> that the biochemical processes on which their life depends are the same. Hence, we can "attribute the same to what is not known as to what is known," and say that potassium cyanide is poisonous to all dogs. Here we assert a relation between the class of "dogs" and the class of "potassium cyanide." Hence we are "taking and giving according to classes." Because of the elliptical nature of the classical Chinese language in which the "Mohist Canons" is written, whether these two methods mean exactly the same thing as deduction and induction in modern Western logic is difficult to say. They do resemble the deductive and inductive procedures of modern logic, although they involve more than a mechanical application of deduction and induction.

"The Mohist Canons" also contains discussions on the method of comparison, the method of analogy, and the method of parallel. The method of comparison is to use one thing to explain another thing which is less familiar to people. For example, by comparing the action of the human heart to a hydraulic pump we can explain the function of the heart. "The use of comparison arises out of the failure of direct statement to be comprehensible. Therefore we borrow for illustration another thing . . . so as to make it clear."[35] The method of parallel consists in comparing two propositions consistently throughout. Thus, for example, if one accepts the proposition "Hunting is cruel," one should also accept the proposition "Fishing is cruel." In the method of analogy, one attempts to show an analogy between two things or situations and argue that one cannot accept one while rejecting the other. For example, "You are so, why should I alone not be so?"[36] The method of parallel and the method of analogy overlap in the "Mohist Canons."

The methodology of the "Mohist Canons" is similar to J. S. Mill's method of experimental inquiry.[37] Mo Zi's "methods of dialectic" are not set formulae to be applied mechanically. The Mohist methodology requires imagination, insight, experience, judgment, as well as a skillful combination of induction and deduction.

d. Criticisms and Opinions.

After the military and political unification of China by Qin Shi Huang Di (221 B.C.), the Mohist school became virtually extinct. Why should a philosophical school which was the first to offer systematic methodological analysis and which was better organized than any others disappear for two thousand years until it was revived by a few Chinese scholars and Christian missionaries in the nineteenth century? The failure of Mohism may be the result of two factors: the political situation of China around 230 B.C., and the content of Mo Zi's ideas. The Mohists took it upon themselves to defend weak states against aggressors. However, the armies of the powerful state of Qin were invincible in the decade of 230-220 B.C. While the Qin armies were conquering one after another of the other six states of China, the Mohists tried in vain to help the attacked states defend themselves. They were slaughtered by the Qin armies. In one instance, one of the Mohist leaders was entrusted with the defense of a small state against Qin's attack. When he realized he was unable to stop Qin's advance, he committed suicide. It is recorded that 181 of his Mohist followers followed the leader by taking their own lives.[38] When Qin completed its conquest, the few remaining Mohists went underground

112

and formed Robin Hood-like bands which roamed the countryside. All the secret societies in China attributed their beginnings to the Mohist organization.

Some of Mo Zi's ideas work against Mohism's chances for survival in China. Mo Zi's denial of the family's special interests and his austere utilitarianism sound hard and cold to most moderate Chinese, especially when compared with Confucianism. Mo Zi's authoritarianism (the principle of shang tong, agreement or identification with the superior) and economic communalism ("enjoy equally and suffer equally") are not compatible with the natural workings of social and political processes. His strict organization, which was a "state within a state," was inevitably perceived by the rulers as a threat and challenge to their authority. While the Confucianists urged the rulers to appoint learned and virtuous scholars as their ministers, Mo Zi suggested that they should turn over their political power to the wise and virtuous men, as the ancient sage kings Yao and Shun did. Perhaps the most fundamental flaw of Mohism is its neglect of basic psychological factors in human behavior.

Mo Zi believed that by proper instruction people can be convinced of the feasibility of the doctrine of universal love and practice it in their daily life. He says: "I feel people will tend toward universal love and mutual aid like fire tending upwards and water downwards."[39] But, as history shows, "to love other people as oneself" is easier said than done. The practice of universal love requires great psychological effort and considerable personal sacrifices. Mo Zi's universal love may be an ideal which cannot be realized except in a strictly disciplined and egalitarian society. The Confucian gradations of love appear closer to human expectations. Mo Zi's argument against music shows that he has no use for any aesthetic expression and does not understand the dynamics of human emotions.

> The people have three worries: that
> the hungry will not be fed, that the
> cold will not get clothed, and that
> the tired will not get rest. These
> three are the great worries of the
> people. Now suppose we strike the
> great bell, beat the sounding drum,
> strum the qin and the she, and blow
> the yü and the sheng, how can the
> material for food and clothing then
> be procured for the people? Even I
> do not think this is possible.[40]

Mo Zi does not believe that music contributes anything
to the benefit of the people. He says musical
instruments such as qin, she, yü, sheng, are not as
useful as the boats or carts. The narrowness of Mo
Zi's utilitarianism is that benefit is to be defined in
material terms only. Apparently for Mo Zi, hardly
anything other than food, clothes, or shelter has any
value. One can agree with Mo Zi that rulers who taxed
the people heavily in order to have beautiful palaces,
and extravagant dances and music are evil. But to
condemn music as evil is going too far. The
Confucianist Xün Zi is correct in his judgment of Mo
Zi: "Blinded by utility, he did not see the value of
refinement."[41] Even if we construe Mo Zi as saying
that no one has the right to enjoy the luxury of music
while some people still suffer from the lack of
necessities such as food, clothes, shelter, Mo Zi is
still wrong. As the Confucianists appreciate it, the
enjoyment of music can satisfy people's psychological
needs and generate tremendous productive energy. Mo
Zi's ascetic inclination and negative attitude toward
music prevent him from seeing this plain truth. If you
deprive people of the enjoyment of music, you also
deprive them of the positive dynamics of their
productive energy. Even from a utilitarian point of

view, one should not say that no one should have a good time simply because some people in the world still suffer from poverty.

In his "three tests of judgments" Mo Zi appeals to logic and intelligence. Yet his doctrine of "identification with superior" (shang tong) says: "What the superior approves all must approve; what the superior condemns all must condemn."[42] One wonders why the Mohists do not apply the three tests of judgments to the superior's statements. The doctrine of "identification with the superior" amounts to the Nazi's Führerprinzip (leader principle); it is irrational authoritarianism and is inconsistent with the spirit of "the Mohist Canons."

Mo Zi was the first philosopher in China to say that all people are created equal and should enjoy equally all the blessings of Heaven. He originated the idea of humanitarian works such as orphanages, hospitals for the poor, and homes for the aged.

> Thus, the aged and widowers will have support and nourishment with which to round out their old age, and the young and weak and orphans will have a place of support in which to grow up. When universal love is adopted as the standard, such are the consequent benefits.[43]

For these concrete programs of universal love, Mo Zi deserves our full recognition. The "love" of Mo Zi's doctrine of universal love is not emotional, but intellectual. We are not to love as we please, but love as we must. Mo Zi's universal love is a rational obligation, the performance of which will benefit all mankind, including oneself. We might call it "enlightened self-interest," although Mo Zi probably would not use this expression.

Mo Zi's doctrine of universal love appeared to some Christian missionaries in China in the nineteenth century akin to Jesus's teaching of love. No doubt, the missionaries' interest in Mo Zi's philosophy was stimulated by their desire to show the Chinese that Christianity is not outlandish, because Mo Zi taught a similar doctrine two thousand years ago in China. The Chinese reformers and revolutionaries in the late nineteenth century and early twentieth century, many of them Western-educated, saw in Mo Zi's universal love an effective tool to break down the clannishness of the Chinese society. They believed that to cause social changes in China they first had to do away with the family-centered attitudes. Mo Zi's anti-fatalistic view has been taken as encouraging the Chinese people to be self-reliant and responsible. In consequence, a strong revival of interest in Mohism is occurring in contemporary China.

Notes

Chapter 4

1. <u>Historical Records</u> (<u>Shi Ji</u>), ch. 124.

2. <u>Mo Zi</u>, ch. 48.

3. Mei Yi-pao, <u>The Ethical and Political Works of Motse</u>, p. 125.

4. <u>Mo Zi</u>, ch. 25.

5. <u>Ibid.</u>, ch. 48.

6. <u>Ibid.</u>

7. <u>Ibid.</u>, ch. 35, "Against Fatalism."

8. <u>Ibid.</u>, ch. 36.

9. <u>Analects</u>, II, 4.

10. <u>Ibid.</u>, XX, 2.

11. Mei Yi-pao, <u>op. cit.</u> p. 180.

12. <u>Ibid.</u>, p. 224.

13. <u>Mo Zi</u>, ch. 46.

14. <u>Mencius</u>, 3, 2, 9.

15. <u>Ibid.</u>, 3, 1, 5.

16. Mei Yi-pao, <u>op. cit.</u>, p. 79.

17. <u>Mo Zi</u>, ch. 44.

18. _Ibid._, ch. 4.

19. _Ibid._, ch. 46.

20. _Zhuang Zi_, ch. 13.

21. _Mencius_, 4, 2, 28.

22. _Ibid._, 1, 1, 7.

23. _Mo Zi_, ch. 42.

24. _Ibid._

25. _Ibid._

26. _Ibid._

27. _Ibid._

28. _Ibid._, ch. 40.

29. _Ibid._, ch. 42.

30. _Ibid._, ch. 48.

31. _Ibid._, ch. 35.

32. _Ibid._, ch. 42.

33. _Ibid._, ch. 45.

34. _Ibid._

35. This explanation is made by the Mohist commentator Wang Fu in his _Jian Fu Lun_, ch. 7.

36. _Mo Zi_, ch. 45.

37. J. S. Mill, _A System of Logic_ (1843).

Furthermore, Mo Zi's ethical statements sound like Jeremy Bentham's and J. S. Mill's.

38. Cf. Lü Shi Qun Qiu.

39. Mo Zi, ch. 16.

40. Ibid., ch. 32, "Anti-music."

41. Xün Zi, ch. 21.

42. Mei Yi-pao, op. cit., p. 56.

43. Mo Zi, ch.16.

Chapter 5

Legalism: The Authoritarian Philosophy of Government

a. Han Fei Zi: The Synthesizer of the Legalist Theories.

Legalism is the philosophy of government which emphasizes the effective use of law as an instrument for the control of the people. The Chinese name of this school of philosophy is Fa <u>Jia</u>--the school of law. However, the Chinese Legalists were not "legalistic" in the sense of being concerned with the letter of the law and its interpretation. <u>Fa</u>, as the Legalists conceived it, is a set of clearly prescribed rules and regulations. Violation of <u>fa</u> will incur severe punishment, while observance of <u>fa</u> will lead to praise and material reward. Those we now call the Legalists made no conscious effort to form an independent school of thought; it came into being as a result of the Chinese historians' grouping together the writings of those who emphasized the importance of law as the sole means of obtaining efficiency in government and orderliness in society. The most comprehensive presentation of the Legalist ideas is <u>Han Fei Zi</u>, written by Han Fei Zi (died 233 B.C.). The book contains 55 chapters which are independent treatises. The book presents a system of methods and principles for the operation of the state. This system represents a synthesis of the ideas of the Legalists before Han Fei Zi. Han Fei Zi's background tells us much about the Legalist philosophy. He was a prince of the royal family of the state of Han. The state of Han was situated in central China in the region east of the state of Qin. Han Fei Zi was born about 280 B.C. He studied under the eminent Confucian scholar Xün Zi who, we recall, believed that human nature is originally evil. One of Han Fei Zi's fellow students was Li Si who later became the prime minister of Qin Shi Huang Di (the first emperor of the Qin dynasty). While they were fellow students under Xûn Zi, Li Si was said to be jealous of Han Fei Zi, for he knew that Han Fei Zi's intellect was superior to his own.[1] If Han Fei Zi was the Legalist theoretician, Li Si was the Legalist practitioner who had the ability and opportunity to put the Legalist philosophy into practice.

Han Fei Zi had a handicap--he stuttered badly. This handicap did not prevent him from making subtle and perceptive observations of social-psychological phenomena. He expressed his thought by writing. In one of his letters to the king of Han, Han Fei Zi warns the king to guard himself against glib politicians. The king of Han ignored Han Fei Zi's numerous letters of advice and remonstrance. Two of Han Fei Zi's essays came into the hands of the youthful ruler of the state of Qin who would later conquer all China and assume the title of Qin Shi Huang Di. The king of Qin expressed his great admiration for the author of the essays to his minister Li Si who then revealed to him the identity of the author. In the year 234 B.C. Qin launched a severe attack on the state of Han. In the hope of saving his state from destruction, the king of Han dispatched Han Fei Zi as his envoy to Qin. The king of Qin was delighted to meet Han Fei Zi and contemplated offering Han Fei Zi a position in his government. Li Si, however, intervened and pointed out that Han Fei Zi was a prince of Han so that his loyalty would always be on the side of Han and against Qin. Li Si finally succeeded in persuading the king of Qin to arrest Han Fei Zi and assign law officials to investigate Han Fei Zi's mission. Fearing that the Qin ruler might change his mind (as he later did), Li Si managed to force Han Fei Zi to drink poison while imprisoned. The year was 233 B. C.

Although Han Fei Zi is considered to be a Chinese philosopher, he was not concerned with truth, nor was he interested in ethics or metaphysics. Unlike all the philosophers we have studied, Han Fei Zi was not even concerned with the unfortunate plight of the people. His thought reflects his princely background; he saw things from the point of view of the ruler or the ruling class. In the late Zhou dynasty, the social distinctions between the aristocrats and commoners were no longer clearly demarcated, due to the disintegration of the feudal system. Aristocrats sometimes lost their titles and lands through bad luck or indolence. Commoners sometimes succeeded in becoming socially and politically important through good luck, talent, or hard work. Han Fei Zi maintained that competent persons should be given free access to the channels that lead to government posts and to higher status, since the ruler should use ability as the sole criterion for the selection of officials. The territories of the feudal lords changed frequently because of the wars among them. Because of incessant warfare, governments of the warring states had to find ways to organize their people, strengthen their armies, and increase their agricultural production. Several states instituted reform measures suggested by the early Legalists to strengthen their governments. Han Fei Zi perceived that states which failed to adopt them fell dangerously behind the times. Furthermore, Han Fei Zi noticed that the strength of a government comes primarily from strong leadership and good organization. He believed that the rulers need to gain more effective and direct control of their land and population. Under the old feudal system, a ruler's control of his people or land was neither effective nor direct. According to Han Fei Zi, the rulers need not idealistic programs for doing good for their people, but realistic methods for dealing with the new situations faced by their government.

Han Fei Zi was intellectually indebted to the three previous Legalist groups, in addition to his teacher Xun Zi. One group was headed by Shen Bu-hai (died 337 B.C.) who emphasized the importance of administrative methods, s̲h̲u̲ (術), in government. The second group was led by Shen Dao who was a contemporary of Mencius and who stressed that power, s̲h̲i̲ (势), is central in politics. The third group was headed by Shang Yang (also called Wei Yang or Gong-sun Yang, died in 338 B.C.) who emphasized law or regulations, f̲a̲ (法). Although Han Fei Zi believed that s̲h̲u̲, s̲h̲i̲, f̲a̲ are all indispensable and equally important in practical politics, perhaps Shang Yang exerted the greatest influence on him. Han Fei Zi learned from Xǔn Zi that human nature is originally evil. But while Xǔn Zi believes that education can transform people into virtuous citizens, Han Fei Zi proposes the enactment and enforcement of law to prevent people's evil nature from running its wild course. He places no value on the virtues of individuals. He believes that virtues are accidental and unreliable. In short, while Xǔn Zi tries to make men good through education Han Fei Zi wants to make it impossible for men to do wrong. Han Fei Zi says:

> The strict household has no unruly slaves, but a doting mother is sure to have a spoiled son. From this I know that only awe-inspiring power can suppress violence, while kindness and magnanimity cannot possibly deter the rebellious. The sage, in governing a state, does not trust men to do good of themselves; he makes it impossible for them to do wrong. In an entire state you could not find ten men who can be trusted to do good of themselves, but if you make it impossible for the people to do wrong the whole state can nevertheless be kept in order. A ruler must concern himself with the majority, not with rare individuals. Thus he takes no

account of virtue, but concerns himself rather with law.[2]

b.   The Strategies of Practical Politics.

According to Shen Dao, the ruler obtains his power by occupying his position (shi). He compares the ruler's position with the extraordinary power of the dragon and the flying serpent who take advantage of the clouds and the mist that carry them aloft. Without the clouds and the mist, these mysterious creatures would be no different from ordinary serpents.[3] In his discussion of the ruler's position and function, Han Fei Zi develops the idea of shi as follows:

> Indeed, the possessor of talent who has no position, even though he is worthy, cannot control the unworthy. For example, when a stand of timber is placed on the top of a high mountain, it overlooks the ravine a thousand fathoms below. The timber is not long but its position is high. When Chieh was the Son of Heaven, he could rule over all under Heaven; not that he was worthy but that his position was influential. Yao, when a commoner, could not administer three families; not that he was unworthy but that his position was low. A weight of one thousand chün floats if aboard a ship, but the smallest farthing sinks if overboard. Not that one thousand chün is light and the smallest farthing is heavy, but that the former has a favorable position while the latter does not. Therefore a short thing can look down on the tall because of its position; the unworthy man can rule over the

worthy also because of his position.

The lord of men, because he is supported by all under Heaven with united forces, is safe; because he is upheld by the masses of the people with united heart, he is glorious. The minister, because he maintains his specialty and exerts his ability, is loyal. If a glorious sovereign rules loyal ministers a state of constant enjoyment and meritorious reputation will be achieved, Name and reality, keeping pace with each other, will reach fruition. Form and shadow, coinciding with each other, will take shape. Hence the sovereign and the minister have the same desire but different functions.[4]

The function of the ruler, Han Fei says, is to keep social order. Han Fei Zi does not believe that the sovereigns have any charismatic rights. In fact, he thinks that the sovereign's existence has nothing to do with the will of Heaven. Power, which makes possible the maintenance of social order, is all important. The authority of a sovereign is derived from his position, not from who he is. Regarding shu (method) and fa (law), Han Fei Zi says:

Now Shen Bu-hai speaks of shu while Gong-sun Yang practices fa. What is called shu is to bestow office according to the capability of the candidate; to demand actual performance in accordance with the title of the office held; to hold fast the handles of the power of life and death; and to examine into the abilities of all his ministers; these are the things that the ruler keeps in his own hands.[5]

A wise ruler should closely supervise the performance of his officials. If they have done a good job, they will be rewarded; if not, they will be punished. Han Fei Zi calls reward and punishment "the two handles of the ruler."[6] He believes that they are effective tools for handling men, because the nature of men is to seek profit and to avoid harm. Law is to a ruler what measures are to a carpenter. As a carpenter cannot build without the help of measures, a ruler cannot rule without law. Law should be just and fair; but whatever the law is, once instituted, it should be enforced equally, on the aristocrats as well as the commoners. Law should be made exact and clear so that people would know what to do and what to avoid. More importantly, law without strict enforcement is just empty words. Both reward and punishment should be administered promptly so as to maximize their effect.

The emphasis on actual performance spares the necessity of searching for motives which are difficult to ascertain. To increase efficiency, government should be made into an impersonal, mechanistic system which functions on a set of rules. Han Fei Zi relates with apparent approval an anecdote about Shen Bu-hai and the ruler of Han (Marquis Zhao):

> Marquis Zhao of Han once said to Shen Zi [Shen Bu-hai, who was once chancellor of Han], "Method is not easy to practice." "What is called method," said Shen Bu-hai, "is to examine achievement as a basis for giving rewards, and to use ability as the basis upon which to bestow office. Now your Highness establishes method and yet grants his attendant's requests. This is the cause of the difficulty in practicing method."

> "From now on," said Marquis Zhao, "I
> will know how to practice method. I
> will not grant requests." One day
> Shen Zi asked the Marquis to appoint
> his elder cousin to an official post.
> Marquis Zhao said: "This is not what
> I learned from you. If I grant your
> request, I nullify your teaching. It
> would be better not to allow your
> request." Shen Zi withdrew to his
> residence for his fault.[7]

Statecraft implies the utilization of human resources.
How does a ruler select officials for the offices of
his government? If someone claims that he has a
certain talent or ability or is known to have it, a
wise ruler will give him work according to his supposed
ability but will hold him entirely responsible for
accomplishing the work. If the work is faithfully
completed, he will be rewarded and retained; if not, he
will be punished and dismissed. This simple procedure
involves more than just trial and error, for the
application of reward and punishment serves the purpose
of reinforcement. If this procedure is followed
consistently, Han Fei Zi says, the competent people
will be retained or promoted, the marginally competent
people will give their best to complete the assignment,
and the incompetent will be weeded out. It may not be
necessary to weed out the incompetent, for they will
not dare to accept the appointment even if offered.
The ruler need not personally supervise all the
officials in his government. He can appoint
supervisors, but the supervisors will be held
responsible for their work. Note Han Fei Zi's warning
against cost overrun of government projects:

> The ruler of men is sometimes misled
> in undertakings and blinded by words.
> These are two dangers which he must
> not fail to consider carefully.

Ministers come blithely forward with a proposal for an undertaking and, because the funds they ask are small, the ruler is duped by the proposal; misled as to its true nature, he fails to examine it thoroughly, but instead is filled with admiration for the men who made it. In this way ministers are able to use undertakings to gain power over the ruler. This is what it means to be misled in undertakings, and he who is so misled will be beset by hazard. If, when a minister comes forward with a proposal, he asks for meager funds but, after he has retired to put it into effect his expenditures are very large, then although the undertaking may produce results, the proposal was not made in good faith. He who speaks in bad faith is guilty of a crime and, though his undertaking has achieved results, he should receive no reward. If this rule is obeyed, then the ministers will not dare to dress up their words in an effort to delude the sovereign.[8]

Adopting the Confucian doctrine of the rectification of names and the dialectician's doctrine of the correspondence of names and actualities, Han Fei Zi insists on "holding the actualities responsible for their names."[9] For the school of names (Chapter 7), the terms "names" and "actualities" are semantical or logical terms, but Han Fei Zi ignores the abstract philosophical aspects of these two terms and gives them an exclusively political interpretation. By "name" he means the name of the office a man holds, the list of duties he is expected to perform, or the proposals he makes; by "actuality" he means the actual performance of the man in office. Han Fei Zi insists that only when "names" and "actualities" coincide exactly can the official be rewarded as doing his job properly. If, for example, a tax collector collects either too little or too much tax, he has not done his job properly and should be punished.

As a corollary of the doctrine of the correspondence of names and actualities, Han Fei Zi believes that people should respect and obey the ruler but there should be no love or affection between the ruler and the people. He tells the story of a duke of Qin and the people who loved him. The duke of Qin was ill. Some of his people sacrificed an ox for his recovery. When the duke recovered from his illness and learned of what the people had done for him, he punished them. It is inappropriate for the subjects to love their ruler; moreover, love between the ruler and the subjects can interfere with the functioning of the government. Therefore, it should be discouraged as soon as possible.[10] Similarly, when Shang Yang became the prime minister of Qin, he promulgated many harsh laws. At first, the people of Qin resented these harsh laws and criticized them. Shang Yang punished both those who criticized the laws and those who violated them, including the crown prince. The crown prince had violated the law. Shang Yang wanted to make an example of it; so he ordered that the crown prince's teacher be branded, presumably on the ground that the teacher did not do a good job. Because of the close relationship between teachers and students in China, the crown prince was seriously humiliated. Thereafter everyone obeyed the laws, and the whole state became orderly. Then some people praised Shang Yang and his laws. When Shang Yang learned of their praise, he banished them to the frontier for daring to comment on the laws. For the Legalists, people are to obey the laws, not to make comments on them. Even if laws appear strange or ridiculous, people should obey them. Once Shang Yang drew up a decree but did not make it public, for fear that people might not have confidence in him.

> He therefore had a pole thirty feet long placed near the south gate of the capital. Assembling the people, he said that he would give ten measures of gold to anyone who could move it to the north gate. The people marveled at this, but no one ventured to move it. Shang Yang then said, 'I will give fifty measures of gold to anyone who can move it.' One man then moved it, and Shang Yang immediately gave him fifty measures of gold, to demonstrate that he did not practice deception.[11]

Of the ruler-official relationship Han Fei Zi says that it should be contractual, like the employer-employee relationship. The Confucian notion that the ruler-official relationship is familial is a mistake. In any event, comparing a ruler to a father is wrong, because a ruler loves neither his subjects nor his officials. Han Fai Zi compares the ruler-official relationship to that of master and hired hand. A reciprocity may exist between master and hired hand, but no love exists between them. The hired hand, expecting good food and generous wages from his master (employer), would work hard, and the employer, expecting good service from the hired hand, would treat him well. "Thus, in the master's treatment of the workman and the workman's service to the master the comparison of father and son seems to exist. But really their minds are attuned to utility since they both cherish self-seeking motives."[12] Here we are to understand that the first concern of any individual is always his own interest. According to Han Fei Zi, a state can be kept in good order only if the familial relationship is replaced by calculations of mutual profit.

The enlightened sovereign . . . learns what the people want in order to gain service from them; he bestows ranks and emoluments to encourage them. [Similarly] he learns what the people dislike in order to prevent them from committing villainy; he inflicts punishment to overawe them. As rewards are sure and punishments are definite, the ruler can promote meritorious persons to office, and no malefactor is used in the government. . . . Moreover, ministers in bartering with the ruler offer their full strength; the ruler in bartering with the ministers dangles ranks and emoluments before them. Thus, the relationship of ruler and ministers is not as intimate as the bond of father and son; it is an outcome of mutual calculation.[13]

Han Fei Zi then argues for the uselessness of the familial concept of state as follows:

In these days the Confucianists and the Mohists all say that the former kings practiced impartial love for the world, that is, they looked upon the people as parents [look upon their own children]. . . . If one supposes that when ruler and subjects act like father and son there must always be order, this implies no disorder ever occurs in the relationship between father and son. In human nature, nothing surpasses the affection of parents. Nevertheless, <u>even</u> <u>when</u> both parents

132

> show love for their children order
> does not necessarily result.
> Similarly, even though the ruler
> should deepen his love for his
> subjects, how could one expect
> disorder thereupon to end?[14]

Love in the family does not preclude conflict or disharmony in the family. Han Fei Zi believes that even within the family, calculation of profit and self-seeking is the rule. He says that children who did not receive good care from their parents would not provide for their well-being when they grow up. The parents would then grow angry and reprimand them.

> When a boy is born, the father and
> mother congratulate each other, but
> if a girl is born they put it to
> death. . . . The reason for this
> difference in treatment is that the
> parents are thinking of their later
> convenience, and calculating what
> will ultimately bring them profit.
> Thus even the attitude of parents
> toward their children is marked by
> the calculation of gain. How much
> more must this be the case with
> relationships which are not
> characterized by the affection that
> exists between father and child.[15]

Girls were considered unprofitable primarily because they would be married off to other families when they grew up, and so would not take care of their parents.

Because Han Fei Zi has such a low opinion of human nature, in politics one cannot rely, according to him, on human virtues such as trust, loyalty, and compassion. He believes that subjects and officials naturally tend to supplant their superiors, by murder if necessary. They would steal the wealth and power of their superiors if they knew they could get away with it. The proper way of handling such a tendency is not to try to enlighten them or be kind to them, but to suppress them and put them under constant surveillance. A ruler must realize that he cannot trust his friends, relatives, or advisers, not even his own wife or children, for they all have something to gain from his death.

> Moreover, whether one is a ruler of a state of ten thousand chariots or of a thousand only, it is quite likely that his consort, his concubines, or the son he has designated as heir to his throne will wish for his death. How do I know this is? A wife is not bound to her husband by any ties of blood. If he loves her, she remains close to him; if not, she becomes estranged. The saying goes, "If the mother is favored, the son will be embraced." But if this is so, the opposite must be, "If the mother is despised, the son will be cast away." A man of fifty has not yet lost interest in sex, and yet at thirty a woman's beauty has already faded. If a woman whose beauty has already faded waits upon a man still occupied by thoughts of sex, then she will be spurned and disfavored, and her son will stand little chance of succeeding to the throne. This is why consorts and concubines long for the early death of the ruler.[16]

Therefore, a ruler must be constantly on his guard against deception from all quarters, and reveal his innermost thoughts and desires to no one. Statecraft for the rulers is the art of survival and prosperity. Any means to the end of political security and prosperity is justified, including bribes, threats, kidnapping, and murder. The following example conveys Han Fei Zi's point about the danger of trust in politics and the necessity of constant alert.

> In ancient times Duke Wu of Cheng wanted to attack the state of Hu, and so he first married his daughter to the ruler of Hu in order to fill his mind with thoughts of pleasure. Then he told his ministers, "I want to launch a military campaign. What would be a likely state to attack?" The high official Guan Qi-si replied, "Hu could be attacked," whereupon Duke Wu flew into a rage and had him executed, saying "Hu is a brother state! What do you mean by advising me to attack it!" The ruler of Hu, hearing of this, assumed that Cheng was friendly toward him and therefore took no precautions to defend himself from Cheng. The men of Cheng then made a surprise attack on Hu and seized it.[17]

Examples such as this fill the pages of the Legalist writings. Han Fei Zi cites history often, but only to impress on his readers human treacheries and follies. When it became clear that Qin was the most powerful state in China, the other six states formed a common alliance against Qin for fifteen years. This alliance stopped Qin's advance toward the east until the alliance was broken by Qin's covert actions. Li Si, Qin's chief minister, sent out secret agents well supplied with gold and precious stones to the other states. They bribed those ministers and rulers who could be bribed to leave the alliance, and assassinated those who could not be bribed. The secret agents created such an atmosphere of suspicion and mistrust among the six states that the alliance finally collapsed. Moreover, several of the states began to fight among themselves. The Qin ruler then sent his well trained armies and excellent commanders to conquer all of them.[18]

No doubt Han Fei Zi believes the end justifies the means. He quotes Shang Yang as having said, "Small faults should be punished severely; then if small faults are inhibited, great crimes will not appear. This is called using punishment to get rid of punishment."[19] Throwing ashes into the street is a small offense, but the law of Shang Yang states that the offender will have his hand cut off. The Legalists agree that cutting off the hand is very hard on the offender. However, since this kind of punishment has an exemplary effect on the whole population, it is justified. It is more effective than trying to explain to the people that throwing ashes into the street can interfere with the traffic and can be hazardous to the people's health. Shang Yang's expectation is that repeated harsh punishments will ultimately frighten the people into obeying all the laws and regulations. Han Fei Zi claims that the ruler punishes the people whenever they break his laws only to benefit the people themselves. Lancing a boil will cause pain but it is good for the patient. Similarly, punishing the people for their violation of laws serves the purpose of saving them from greater evil. The ordinary people, through their ignorance, will resent the harsh laws and hate the men who made such laws. That is why a ruler should protect himself with tight security measures. A team of bodyguards is a necessity.

> The ruler of men must be enlightened
> enough to comprehend the way of
> government and strict enough to put
> it into effect. Though it means

going against the will of the people, he will enforce his will. In proof of this, we may note that Lord Shang, when he came and went at court, was guarded by iron spears and heavy shields to prevent sudden attack. Similarly, when Guo Yen instituted his new policies in Jin, Duke Wen provided him with bodyguards, and when Guan Zhong first began his reforms in Qi, Duke Huan rode in an armored carriage. All these were precautions against danger from the people. For the people, in their stupid and slovenly way, will groan at even a small expenditure and forget the great profits to be reaped from it.[20]

The Legalists hold that in order to make the ruler politically powerful and the state militarily strong, some classes will be forced to change their vocations or eliminated. These include hereditary aristocrats, those artisans whose main business is to produce luxury goods, hermits, innkeepers, merchants, scholars, soothsayers, philanthropists, and swashbucklers. A brief explanation is in order for this long list.

No hereditary privileges, except the hereditary kingship, shall exist. Titles of nobility are not inheritable but are awarded on the basis of merits. Shang Yang proposed that military merit is the only criterion. Han Fei Zi expanded this criterion to include ability and diligence in administrative works. Han Fei Zi also pointed out that good soldiers are not necessarily good administrators, and vice versa. The Legalists did not challenge the hereditary kingship. This sacrifice in logic is called for by their need to obtain the approval of the king. Although often logical, the Legalists would readily abandon logic if necessary, since their philosophy is based on stronger forces than reason. Artisans such as carpenters and weapon manufacturers are deemed useful workers. But craftsmen such as makers of fine tissues, brocades, and embroideries, artistic carvers, and painters are considered useless. Hermits who live in the forests and inaccessible caves do not contribute anything to the society and ought to be eliminated. Inns and innkeepers should be abolished because they make it possible for people to travel around the country. To the Legalists, travel is unproductive; moreover, people who travel are likely to be troublemakers, restless, or engaged in secret plots. Shang Yang says that if people cannot travel, they would stay in their home village and work the land. This would help agriculture in the state. Merchants were a relatively new class in the late Zhou dynasty. They travel a lot. Though they do not work the land or make anything, they make huge profits by manipulating the market. Merchants are cunning and treacherous. Their existence is a threat to the ruler because they often acquire considerable power through the accumulation of wealth. The Chinese had a well-known prejudice against businessmen until recent times. But while the Confucianists and the followers of the other philosophies looked down upon merchants, the Legalists wanted to eliminate them. The Legalists believe that people become rich through hard work and thrift, but become poor through idleness and extravagance. Yet the philanthropists want to help the poor by giving them money and land. If the ruler listens to the philanthropists and decides to help the poor, he can do it only by taxing the rich. This penalizes the industrious and thrifty while encouraging idleness and extravagance. Can we expect the people to work hard and practice economy if the philanthropists have their way? For the Legalists, poverty is not a problem, but the unwillingness of people to work hard enough is a problem.

Han Fei Zi believes that all book-learning is

useless. He has a contempt for "useless scholars" who busy their little heads with irrelevant antiquity or trivial discussions. Time can be better used to raise food or other necessities. Yet, Han Fei Zi complains, rulers too often compete with each other to honor scholars by giving them high positions or material rewards. This encourages people to become scholars. But the more people who study, the fewer people will work the lands or be trained as soldiers. Scholars should be persecuted because they talk too much and have a propensity to criticize the ruler and his government. Their criticisms can lead to dissension and discontent which in turn may weaken the ruler's control of the people, induce revolts and even the overthrow of the sovereign. Han Fei Zi maintains that even the study of the Legalist treatises or military textbooks should be discouraged and restricted to a select few.

> Today, everyone talks about methods of government and there is not a family that does not possess a copy of the laws of Shang Zi and Guan Zi [two early Legalists]. But despite this, the land grows poorer and poorer. Those who talk about agriculture are many; those who hold the plough are few. Everyone talks about the art of warfare and there is not a family that does not possess a copy of Sun Zi and Wu Zi [two books on military strategy], but our armies grow weaker and weaker. Those who talk about fighting are many; those who put on armor are few.[21]

This anti-intellectualism led to the burning of books and execution of 460 scholars in China in 212 B.C. This was the work of Li Si who proposed to Qin Shi Huang Di in 213 B.C. the following:

139

1. Burn all books in the empire except the official history of Qin state, books on medicine, divination, and agriculture.

2. The imperial professors are authorized to keep books in their respective fields; all others who have books should report to the local authorities and hand to them their holdings, all of which would be burned. Those who dare to discuss among themselves the contents of burned books should be executed in public.

3. Those who dare to criticize the present regime by invoking the ancient writings should be put to death, together with all the members of families. Government officials who know violations have occurred but choose not to prosecute would be regarded as having committed the same crime as that committed by the offenders.

4. If books are not burned thirty days after the issuance of this order, the offenders should have their faces branded and exiled to the northern frontier to build the Great Wall.

One year later (212 B.C.), with the approval of Qin Shi Huang Di, Li Si began his persecution. In the capital, 460 scholars were found to have "slandered the emperor" and "spread heretical ideas to confuse the public," and were buried alive. In the provinces, those who had been accused of committing similar crimes were exiled to the north to build the Great Wall. The book-burning campaign was so thoroughly conducted throughout the empire that many books were permanently lost while others had to be reconstructed from the memory of surviving scholars (Qin dynasty lasted only fourteen years). This is the earliest record of large scale systematic book-burning in human history.

The Legalists, being realistic politicians, understandably condemn any reliance on supernatural guidance. Soothsayers thus come under attack. Han Fei Zi warns: "that a state should use time and days, serve ghosts and spirits, trust in divination by tortoise or by the yarrow-stalks, be addicted to prayers and sacrifices, is a portent of doom."[22] It is difficult, if not impossible, for anyone to get rid of all supernatural beliefs; and no society has ever completely eliminated all types of soothsayers. Ironically, Qin Shi Huang Di was interested in soothsaying and in obtaining the elixir of immortality. When Li Si burned books, he made an exception of divination books, probably in deference to the emperor's interest.

Finally, the swashbucklers are troublemakers. They engage in personal vendettas and take the law into their own hands. Sometimes they champion the cause of the oppressed and rob the rich to help the poor. But one is not sure that they do not also rob the rich to enrich themselves. In any case, they have no respect for the law. The Legalists therefore want to eliminate them.

The Legalists claim, with some justification, that they are the social and political innovators. They conceive of history as a process of change; each age has new problems which must be solved by new methods. They do not believe in looking back to the past for guidance. New ideas must be tried;, and new circumstances must be taken into account. Shang Yang says: "When the guiding principles of the people become unsuited to the circumstances, their standards of values must change. As conditions in the world change, different principles are practiced."[23] During his tenure as the chief minister of Qin, Shang Yang introduced a host of new measures which laid the foundation for Qin Shi Huang Di's conquest of all

China. Among other things, he advocated private ownership of land and legalized land transaction between individuals; offered ownership of virgin lands and exemption from military service to attract immigrants from the east; organized the state's population into groups of five or ten households, each household being held responsible for the deeds of other households within the group; broke up the age-old institution of patriarchial family by putting an extra tax on any family which includes two or more adult males. Han Fei Zi has nothing but contempt for those who adhere to the tradition and custom and are unable to adapt to the new circumstances. He tells the following story:

> A farmer of Song tilled the land, and in his fields was a stump. One day a rabbit, racing across the field, bumped into the stump, broke its neck, and died. Thereupon the farmer laid aside his plow and took up watch beside the stump, hoping that he would get another rabbit in the same way. But he got no more rabbits, and instead became the laughing stock of Song. Those who think they can take the ways of the ancient kings and use them to govern the people of today all belong in the category of stump-watchers.[24]

Han Fei Zi's idea of a strongly centralized government operating mechanically in accordance with a set of rigid and fixed laws has since become the model of Chinese government. Thanks to the Legalists, China has had a relatively strong government since Qin dynasty. The Legalists have left their indelible marks on the structure and function of Chinese government, even though Legalism as a school of thought ceased to exist a long time ago.

c. Comparisons and Criticisms.

The Legalists derived their ideas from Confucianism, Daoism, Mohism, and the school of names. From a philosophical point of view, the Legalists have not offered any new ideas in metaphysics, epistemology, ethics, or logic. Although Han Fei Zi is often critical of the other schools of thought, he shares some common grounds with them. The early Legalist Shen Dao was a Daoist as well as a Legalist. Han Fei Zi criticized Daoism the least. This at first is puzzling, for the Legalist and the Daoist philosophies of life are poles apart. The Daoist hold that human nature is originally innocent, but the Legalists maintain that human nature is evil through and through. The Daoists value spontaneity and individual freedom, but the Legalists stress social control and discipline. The Daoists condemn war and oppressive government, but the Legalists glorify them. However, the Daoists and the Legalists find the common ground in the idea of transcendence of good and evil and wu-wei (non-action). A Daoist identifies himself with nature and thus transcends good and evil; an enlightened ruler identifies himself with the laws of practical politics and thus is beyond good and evil. The Legalists adroitly use Daoism as a metaphysical foundation for their amoral authoritarian politics by discarding other aspects of Daoism that do not suit their purpose. Thus Han Fei Zi says:

> Just as the sun and moon shine forth, the four seasons progress, the clouds spread, and wind blows, so does the ruler not encumber his mind with knowledge, or himself with selfishness. He relies for good government or disorder upon laws and methods (shu); leaves right and wrong to be dealt with through rewards and

punishments; and refers lightness and
heaviness to the balance of the
scale.[25]

In other words, just as a Daoist sage adopts a course
of quietude and refrains from all forced or unnatural
activity, a Legalist ruler sets up the machinery of
government and then allows it to run by itself. This
is the Legalist construal of Lao Zi's proposition, "Dao
invariably takes no action, and yet there is nothing
left undone."[26]

The concept of wu-wei is not easy to understand.
In the Daoist context, the concept can be explicated
and defended without much difficulty. However, the
Legalist construal of wu-wei is implausible. For,
according to Han Fei Zi, a ruler cannot trust anyone
and must supervise his ministers' work closely. Hence
he cannot withdraw and let things take care of
themselves. Furthermore, the Legalists often talk
about fa (law) as if it were the Dao of human society.
But, while Dao is the way of nature for the Daoists,
the Legalist fa is a man-made law. As Han Fei Zi often
stresses, human nature is incorrigibly evil, and the
administration of law requires social control and
coercion. Thus, fa is the antithesis of wu-wei. Lao
Zi puts it this way:

> The more taboos and prohibitions
> there are in the world, the poorer
> the people will be. The more sharp
> weapons the people have, the more
> troubled the state will be. The more
> cunning and skill man possesses, the
> more vicious things will appear. The
> more laws and orders are made
> prominent, the more thieves and
> robbers there will be.[27]

The Legalists have also utilized some of the Mohist
doctrines. The Legalists share with the Mohists their

contempt for rituals and their emphasis on utility. Mo Zi insists on discipline and on the doctrine of shang tong (identification with the superior). We find much the same demand in the Legalist writings. The doctrine of shang tong demands that what the superior considers right, all must accept as right,; what the superior considers wrong, all must accept as wrong. In addition, it requires that all members report good deeds or evil deeds of others to the superior. Those who report the good deeds of others will be rewarded as if they themselves had done the good deeds; those who fail to report the evil deeds of others will be punished as if they themselves had done the evil deeds. We recall that Shang Yang organized the people into groups of five or ten families; members of each group are mutually responsible for each other and are obliged to denounce each other's crimes. Anyone who fails to do this is to be punished as though he himself had committed the crime. We also detect a tendency in Mohism and Legalism to carry principles to their logical conclusion without regard for mitigating circumstances.

The Mohists and the Confucianists believe in the golden age of the past: the times of Yü, Yao, and Shun. In their view, the movement of history since the golden age has been one of progressive degeneration. Therefore, social and political reform aims at returning the society to its uncorrupted form. For the Legalists, however, the golden age lies in the future, not in the past, and we have to work hard to bring it about. Han Fei Zi concedes that life in the ancient times may in some respects be better than the present, but this is due to the difference in material circumstances rather than to the difference in the character of the people.

> In ancient times husband did not have
> to till fields, for the seeds of
> grass and the fruit of the trees were

145

enough for people to eat. Wives did
not have to weave, for the skins of
birds and beasts provided sufficient
clothing. No one had to struggle to
keep himself supplied. The people
were few, goods abounded, and so no
one quarrelled. . . . But nowadays no
one regards five sons as a large
number, and these five sons have five
sons each, so that before the
grandfather has died, he has twenty-
five grandchildren. Hence the number
of people increases, goods grow
scarce, and men have to struggle and
slave for a meager living. Therefore
they fall to quarrelling.[28]

Han Fei Zi urges the rulers to recognize that material
circumstances change over time. New circumstances
generate new problems which require new measures to
solve them. "For the sage does not try to practice the
ways of antiquity or to abide by a fixed standard, but
examines the affairs of the age and takes what
precautions are necessary."[29] Those who "practice the
ways of antiquity or abide by a fixed standard," are
like the "stump-watcher" who waits by the tree stump,
hoping that another rabbit would bump into the stump
and kill itself.

Insofar as the Confucianists deny hereditary class
distinctions and advocate a strong centralized
government, Legalism agrees in part with Confucianism.
However, the differences between the two ways of
thought are greater than their similarities. The
Confucian ideal of government is benevolent government
(ren zheng) according to which the benevolence and
wisdom of the ruler evoke loyalty and moral conduct in
the people, so that laws and sanctions become
unnecessary. We have seen that the Legalists eschew
moral consideration and concentrate on laws and

sanctions. The Confucianists hold that the conduct of the aristocrats and the commoners alike should be governed by <u>li</u> (propriety), whereas the Legalists insist that the laws of rewards and punishments be applied to both the aristocrats and the commoners. The Confucianist ideals are idealistic but those of the Legalists are "realistic" (some would say cynical).

Some writers use "the realist school" to refer to the Legalists. Since the Legalists are not interested in the epistemological issue of the nature of ultimate reality but stress laws and sanctions, I call them Legalists. Moreover, a doctrine which is so one-sided in its analysis of the human <u>psyche</u> is really unrealistic. "The Legalist School" is also the most commonly used name. One basic assumption of the Legalist psychology is that people are always selfish. The statement "People are always selfish" is like the statement "We always do what we want to do," which is easily construed as a tautology. One could stretch the meaning of "selfish" so far that everyone is selfish all the time. Suppose that someone helps a stranded traveller but refuses to accept anything in return. Our Legalists might say that that is because the good Samaritan in question <u>enjoys</u> helping other people. It is for his enjoyment. Therefore, it is still a "selfish" act. But if someone does things to benefit other people because these are things he wants to do or because doing these things enhance his self-respect, it is more reasonable to consider him benevolent or compassionate rather than selfish. We have heard stories about little old ladies who are kind to animals and children because they believe that being kind to children and animals will facilitate the fulfillment of their desire to enter heaven. If one says that the little old ladies act out of "selfish" motive, it is still a misuse of the word. Being selfish implies both the desire to benefit oneself and the disregard of other people's well-being. All men are motivated by desire. But they may desire all sorts of things. In

147

this connection, the Confucianists firmly believe, unlike the Legalists, that through education men can learn to desire to be truthful and benevolent.

The Confucianist and the Legalist views contrast on the conflict between filial piety and loyalty to the state. The Confucianist view is discussed in Chapter 2. We shall now examine the Legalist view. The story of a son who bore witness against his father for stealing a sheep (cf. Analects XIII, 18) is told again in Han Fei Zi, with the criticisms of Confucius and the added detail that the son was later sentenced to death by the authorities on the ground that the son's loyalty to the ruler was outweighed by the resulting lack of filiality to his father.

> In the state of Qu there was a man named Honest Gong. When his father stole a sheep, he reported the theft to the authorities. Yet the local magistrate, considering that the man was honest in the service of his sovereign but a villain to his own father, replied, "Put him to death!", and the man was accordingly sentenced and executed. Thus we see that a man who is an honest subject of his sovereign may be an infamous son to his father.

> A man of Lu accompanied his sovereign to war. Three times he went into battle, and three times he ran away. When Confucius asked him the reason, he replied, "I have an aged father and, if I should die, there would be no one to take care of him." Confucius, considering the man filial, recommended him and had him promoted to a post in the government.

> Thus we see that a man who is a
> filial son to his father may be a
> traitorous subject to his lord. The
> magistrate executed a man, and as a
> result the felonies of the state were
> never reported to the authorities;
> Confucius rewarded a man, and as a
> result the people of Lu thought
> nothing of surrendering or running
> away in battle![30]

Han Fei Zi disagrees with the Confucian view. As Han
Fei Zi insists, the administration of law is not
primarily concerned with the individuals to whom the
law is applied but with the effect upon the whole
society. He sees that the Confucian view and practice
put the individuals over the whole society. According
to Han Fei Zi, the effect of the Confucian view on the
whole state can be disastrous, for Confucianism
indirectly encourages (or does not discourage, in the
above examples) stealing, treason, and other vices. If
reporting a crime is itself a crime to be severely
punished, who would report it? And if no one reports
crimes, then the enforcement of laws is undermined.
The Confucianists, however, allow that in some cases an
individual should follow a higher law than the law of
the state. According to Li Ji (Ritual Records), if a
man's mother or father has been slain, the task of
avenging his parent falls on the man, not the state.[31]
The duty to avenge applies in a lesser degree to the
killing of one's brothers, sisters, and in some cases
even teachers and employers.[32] Han Fei Zi's reaction
to such Confucian principles is very unfavorable.

What Han Fei Zi cites as a story became an
established law in China. As early as the Han dynasty,
Chinese were allowed to conceal the crimes of their
close relatives without legal penalty, and the
government could not compel them to testify in court
against their close relatives. For two thousand years,

from Han times to Qing (Manchu) dynasty,

> a son who brings an accusation of
> parental wrong-doing before the
> authorities is thereby [judged]
> unfilial and hence subject to heavy
> punishment. Under the Qing code, for
> example, such an accusation, if
> false, was punished by strangulation,
> but even if true, it brought three
> years of penal servitude plus 100
> blows of heavy bamboo. . . . A
> notable exception . . . [is] in cases
> of treason or rebellion.[33]

One can sympathize with Han Fei Zi's complaint,
although Han Fei Zi went to the other extreme. Imperial
China was probably the only country where reporting a
crime could itself be a crime. The exception made for
treason or rebellion shows that when it came to the
survival of the emperors, the Confucianists were
willing to sacrifice the claim of the priority of
filiality over loyalty to the emperor.

The Chinese practice of punishing a son who
reports his parents' criminal act is the opposite of
the practice of plea-bargaining in which a guilty
criminal may be granted immunity from prosecution by
reporting or bearing witness on criminal activities
(including his own). The American legal practice that
a wife cannot be compelled to testify against her
husband seems to have taken into consideration the
special relationship between husband and wife and also
the need of witnesses in a court of law. It strikes a
reasonable medium between the two extremes of the
Confucianist and the Legalist principles.

A common criticism of Han Fei Zi and other
Legalists is that they are ruthless. The Legalists not
only do not attempt to season justice with mercy but

they condemn the very concept of mercy. Either the Legalists have overestimated their ability to manipulate people or underestimated the ability of people to rise against brutality and oppression. By following the Legalist doctrines, Qin Shi Huang Di succeeded in unifying China in 221 B.C. and instituting the tight regimentation of life and thought of the people. But the Qin dynasty lasted only fourteen years, the shortest in Chinese history. Heavy punishments did not always have the effect that the Legalists expected. In 209 B. C. two obscure farmers Chen Sheng and Wu Guang, were ordered to report for work at Yüyang, many miles from their home. After a heavy storm the roads were destroyed by the subsequent flood. Chen and Wu realized that they could not possibly arrive in time. According to the Qin code, the penalty for late arrival in corvee assignment was death, with no possibility of clemency, no matter how extenuating the circumstances. By pointing out to their fellow conscripts that they had to choose between certain death and rebellion, it did not take them long to persuade the other conscripts to start a revolt and fight for their life. The revolt caught the Qin regime by surprise and it spread like wildfire. Although the revolt was finally put down by the Qin army, the country was in chaos, and the Qin dynasty ended shortly thereafter. All the three important Legalist philosophers-administrators (Shang Yang, Han Fei Zi, and Li Si) met their death violently. When Qin Xiao Gong (the duke of Qin) died, the crown prince, whose teacher Shang Yang had punished, succeeded to the throne.[34] Shang Yang fell into disfavor and tried to flee the state. He was captured and killed by being quartered by chariots. As mentioned earlier, Han Fei Zi was forced by Li Si to drink the poison. After the death of Qin Shi Huang Di (210 B.C.), Li Si got involved in a palace intrigue and his co-conspirator later ordered that Li Si be executed by being cut into two pieces at the waist.

It appears that, for the Legalists, the objective of establishing a totalitarian government is unqualified and unquestioned. To achieve this objective, the Legalists are willing to use whatever means necessary. The Legalist goal of political power and stability is a highly questionable one, and the difficulty with "the end justifies the means" argument is that it presupposes that the identity of the means is irrelevant to the context of the end. History has shown that the means do not merely lead to the end, they often become the end. Shang Yang said that he wanted to use punishment to get rid of punishment.[35] The twentieth-century totalitarian dictators say that the reason they countenance violence and slavery is that they want to attain peace and freedom. The fact is that their end never comes, but the means they use destroy millions of lives.

After the fall of the Qin dynasty, Legalism has been a despised term in China, despite the Legalists' contribution to the organization of the Chinese government. The Legalist "law" in effect represents nothing but an instrument of control for the rulers. Chinese scholar-administrators with the Legalist bent have learned to carefully put their Legalist ideas in Confucian clothes. Unlike Western law, where the Roman concept of law as an embodiment of some higher order of God or nature is present, the Legalists offer no concept of civil law to protect the citizens. Until the establishment of the Republic of China, Chinese law largely contained administrative and penal regulations--the sort of things people wanted to stay away from.

Over the course of Chinese history since the Qin dynasty, Legalism and Confucianism have maintained a precarious balance. The Confucian ideal of benevolent government is a government by virtuous men in which the superiors personally know their subordinates. In the pre-Confucian feudal system where the feudal lords had small domains, government by virtuous men had its advantages. But as the states grew larger and economic activity became more complex, the business of government inevitably demanded more special knowledge and skills. Those who had a good knowledge of the Chinese classics did not always make good administrators. Knowledge of fa (law) and administrative technique(shu) had become a necessary qualification of a good administrator. The state could no longer be just an extended family. To rule over a vast mass of people, the rulers of the imperial China had to incorporate some Legalist elements into their official Confucianism in practice. This combination of Legalism and Confucianism contributed much to the political stability in imperial China.

Notes

Chapter 5

1. Cf. Si-ma Qian, Historical Records (Shi Ji). ch. 63.

2. Han Fei Zi, ch. 19.

3. Cf. Chūn Shu Zhi Yao (ch. 37.7), contained in Si Bu Chong Kan.

4. Han Fei Zi, ch.8.

5. Ibid., ch.17.

6. Ibid., ch. 7.

7. Ibid., ch. 11.

8. Ibid., ch. 18.

9. Ibid., ch. 43.

10. Cf. Han Fei Zi, chs. 14 and 18.

11. Si-ma Qian, Historical Records, ch. 68.

12. Han Fei Zi, ch. 11.

13. Ibid., ch. 15.

14. Ibid., ch. 19.

15. Ibid., ch. 18.

16. Ibid., ch. 17.

17. Ibid., ch. 12. This event occurred, according to

Bamboo Annals, in 763 B.C.

18. Cf. Si-ma Qian, Historical Records, ch. 87.

19. Wang Xian-shen, Han Fei Zi Ji Jia, 9, 10b, quoted by H. G. Creel in Chinese Thought, p. 128.

20. Han Fei Zi, ch. 18.

21. Ibid., ch. 49.

22. Ibid., ch. 15.

23. Book of Lord Shang, II, 7.

24. Han Fei Zi, ch. 49.

25. Ibid., ch. 29.

26. Dao De Jing, ch. 37.

27. Ibid., ch. 57.

28. Han Fei Zi, ch. 49.

29. Ibid.

30. Ibid.

31. Li Ji, books I-III.

32. The story of 47 Ronin (wandering samurai) in Japan is a classic example of this kind of conflict between the Confucian principle and the state law. Cf. G. B. Sansom, Japan, A Short History, (New York, Appleton-Century-Crofts, 1962), pp. 498-500.

33. Derk Bodde, Essays on Chinese Civilization, p. 188.

34. Because of the powerlessness of the late Zhou dynasty, the duke of Qin was a <u>de facto</u> king.

35. Cf. note number 19 above.

Chapter 6

The Naturalism of the Yin-Yang School

a. The Concepts of Yin and Yang and the Principle of
    Complementarity.

Yin and yang are the terms the Chinese use to
refer to the two complementary creative forces in
nature. Yin is female, passive, negative, dark, cold,
soft, wet; yang is male, active, positive, light, hot,
hard, dry. Here "positive" and "negative" do not have
any connotation of good or bad, desirable or
undesirable, but are used in much the same sense that
physicists speak of positive or negative electrical
charges of particles. Yin and yang symbolize the
eternal and profound duality in nature. Although yin
and yang are opposites, they counterbalance and
complement each other. Thus, if we consider the yin-
yang philosophy dualistic, it is not the antagonistic
dualism such as between good and evil or spirit and
matter. The ideas of yin and yang probably first
emerged in China about the fourth century B.C. In the
Guo Yü (Discussions of the States, c. 400-300 B.C.) we
find one of the earliest references to yin and yang:
"One must make use of the regularities of the yin and
yang, and comply with the regularities of Heaven and
Earth; be soft yet not yielding, strong yet not hard.
. . . "[1] Guo Yü explains the earthquake of 780 B.C. in
this way: "When the yang is concealed and cannot come
forth, and when the yin is repressed and cannot issue
forth, then there are earthquakes."[2] In Yi Jing (The
Book of Changes), yin and yang are used in a
philosophical sense. "The Tai Ji (supreme ultimate) at
the beginning of time, engenders the two primary modes
of yin and yang, which in turn engender the four
secondary forms, which in their turn give rise to the
eight elements, and the eight elements determine all
good and evil and the great complexity of life."[3] "One
yin and one yang, that is the Dao."[4] In the Zuo Zuan

157

Commentary on the Spring and Autumn Annals (Qun Qiu)[5], the terms yin and yang are used to explain the good and bad fortune of the state of Lu in 644 B.C. Although the theory of yin-yang and the theory of the five agents (wu xing) are often mentioned by the Chinese in the same breath (as yin-yang wu-xing), the two theories developed separately about the same time. The two theories were gradually combined to form an independent school of thought. It is possible to explain human and physical phenomena in terms only of yin-yang or only of the five agents. But when the two theories were combined, the explanatory power was markedly increased. The fusion of the yin-yang theory and the five agents theory apparently took place before the time of Si-ma Tan (Si-ma Qian's father, died 110 B.C.), so that in the Historical Records, the two theories are grouped together under the heading of the Yin-Yang School (Yin-Yang Jia). Zou Yen (305-240 B.C.), the greatest synthesizer of the Yin-Yang School, is credited with having combined the two theories into one. This synthesis produced a dialectical monism with the concept of rotation, that is, things succeed one another as the five agents take their turn. The five agents are metal, wood, water, fire, and earth. The rotation of the five agents is discussed in the next section. The five "agents" stand for five kinds of processes or actions rather than substances or chemical elements. The Yin-Yang School originated in the peripheral coastal states of Yen and Qi, a region famed for its occultists. Zou Yen lived in the state of Qi (present Shandong province). He was interested in astronomy (and astrology), geography, and history. Liu Xin may well be right about the origin of the Yin-Yang School. He says:

> Those of the Yin-Yang School had their origin in the official astronomers. They respectfully followed luminous heaven, and the successive symbols of the sun and

moon, the stars and constellations, and the divisions of times and seasons. Herein lies the strong point of this school.[6]

All things may be classified as partaking of the yin or the yang. For example, heaven, the sun, and fire are yang; earth, the moon, and water are yin. When a Chinese says that something is yin, let us say, he means that the yin force is dominant in that thing; he does not mean that the thing is absolutely yin and contains no yang at all. Everything has both yin and yang aspects, but not equally. A good example is men and women. A man is not devoid of feminine (yin) qualities, but his masculine (yang) qualities are dominant. Similarly, a woman has some masculine qualities, but her feminine qualities are dominant. Yin and yang are relative terms. Thus, a man is yang in relation to his wife, but yin in relation to his father. Relative to heaven (Tian), earth is yin. But like everything else, the earth has both the yin and yang aspects. Rivers and lakes are said to be yin; mountains and plains can be said to be yang. Relative to land, humans are yang. Among humans, there are men (yang) and women (yin). The interior of the human body is yin and the exterior is yang. Thus, by continuous dichotomy, we can predict the relative yin-yang aspects of a thing. This process of successive dichotomy of yin-yang is analogous to dividing a magnet into two smaller ones. The north and south poles of a magnet are reproduced when it is cut in two. This reproduction of the north and south poles continues as long as we can divide a magnet in two, no matter how many times. The relationship between the yin-yang principles has been ingeniously symbolized as follows:

The whole circle represents the harmony of yin and yang. The dark area represents yin and the light area represents yang. Notice that yin and yang each invades the other's hemisphere and in the very center of a hemisphere there exists an element of the opposite. Because yin and yang are mutually complementary and balancing, the greater yang grows, the sooner it will yield to yin, in order to restore the balance. The mutual dependence of yin and yang fits in with Lao Zi's proposition that reversal is the movement of Dao. The twenty-fourth hexagram in Yi Jing is titled Fu (return). The darkest hour of the night is also the beginning of the dawn. In a circle there is no beginning or end: the end is also the beginning and the beginning is also the end. The balanced symmetry of the above symbol of the yin-yang principles represents the rhythms of life: day and night, summer and winter, hot and cold, dry and wet, on and off, up and down, and the opposite but balancing roles of male and female. Indeed, people claim that meditation on this profound symbol will yield insights more valuable than any book can afford.

In the Appendices (the so-called "ten-wings") of Yi Jing (The Book of Changes), we read that the law of the universe is the law of change; change keeps the universe living and dynamic. However, change does not occur in a random fashion; it follows a regular pattern, that is, the pattern of the Eight Trigrams (Ba Gua). In the symbolism of Yi Jing, an unbroken line (——) is used to represent the yang force, and a broken line (— —) is used to represent the yin force. A trigram consists of three unbroken or broken lines in various combinations and represents the proportion of the yin-yang forces. Since we use two different kinds of lines (broken and unbroken) to put them in groups of three, we have eight trigrams (2^3 = 8). The yin and yang interact in accordance with the form provided by one of the eight trigrams. The first trigram is Qian (☰). It is the purest yang. Here the yang force so completely dominates the yin that yin does not appear. Qian represents Heaven or father. The second trigram is Kun (☷). It is the purest yin, representing Earth or mother. The six remaining trigrams are as follows:

Trigram	Name	Significance
☳	Zhen	thunder
☵	Kan	moon, fresh water
☶	Gen	mountain
☴	Sun	wind
☲	Li	lightening, sun
☱	Dui	sea, sea-water

By combining any two of the eight trigrams into diagrams of six lines each, we have 64 different combinations (8^2 = 64). These are known as the 64 hexagrams. In the Book of Changes, one hexagram is usually followed by another which is opposite in character. The first four hexagrams appear as follows:

161

The Book of Changes contains a description of the 64 hexagrams and the interpretations of their symbolic meaning. It was initially a book of divination. The old tradition placed the invention of the eight trigrams as early as Fu Xi, a legendary culture hero who is said to have lived around 3000 B.C. Modern research suggests that the eight trigrams was first devised by the early Zhou diviners. The system represents a marked improvement over the old method of interpreting the irregular cracks of oracle bones. The philosophical discussions contained in the Appendices of the Book of Changes were added by later scholars. The hexagrams may be considered an early form of binary or dyadic arithmetic. If we take the unbroken lines to represent 1, and the broken lines to represent 0, the Yi Jing hexagrams could be interpreted as another way of writing numbers according to the binary system.[7]

The Book of Changes purports to explain the observable changes in the world in terms of the harmonious and organic interplay of the complementary forces of yin and yang. It does not mention the five agents (wu xing) at all. Since the 64 hexagrams represent fluctuations in nature that correspond to changes in human affairs, they became models for decision-making. In the past, Yi Jing was frequently consulted by people who had to make important decisions. The answer one may find in Yi Jing is not a simple yes or no, but a series of images, often obscure but suggestive. Some are quite enigmatic, for example, "A young fox wets his tail crossing a stream." The method of consulting the Yi Jing is to draw stalks of the milfoil plant to select a specific trigram or hexagram. The process of drawing stalks is similar to tossing three coins six times, which most people do these days when they "play" the hexagram game. Let us say heads gives you the number 2, tails gives you the number 3. For each toss you add up the heads and tails of the three coins. If you get two tails and one head, your sum is eight. The possible sums include six, seven, eight, or nine. Each of these numbers represents a line: the even numbers give broken _yin_ lines; the odd numbers are unbroken _yang_ lines. You end up with six lines or a hexagram, which is "read" from the bottom up, that is, the first line on the bottom represents the result of your first toss, the top represents your last toss. A possible hexagram determined by your tossing three coins six times may look as follows:

$$
\begin{array}{ll}
\underline{\quad\quad} & 7 \\
\underline{\quad\quad} & 9 \\
\underline{\;\; \;\;} & 6 \\
\underline{\quad\quad} & 7 \\
\underline{\;\; \;\;} & 6 \\
\underline{\;\; \;\;} & 8 \\
\end{array}
$$

Having selected your hexagram by tossing coins or drawing stalks, you then find the interpretation or judgment of your hexagram in the Book of Changes. The "judgments" of the Book of Changes are credited to the Duke of Zhou, the illustrious son of King Wen of the Zhou dynasty. King Wen and the Duke of Zhou insisted that in every situation there was a right course of action and a wrong course of action. They thus changed the Yi Jing from a divination book which tells you that you are going to win a lottery ticket prize or die in a traffic accident, to one which allowed for choice, for your deliberation on correct action. This gives the person consulting the Yi Jing an active role in his own future. For an example, let us look at the second hexagram Kun.

$$
\begin{array}{l}
\;\; \;\; \\
\;\; \;\; \\
\;\; \;\; \\
\;\; \;\; \\
\end{array}
$$

The text tells us about its significance: " . . . the dark, yielding, receptive primal power of yin. . . . It represents earth in contrast to heaven, space as against time, the female-maternal as against the male-paternal." The "judgment" is as follows:

> The receptive brings about sublime success,
> Furthering through the perseverance of a mare.
> If a superior man undertakes something and tries to lead,
> He goes astray;
> But if he follows, he finds guidance.
> It is favorable to forego friends in the east and north.
> Quiet perseverence brings good fortune. [8]

The Book of Changes, with its hexagrams and judgments, is a response to the basic and continuing need to make sense of human lives, to understand how and why things happen, and to find judicious guidance for human action. The highest achievement of man, the Book of Changes says, is harmony in one's self and human society. The highest achievement of Heaven is Supreme Harmony, which permeates the entire universe. The supreme virtue of Heaven is to create. All created beings partake of the yin and yang which are opposite forces operating complementarily to maintain balance and harmony. The idea that different, even opposite things can co-exist peacefully and productively without losing their individual identity is the Yin-Yang School's contribution to Chinese philosophy. "How vast is the originating power of [the hexagram] Qian. . . . Unitedly to protect the Supreme Harmony: this is indeed profitable and auspicious."[9]

b. The Theory of the Five Agents (W̲u̲ X̲i̲n̲g̲).

X̲i̲n̲g̲ means movement, action, or operation. W̲u̲
X̲i̲n̲g̲ means five actions. Therefore the name "five
agents" is to be preferred over "five elements." The
five agents--metal, wood, water, fire, and earth--stand
for five kinds of actions rather than atomistic
elements. For this reason, they are also referred to
as the five powers (w̲u̲ d̲e̲). The five agents are five
powerful forces in ever-flowing cyclical motion, and
not passive fundamental substances. We may take them
as the basic properties of material things. These
properties manifest themselves when they are undergoing
change. Nevertheless, the Chinese theory of the five
agents bears resemblance to the ancient Greek theory of
the four elements (earth, fire, air, and water). The
ancient Greek philosopher Anaximander (c. 560) thought
that a fifth, namely, a̲p̲e̲i̲r̲o̲n̲ (the non-limited), exists
as a substratum of the other four elements. Since the
Chinese five agents are often regarded as the immediate
products of the y̲i̲n̲-y̲a̲n̲g̲ interaction, the similarity
between the Chinese and the Greek theories is striking.
The metaphysical ground of the y̲i̲n̲ and y̲a̲n̲g̲ is T̲a̲i̲ J̲i̲
(the supreme ultimate) which is akin to Anaximander's
a̲p̲e̲i̲r̲o̲n̲. Both theories are attempts to explain the
bewildering complexity of things in the world in terms
of a few simple familiar elements or forces.

Through the combinations of the five agents, more
complex things are created, such as trees and rivers.
In each of the things created by the five agents, one
of the agents has a more dominating position than the
others. The trees, for example, have a "wood power"
(m̲u̲ d̲e̲), and the rivers, "water power" (s̲h̲u̲i̲ d̲e̲). In
the process of change, the five agents successively
produce and destroy one another; no agent can maintain
its present status indefinitely. The enumeration
orders of the five agents, so important in this theory,
are the orders in which the five agents are named in
the discussions of the subject. Four different

enumeration orders exist. If we use the following convenient notations: w (water), W (wood), F (fire), M (metal), E (earth) we can list the enumeration orders as follows[10]:

   (1)   The cosmogonic order: w F W M E.

   (2)   The mutual production (<u>xiang seng</u>) order: W F E M w.

   (3)   The mutual conquest (<u>xiang sheng</u>) order: W M F w E.

   (4)   The "modern" order: M W w F E.

We shall now discuss the significance of these orders.

   (1)   The cosmogonic order (w F W M E).

   This is the evolutionary order in which the agents were supposed to have come into being. This sequence reflects the speculation that water starts the cycle of change. Here we find a parallel in the ancient Greek philosopher Thales (c. 624-546 B.C.) who said that everything comes from water and to it everything returns. Water and fire feature prominently in many of the world's creation myths.

   (2)   The mutual production order (W F E M w).

   This is the order in which the five agents are supposed to produce each other (see the diagram below).

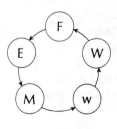

166

W produces F (by supporting it), F produces E (by giving rise to ashes), E produces M (by fostering the growth of metallic ores within its rocks), M produces w (by attracting dew when metal mirrors are exposed at night, or else by its property of liquefying), and w produces W (by making possible the growth of wood). The production order corresponds to the order in which Chinese give the four directions and to the sequence in which the agents come into being at the successive seasons of the year. Wood appears in spring (east), fire appears in summer (south), metal appears in autumn (west), and finally water appears in winter (north). Earth is left out here because it is believed to occupy the central position of the cycle of the five agents. Earth's season of domination is said to be a brief interim between summer and autumn. South and summer are associated with fire because south is the direction and summer the time in which the agent of fire (heat) is dominant. (China is situated in the Northern Hemisphere). North and winter are associated with water because north and winter are cold and water is associated with ice and snow, which are cold. East and spring are associated with wood because spring is the time when plants begin to grow and the east is correlated with spring and sunrise. West and autumn are associated with metal because metal is regarded as hard and harsh, and autumn is the bleak time when growing plants reach their end, and the west is correlated with autumn.

(3) The mutual conquest order (W M F w E).

This is the order in which the five agents are supposed to conquer (destroy) each other (see the diagram below).

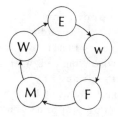

This order is the best known one because it was expounded by the master Zou Yen himself. Wood conquers earth because tree roots or wooden plow penetrate earth. Earth conquers water because it soaks up water or dams the course of water. Water conquers fire because it extinguishes fire. Fire conquers metal because it can melt down metal. Metal conquers wood because it can cut or carve wood. Thus the cycle is again completed.

(4) The "modern" order (M W w F E)

This is the order in which the modern and contemporary Chinese enumerate the five agents. The reason behind this order is obscure, no logical explanation is evident. Some scholars suggest, plausibly, that this modern order is just another variation of the mutual conquest order. W. Eberhard suggests that it may derive from an ancient mnemonic rhyme. [11]

Two secondary principles have been derived from the mutual production and mutual conquest orders to increase the explanatory power of the five agents theory. They are the principle of control (<u>xiang zhi</u>) and the principle of masking (<u>xiang hua</u>).

(a) The principle of control.

This principle is derived from the overall consideration of the mutual conquest order. A given process of destruction is said to be "controlled" by the agent which destroys the destroyer. For example, fox eats rabbits, but wolves eat fox. Thus we may say that fox destroys (conquers) rabbits, but wolves "control" the process (of fox's destroying rabbits). In terms of the five agents, the following can be stated:

W destroys (conquers) E, but M controls the process.

M destroys (conquers) W, but F controls the process.

F destroys (conquers) M, but w controls the process.

w destroys (conquers) F, but E controls the process.

E destroys (conquers) w, but W controls the process.

These follow easily if we take a look at the diagram for the mutual conquest order.

   (b)   The principle of masking.

   This principle is derived from the overall consideration of the mutual conquest order and the mutual production order. A process of change is said to be "masked" by another process if the second process can produce more of the substrate or produces it faster than it can be destroyed by the first process. For example, if in a certain region, the population of fox increases despite the presence of wolves, because of the increase in the population of rabbits, we can say that wolves conquer (destroy) fox, but the increasing population of rabbits "masks" the process. Similarly, if the population of a country keeps increasing despite continuing warfare, because of improved food supply and medical care, we say that the wars destroy the people but are masked by the improved food supply and medical care. Many good examples of competing processes which illustrate the principles of control and masking can be found in the ecological balance of animal species or the effects of drugs on the functions of the human body. In terms of the five agents, the following can be stated:

W destroys (conquers) E, but F masks the process.

F destroys (conquers) M, but E masks the process.

E destroys (conquers) w, but M masks the process.

M destroys (conquers) W, but w masks the process.

w destroys (conquers) F, but W masks the process.

The principles of control and masking are designed to answer questions which are not answerable in terms of the simple production and conquest orders alone.

Perhaps the earliest record of the theory of the five agents is the Hong Fan (Grand Norm) which is contained as a section (part V, book 4) of the Book of History (Shu Jing) which was written between the fourth and third century B.C. Hong Fan is said to be the record of a speech delivered by the Viscount of Qi, a prince of Shang conquered by King Wu of Zhou dynasty at the end of the twelth century B.C. The Viscount of Qi in turn attributed the idea of the five agents to the "Great Yü (the traditional founder of the Xia dynasty, living around 2200 B.C.) The idea is quite old. In the Hong Fan, the idea of the five agents is still crude. There the five agents are often thought of as actual substances, water, wood, metal, etc., rather than abstract forces or properties, as they later came to be regarded. By the time of the middle or late Zhou dynasty, the five agents theory had become more than a naturalistic explanation of the physical world; it had

come to include an assumption about the close relation
between natural phenomena and human affairs, especially
those of the ruling class. Yüe Ling[12] (Monthly
Commands), another important document of the Yin-Yang
School, is full of advice about being sensitive to
natural occurrences and retaining harmony with the
forces of nature.

c. Heaven, Man, and Nature.

   The Yin-Yang School was initially concerned with
cosmology and cosmogony. The school developed as a
result of man's curiosity about nature--its functions
and its structure. For this reason, we call members of
this school naturalists. The theory of the five agents
is an answer to the question about the structure of the
universe, while the yin-yang theory is a result of
speculations about the origin of the universe. Later,
with the addition of the doctrine of "the mutual
influence between nature and man" this school became
deeply involved with human affairs. Zou Yen developed
the ideas that historical changes correspond to the
revolutions and transformations of the five agents and
that a mutual influence subsists between nature and
man. According to Lü Shi Qun Qiu,

> Whenever an emperor or king is about
> to arise, Heaven must first manifest
> some favorable omen to the common
> people. In the time of the Yellow
> Emperor, Heaven first made huge
> earthworms and mole crickets appear.
> The Yellow Emperor said: "The force
> of Earth is in its ascendancy."
> Therefore he assumed yellow as his
> color and took Earth as the pattern
> for his affairs. In the time of Yü
> [founder of the Xia dynasty] Heaven
> first made grass and trees appear
> which did not die in the autumn and

171

winter. Yü said: "The force of Wood
is in ascendancy." Therefore he
assumed green as his color and took
Wood as the pattern for his
affairs.[13]

The rise of the Shang dynasty was similarly correlated
with Metal (white), while the rise of the house of Zhou
was correlated with the ascendancy of Fire (red). It
follows deductively that the next dynasty will be
correlated with Water (black). Before the next dynasty
takes over, Heaven will first make the ascendancy of
water manifest. When the cycle is completed, the next
cycle begins with the ascendancy of Earth. As it
happened in Chinese history, the first emperor of Qin,
who established Qin as the successor of Zhou, believed
that the force of Water was in ascendancy. He
therefore "took Water as the pattern for affairs, black
as his color . . . and changed the name of the Yellow
River to that of Power Water, because it was supposed
to mark the beginning of the power of Water."[14] The
following table shows the correspondence of the five
agents, five colors, five directions, and five seasons.

agent	color	direction	season
M	white	west	autumn
W	green	east	spring
w	black	north	winter
F	red	south	summer
E	yellow	center	summer-autumn

The Hong Fong (Grand Norm) also says that improper conduct of a ruler will induce Heaven to send down natural calamities such as unseasonable heat, cold, wind, or rain. On the other hand, a ruler's good conduct will bring about seasonable and moderate sunshine, rain, wind, etc.[15] The question arises, how are these "mutual influences between nature and man" effected? The yin-yang naturalists offered two theories, teleological and mechanistic. The teleological theory maintains that a Supreme Ruler would be angered by the improper conduct of a sovereign on earth and pleased by the correct behavior of a sovereign. His anger results in harmful natural phenomena which represent his warnings to the sovereign; his pleasure results in favorable natural conditions on earth which represent his approval. The mechanistic theory holds that the whole universe, including human societies, is a mechanism, such that when one part of it is out of order, the other parts will automatically be affected in a naturalistic and mechanistic manner. The wrong conduct of a sovereign reveals a disturbance of the yin-yang forces which automatically produces harmful natural phenomena. The yin-yang naturalists vacillated between the two theories. In any case, the yin-yang naturalists such as Zou Yen were able to use these quasi-scientific theories to frighten, console, or ingratiate the feudal lords and the kings as the situations allowed. Dong Zhong-shu, the eminent Han Confucianist, made a science out of the supposed "mutual influence between nature and man." Although Dong Zhong-shu is generally considered to be the greatest of the Han Confucian scholars, he was an eclectic, as most of the Han Confucianists were. He borrowed substantially from the ideas of the yin-yang naturalists and the Daoists to write his book, Qun Qiu Fan Lu (Luxuriant Dew from the Spring and Autumn Annals).[16] The book is a masterpiece of philosophical synthesis in which Dong Zhong-shu attempts to justify Confucian doctrines with the help of the teachings of the Yin-Yang School. Dong Zhong-

173

shu made an exhaustive study of natural phenomena such as floods, eclipses, and earthquakes which occurred in the "Spring and Autumn" period (722-481 B.C.) and the political events that preceded them. He concluded that these two sets of events are connected, however mysterious the connection may appear, and that an understanding of the connection enables us to know the reason of an abnormal natural occurrence and even the remedy for it. The following passage illustrates how Dong Zhong-shu used the yin-yang and the five agents theories to develop his ethics:

> Heaven has five forces, namely wood, fire, earth, metal, and water. Wood is first and water last, with earth in the middle. This is their Heaven-ordained sequence. Wood gives birth to fire, fire gives birth to earth [ashes], earth gives birth to metal, metal gives birth to water, and water gives birth to wood. This is their father-son relationship. Wood occupies the left, metal the right, fire the front, water the rear, and earth the center. This is the order in which, as fathers and sons, they receive from and transmit to each other. Thus, wood receives from water, fire from wood, earth from fire, metal from earth, and water from metal. As transmitters they are all fathers, as receivers, sons. Constantly to rely upon one's father in order to provide for one's son is the way of Heaven.
>
> Therefore, wood, living, is nourished by fire; metal, when dead, is buried by water. Fire delights in wood and nourishes it by means of the yang [solar?] power; water overcomes

metal [its "father"], yet mourns it
by means of the yin power. Earth, in
serving Heaven, shows the utmost
loyalty.   Thus   the   five   forces
provide a pattern of conduct for
filial sons and loyal ministers. ...
The sage, by understanding this, is
able to increase his love and lessen
his severity, to make more generous
his support of the living and more
respectful his performance of funeral
rites for the dead, and so to conform
with the pattern established by
Heaven.   Thus, as a son he gladly
cares   for   his   father,   as   fire
delights in wood, and mourns his
father, as water overcomes metal. He
serves his ruler as earth reverences
Heaven.   Thus he can be called a man
of "force."   And just as each of the
five forces keeps its proper place
according to their established order,
so officials corresponding to the
five forces exert themselves to the
utmost by employing their abilities
in their respective duties.[17]

For Dong Zhong-shu, man is the universe in miniature:
man is the microcosm, nature the macrocosm.   They are
governed by the same laws of the yin-yang forces and
the five agents.   Following Dong Zhong-shu's all too
human interpretation of the theory of the five agents,
later Confucianists made use of the "principle of
control" in the mutual conquest order to support the
claim that a son has the right (and obligation) to take
revenge on the killer of his father.   We recall that
when the principle of control is introduced to the
mutual conquest order, the "controlling" agent is
always that one produced by the destroyed agent (cf.
the diagrams for mutual production and mutual conquest

orders). Thus, it is only natural for a son, who was produced by his father, to avenge himself of the killing of his father.

In the Yin-Yang School, the universe is conceived of as a well-coordinated system where everything is causally connected with everything else. In particular, as Dong Zhong-shu and Zou Yen believed, natural phenomena and political events can influence (activate) each other. The Book of Changes takes the universe as an endless process of transformation which can be represented in the arrangement of trigrams and hexagrams. Man is an integral part of the cosmic system and goes through the same cycles of change that can be observed in the larger whole. The Book of Changes, however, emphasizes the connectedness of events and things rather than causal relationship. This is, in part, why the judgments of the hexagrams cannot be explained satisfactorily in any scientific sense. According to the Book of Changes, the cycles of changes are governed by the natural laws and are thus outside of man's control. Yet the operative conditions in any situation do not uniquely determine only one outcome. Within the constraints of the pre-existing conditions, a person still has the choice of taking a right course of action or a wrong one. Thus, whatever we do, we are responsible for our actions. Some people may point out that the "judgments" in the Book of Changes are so vague and ambiguous that they do not assert anything and therefore cannot be said to be either true or false. I agree with this judgment on "the judgments." Nevertheless, insofar as the Book of Changes' emphasis is on finding peace by being in harmony with the world, reading of the "judgments" may well clarify one's confusion of desire and guilt, fear and ambition. Consequently, chances are good that reading of the Book of Changes would help one make the right choice.

176

d. The Influence of the Yin-Yang School.

That the design of the flag of the Republic of Korea consists of the yin-yang symbol and the eight trigrams shows the profound influence the Yin-Yang School has exerted in East Asia. The eight trigrams and the circular symbol of the yin-yang are frequently portrayed in East Asian art. In China, the ideas of the yin-yang interaction and the rotation of the five agents were adopted by all the schools of thought. The Neo-Confucianists utilized the ideas of the Yin-Yang School to establish a metaphysical foundation for the ethical and social teachings of Confucius. The yin-yang and the five agents theories have been so widely and deeply believed by the Chinese that almost every aspect of Chinese life (medicine, marriage, politics, art, even metallurgy and cooking) has been affected by them. Indeed, whenever harmony is sought, people talk about the yin and yang; and people talk about the rotation of the five agents when important changes in their life are taking place. Although the Yin-Yang School has generated many superstitious beliefs and practices, it marked the beginning of Chinese science, mathematics, and technology. From a historical point of view, to call the Yin-Yang School pseudo-scientific is unfair. "Proto-scientific" is more appropriate for the Yin-Yang School. The Yin-Yang School shares with twentieth-century science the desire to interpret nature in a naturalistic manner and to use the knowledge thus acquired to serve people. What went wrong in some sections of the Yin-Yang School was their dogmatic attitude toward the authority of the ancient writings. They ignored experimental evidence and turned their attention exclusively to their masters' interpretations of the classics. No doubt, chemistry and astronomy have benefited enormously from the activity of the alchemists and astrologers. But speculation without empirical evidence does not lead to science. What distinguish science from pseudo-science are the critical spirit and open-mindedness. Dogmatism is the antithesis of science.

Chinese medical theory is based on the yin-yang theory, with significant emphasis on the psychic balance of a person. The central concern is the proper circulation of qi (vital energy, living force) in the maintenance of the harmony of the yin-yang forces and the five agents. Acupuncture and herbal pharmacology are two examples of the application of the yin-yang theory. The five agents are correlated with the five internal organs; the medicinal properties of herbs are classified in terms of the five agents. Water overcomes fire. So watermelon is good for patients who have a fever. On the other hand, hot ginger soup is often prescribed for cold or chill. This kind of common sense approach is still being followed by the Chinese.

Several belief systems have been associated with the Yin-Yang School, although their origins are obscure; among them are astrology, alchemy, almanacs, geomancy, physiognomy, glyphomancy, numerology, cheiromancy, chronomancy, and oneiromancy. Physiognomy is the belief that the fortune of an individual could be foretold by examination of his physical characteristics, facial appearance, bodily form, especially the bone structure. Glyphomancy is the art of analyzing the significance of a person's name. Numerology is a system that proports to explain the occult influence of numbers. Cheiromancy is palmistry, the art of palm-reading. Chronomancy is the belief that there are lucky and unlucky days, based on the phases of the moon. Oneiromancy is the art of making predictions on the basis of dreams. Among the rural Chinese, geomancy still has its hold. The Chinese term for geomancy is feng shui, which means wind and water. Feng shui means the belief that since man is the product of the yin-yang forces and the five agents, his living quarters and burial place must be located and arranged as to be in harmony with "wind and water" (natural forces). Harmony between the ancestors' grave sites and the "wind and water" would bring about good fortune and success; whereas disharmony with the feng shui may result in one's misery and misfortune in life. The belief in feng shui is responsible for the concern many Chinese have regarding their ancestors' and their own burial sites. The location of one's living quarters and arrangement of the furniture are also significant. The location and direction of the bed are believed important to conjugal harmony. Couples who suffer from marital discord are sometimes advised by the feng shui "doctors" to relocate their bed and re-arrange their furniture. For depression, a feng shui "doctor" may suggest that the patient change the location of a certain mirror in the house. Why? A scientific answer for the question is lacking. A rational explanation might be the following: The mirror was placed in such a way that the patient unconsciously looked at himself in the mirror every time he came back home from work. Since at this time of the day he often looked tired and run down, the image of himself in the mirror slightly irritated him when he looked at it. Over a long time, this irritating habit developed into a depression. Removal of the mirror broke a crucial link in the causal chain which ended in the depression. But given the assumptions of the Yin-Yang School, this kind of practice follows some kind of logic--a logic perhaps compatible with the logic of scientific explanation.

Another practice which had high sociological significance was the exchange of birth information in the arrangement of a marriage. In the past, Chinese parents of the prospective groom or bride insisted on getting the hour, day, month, and year of the birth of the young man or woman in order to decide whether the proposed marriage was going to be a good one. The twelve annual signs of the Chinese zodiac are: rat, ox, tiger, rabbit, dragon, serpent, horse, lamb, monkey, cock, dog, and pig. Other things being equal, a woman

born in the year of the tiger would have limited
choices. She could not marry a man born in the year of
the Lamb because she would swallow (dominate, injure)
him. But a man born in the year of the Monkey would
be able to live with her because a monkey could jump
onto the back of a tiger. Regrettably, many
potentially happy marriages were ended right after the
exchange of the birth information. Occasionally,
people had disagreements on the compatibility or
incompatibility of the prospective couple based on the
birth information. Debates on such matters sometimes
are quite amusing. Debaters usually cite ancient texts
(the older the better) and the great masters'
interpretations to support their arguments.
Considerable amount of time and energy could be spent
on such debates, usually without decisive outcome. The
clash of two dogmas does not produce new knowledge. In
this kind of debate, the question of verifiable
empirical evidence is left out of discussion. This is
one of the reasons the Chinese failed to develop the
Yin-Yang School into a bona fide science.

Notes

Chapter 6

1. Quoted by Feng You-lan, in A History of Chinese Philosophy, p. 33.

2. "Zhou Yü", I, 10, quoted by Feng You-lan, op. cit., p. 138.

3. Yi Jing, Appendix I, section II. The Appendices of Yi Jing were written about 4000-3000 B.C.

4. Ibid., Appendix V, section V.

5. Qun Qiu (Spring and Autumn Annals) is an official history of the state of Lu during the Spring and Autumn Period (722-481 B.C.) The Zuo Zuan commentary was not written until the fourth century B.C.

6. Quoted by Feng You-lan in A Short History of Chinese Philosophy, p. 33.

7. For a discussion of the possible connection between the Yi Jing hexagrams and the binary arithmetic of G. W. von Leibniz, cf. J. Needham, Science and Civilization in China, vol. II, pp. 340-345.

8. Appendix I, Yi Jing.

9. Ibid.

10. This list is taken from J. Needham's Science and Civilization in China, vol. II, p. 253.

11. W. Eberhard, "Beiträge zur kosmologischen Spekulation Chinas in der Han Zeit" in Baessler

Archiv, 1933.

12. Yüe Ling is first found in the Lü Shi Qun Qiu (Mr. Lü's Annals on the Qun Qiu Period) which was written in the late third century B.C. Later it was included in Li Ji (Ritual Records).

13. Book XIII, 2. Zou Yen's name is not explicitly given here but this section of the book deals with Zou Yen's ideas.

14. Historical Records, ch. 6.

15. Cf. Feng You-lan, A History of Chinese Philosophy, p.164.

16. Dong Zhong-shu's Confucianism is sometimes called yin-yang Confucianism.

17. Luxuriant Dew from the Spring and Autumn Annals, ch. 42.

Chapter 7

The School of Names

"The school of names" is the literal translation of the Chinese term <u>Ming Jia</u>. It refers to a group of philosophers who were like the Sophists of ancient Greece. They are more aptly called debaters or dialecticians than logicians in the modern Western sense, although they were interested in analyzing the meaning of words and avoiding the logical pitfalls of language. Except portions of <u>Gong-sun Long Zi</u>, all the dialecticians' writings have been lost, which is highly indicative of the general Chinese attitude toward this school. Our knowledge of this school of philosophy comes indirectly through the writings of the other schools, notably the writings of Zhuang Zi, Xün Zi, Mo Zi, and Han Fei Zi. Thus, we should remember that philosophers of the other schools usually discussed the dialecticians' ideas with the purpose of criticizing them. Zhuang Zi was a friend of the master dialectician Hui Shi (fl. 350-260 B.C.), yet his opinion of Hui Shi's philosophic activity is a negative one.

> Hui Shi used to deliver his views leaning against a dryandra tree. ... He diffused himself all over the world of things without satiety, till in the end he had the reputation of being a skillful debater. Alas! Hui Shi, with all his talents, vast as they were, made nothing out; he pursued all subjects and never came back [with success]. It was like trying to shout down an echo, or running a race with one's own shadow. Alas![1]

Zhuang Zi also quoted Gong-sun Long (fl. 284-259 B.C.), one of the leaders of the school of names, as having said:

> I have unified similarity and difference, and separated hardness and whiteness. I have proved the impossible and affirmed what others deny. I have controverted the knowledge of all the philosophers, and refuted all the arguments against me.[2]

Historian Si-ma Tan says: "The School of Names conducted minute examinations of trifling points in complicated and elaborate statements, which made it impossible for others to refute their ideas."[3] Hui Zi and Gong-sun Long are the two great masters of this school. Lesser dialecticians include Deng Xi Zi, who was a lawyer. A story about Deng Xi Zi follows. A wealthy man was drowned during a flood of the Wei River. His body was picked up by a boatman. But when the family of the drowned rich man went to get the body, the boatman demanded a huge reward. Thereupon the members of the family went to Deng Xi Zi. He told them: "Just wait. Nobody else besides yourselves wants the body." The family took the advice and waited, until the boatman became much troubled and went to Deng Xi Zi. Deng Xi Zi said to him: "Merely wait. Nobody else exists but you from whom they can get the body."[4] A negative overtone is evident in this story about the dialecticians.

While Hui Shi discussed the relativity of concrete particulars things, Gong-sun Long's interest is mainly in the immutable universals. In the sentence "Fido is a dog," "Fido" is a particular creature, and "dog" is a universal. Fido, as a particular creature, may come and go; but the universal or name "dog" is absolute and permanent, according to Gong-sun Long. Both Hui Shi and Gong-sun Long engaged in the discussion of paradoxes or bizarre statements. Both men contributed to the purely theoretical field of epistemology and both were pacifists. Any language is capable of generating paradoxes. The nature of the classical Chinese language exacerbates the problem of ambiguity in the use of the language. The Chinese language is non-inflexional; its grammar does not have tense and does not express the difference between singular and plural, the concrete and the abstract, active and passive voices. In addition, the classical Chinese does not have punctuation marks. In a sense, dialecticians may be taken as experts in the exploitation of semantical difficulties. The following story about Gong-sun Long is an example.

> The states of Zhao and Qin entered into an agreement which said: "From this time onward, in whatever Qin desires to do, she is to be assisted by Zhao, and in whatever Zhao decides to do, she is to be assisted by Qin." But soon after Qin attacked the state of Wei, and Zhao made ready to go to Wei's assistance. The king of Qin protested to Zhao that this was an infringement of the pact, and the king of Zhao reported this to the Lord of Ping Yüan, who again told it to Gong-sun Long. Gong-sun Long said: "We too can send an envoy to protest to the king of Qin, saying: 'According to the pact, each side guarantees to help the other in whatever either decides to do. Now it is our desire to save Wei, and if you do not help us to do so, we shall charge you with infringement of the pact.'"[5]

a. Hui Shi's Relativism.

According to tradition, Hui Shi was a native of the state of Song and once served as premier of the state of Wei. He had a quick mind and was known for his erudition. Unfortunately, Hui Shi's writings are lost; our knowledge of him is derived chiefly from chapter 33 (The World) of Zhuang Zi, where Hui Shi's famous "ten propositions" are preserved along with twenty-one additional paradoxes propounded by unnamed dialecticians. Hui Shi was interested in science as well as semantics and logic, for we read:

> In the south there was a queer man named Huang Liao, who asked why the sky did not fall and the earth did not sink; also about the causes of wind, rain, and rolling thunder. Hui Shi answered without hesitation, and without taking time for reflection. He discussed all things continuously and at great length, imagining that his words were but few, and still adding to them strange statements.[6]

Because Hui Shi was a pacifist and espoused the doctrine of universal love, some scholars consider him a Later Mohist. However, Hui Shi was an individualist, he did not join the Mohist organization, and he did not regard the chü zi (the Mohist leader) as a sage. Hence we may classify him under the group of dialecticians. The main philosophical thesis of Hui Shi is that all things are limited, relative, and constantly changing. This thesis is ordinary, but the manner of Hui Shi's presentation is novel and exciting. He presents his thesis in ten propositions, which suggests that Hui Shi enjoys challenging people's customary beliefs and manipulating terms and meanings. Zhuang Zi acknowledged that Hui Shi had profound and original insights but recorded only the ten propositions without the supporting statements. We have no way of knowing the reasons or the logical steps behind the ten propositions, since logically one and the same conclusion may follow validly from many possible premises. Thus we are free to supply our own premises or explanations for the ten propositions. We shall now list the ten propositions and then discuss them individually.

1. The greatest has nothing beyond itself and is called the Great One; the smallest has nothing within itself, and is called the Small One.

2. That which has no thickness cannot be piled up, but it can cover a thousand square miles.

3. The heavens are as low as the earth; mountains are on the same level as marshes.

4. The sun at noon is the sun declining; the creature born is the creature dying.

5. A great similarity differs from a little similarity. This is called the little-similarity-and-difference. All things are in one way all similar, in another way all different. This is called the great-similarity-and-difference.

6. The South has at the same time a limit and no limit.

7. Going to the state of Yüe today, one arrives there yesterday.

8. Linked rings can be sundered.

9. I know the center of the world; it is north of the state of Yen and south of the state of Yüe.

10. Love all things equally; the universe is one substance.

1. The greatest has nothing beyond itself and is called the Great One; the smallest has nothing within itself and is called the Small One.

This proposition may be taken as a definition of the Great One (the greatest) and the Small One (the smallest), and therefore is analytically true. It does not say anything about what exists in the world. Things in the world are only relatively great or small. A sea is greater than a river; but in comparison with Heaven and Earth, it is small. In Zhuang Zi's words, "If we call a thing great because it is greater than something else, then nothing in the world is not great. If we call a thing small because it is smaller than something else, then nothing in he world is not small."[7] What the definition defines are the two abstract concepts. When we deal with concrete objects, we cannot be sure that they are the greatest or the smallest. "What men know is less than what they do not know. The time they are alive is less than the time they are not alive. . . . How can we know that the tip of a hair is the extreme of smallness, and Heaven and Earth are the extreme of greatness?"[8]

2. That which has no thickness cannot be piled up, but it can cover a thousand square miles.

To be without thickness is to be an ideal geometric plane. It is two-dimensional, so it does not have the dimension of thickness. Hence, it may be considered small. But a geometric plane may be long and wide, so it can cover a thousand square miles. In this sense, it may be called great.

3. The heavens are as low as the earth; mountains are on the same level as marshes.

The proposition expresses the relativity of the high and the low. If we take things as relatively high, then nothing is not high; but if we take them as relatively low, nothing is not low. The difference in altitude between the heaven and the earth, mountains and marshes, are insignificant compared with the immensity of space in the universe.

4. The sun at noon is the sun declining; the creature born is the creature dying.

This proposition applies to astronomy as well as biology and metaphysics. Because everything is constantly undergoing change and "reversal is the movement of Dao," we can say that the sun at noon is the sun declining, and the creature born is the creature dying.

5. A great similarity differs from a little similarity. This is called the little-similarity-and-difference. All things are in one way all similar, in another way all different. This is called the great-similarity-and-difference.

This proposition is unclear and difficult to understand. It has to do with the way we classify things. Feng You-lan[9] believes it refers to the difference between seeing the differences (or similarities) between particular objects (the little-similarity-and-difference) and realizing that in one way all things are different and in another way they are similar (the great-similarity-and-difference).

6. The South has at the same time a limit and no limit.

This sounds like a contradiction. But we cannot take it at its surface meaning. "The South" means the south of China. This paradoxical proposition implies that beyond the bounds of what was then known as the South of China were vast regions of land and water. But, as compared with the immense space of the universe, the apparent limitlessness of the South is rather limited.

7. Going to the State of Yüe today, one arrives there yesterday.

This proposition suggests Hui Shi's recognition of temporal relativity and the existence of different time-scales in different places. Living in an age of jet travel, we easily understand that we can cross the international dateline and arrive at some place a day before we began the journey (according to the calendar).

We can also take this proposition as implying that the meaning of "today" and "yesterday" is relative to contexts. Yesterday was the today of yesterday, today is the tomorrow of yesterday, and tomorrow will be the today of tomorrow. One can leave for the State of Yüe today and arrive on a day which in a different context is referred to as "yesterday."

8. Linked rings can be sundered.

Linked rings can be broken by brute force. But this statement has no philosophical significance. The eighth proposition perhaps means that whatever material connected rings are made of, it will in time decay, break, and perish. To link rings together is an act of construction, but no construction is permanent. The proposition also suggests that connected rings usually have a weak joint and that it can be sundered easily at this joint. Also, topologically, rings can be connected and disconnected without breaking them.

9. I know the center of the world; it is north of the State of Yen and south of the State of Yüe.

Yen was the northernmost state of China, and Yüe was the southernmost state in the period of the Warring states. The ancient Chinese took it for granted that China was the center of the world (Chinese call China Zhongguo, central kingdom); hence, the center of the world, which also was the center of China, lay south of Yen and north of Yüe. Hui Shi challenged this narrow-minded conception, perhaps because of his appreciation of the sphericity of the earth. Si-ma Biao put it very well: "The world has no compass points; therefore [from one point of view] wherever we may happen to be is the center; cycles have no starting-point, therefore whatever period we may happen to be in is the beginning."[10]

10. Love all things equally; the universe is one substance.

This proposition shows Hui Shi's affinity to Mohism and Daoism. "Love all things equally" sounds like the Mohist doctrine of universal love. "The universe is one substance" captures the Daoist idea of the identity of all things.[11] The tenth proposition may be taken as providing a metaphysical foundation of the ethic of universal love. It establishes a link between the Daoist love of nature and the Mohist love of all mankind.

b. Gong-sun Long's Theory of Universals.

Gong-sun Long Zi, or simply Gong-sun Long, was a native of the state of Zhao. Like Hui Shi, Gong-sun Long espoused pacifism and the doctrine of universal love. He liked to make paradoxical statements about abstract "universals" and concrete "particulars." Gong-sun Long maintained that universals, which are referred to by names, are as real as the particular objects and can exist independently of the physical world. Many passages of the surviving portions of Gong-sun Long Zi are too corrupt to convey any clear meaning. But since Gong-sun Long is best known for his outlandish statement that a white horse is not a horse, and his theory of "the separation of hardness and whiteness," we shall discuss these two aspects of his philosophy.

Gong-sun Long reportedly once rode a white horse near a frontier. The frontier guards stopped him and said: "Horses are not allowed to pass." Gong-sun Long replied: "My horse is white, and a white horse is not a horse." Having said that he passed the frontier with his white horse. Presumably, the guards were too astounded to stop him. We find Gong-sun Long's three arguments in support of his statement that a white horse is not a horse in a chapter entitled "Discourse on the White Horse" in Gong-sun Long Zi. In the first argument, Gong-sun Long says that because the intension of the term "white horse" is different from the intension of the term "horse," a white horse is not a horse. The intension of a term (or its intensional meaning) consists of the qualities or attributes that the term connotes. Qualities are connoted by "white horse" but not "horse." The second argument runs as follows:

When a horse is required, a yellow

horse or a black horse may be brought
forward. . . . The term 'horse'
neither excludes nor includes any
color; therefore yellow and black
ones may respond to it. But the term
'white horse' both excludes and
includes color. Yellow and black
horses are all excluded because of
their color. Therefore only a white
horse can fit the requirements. That
which is not excluded is not the same
as that which is excluded. Therefore
I say that a white horse is not a
horse."[12]

This is one of the few passages in <u>Gong-sun Long Zi</u>
which are clear and easy to follow. Here Gong-sun Long
is saying that the extension of the term "horse" is
different from the extension of the term "white horse."
The extension of a term (or its extensional meaning)
consists of the members of the class that the term
denotes. The extension of the term "horse" includes
all horses of different colors, whereas the extension
of the term "white horse" includes only white horses.
The third argument is similar to the first one. Gong-
sun Long simply points out the distinction between the
universals "horseness" and "white-horseness."

Thus, when Gong-sun Long says that a white horse
<u>is</u> not a horse, he is using the word "is" in the sense
of "being identical with." But the word "is" can also
be used to express class-membership (as in "Gong-sun
Long is a dialectician.") or class-inclusion (as in
"The class of white horses is included in the class of
horses.") Most people regard Gong-sun Long's statement
as outlandish because they take it as a denial of the
fact that the class of white horses is included in the
class of horses. By not clarifying the ambiguity of
the meaning of the word "is" at the outset of his
discourse, Gong-sun Long is responsible for the charge

of absurdity. Perhaps he did so deliberately to shock people.

Gong-sun Long was also interested in the problems of perception and cognition. His discourse on the separation of hardness and whiteness shows this interest. By "the separation of hardness and softness" Gong-sun Long means that hardness and whiteness are two unrelated and independent attributes. He has two arguments for the separation of hardness and whiteness. In the first argument he says:

> [Supposing there is a hard and white stone] is it possible to say hard, white, and stone are three? No. Can they be two? Yes. How? When without hardness one finds what is white, this gives two. When without whiteness one finds what is hard, this gives two. Seeing does not give us what is hard but only what is white, and nothing is hard in this. Touching does not give us what is white but only what is hard, and nothing is white in this.[13]

This may be taken as an epistemological argument, for Gong-sun Long is saying that we come to know the whiteness and hardness of a stone through different senses, that is, sight and touch; and without the constructive synthesis of the mind we can only know either a hard stone or a white stone, but not a white and hard stone. Is it true that "seeing does not give us what is hard but only what is white?" Yes. People such as experienced carpenters can often judge the hardness of a piece of wood simply by visually examining it. But such "judgments" are cases of inference based on perception, not perception alone. Moreover, inferences of this kind are often unreliable. A carpenter would be at a loss when he encounters a new type of material. The second argument is a metaphysical one. It says that hardness and whiteness, as universals, do not give us any information as to what sort of things are white or hard. One can think of whiteness without thinking of any white object, although whiteness may be manifested in any white object. Gong-sun Long continues that the universals of whiteness and hardness are independent of the existence of objects that are hard and white. That hardness and whiteness are separate and independent universals is shown by the fact that some objects are white but not hard while some other objects are hard but not white.

Gong-sun Long uses the words zhi for universals and wu for particulars. The literal meaning of zhi is "finger," "pointer," or "to indicate" (as a verb). A universal is what a name points out. Gong-sun Long is a realist when it comes to the ontological status of universals, that is, he believes that universals are not just words or subjective ideas in the mind, but rather permanent and immutable entities.

c. The Paradoxes and Bizarre Propositions.

In chapter 33 ("The World") of Zhuang Zi, we find twenty-one paradoxes or bizarre propositions. Some of them are fascinating. Evidently some are based on the ideas of Gong-sun Long, while some are related to the ten propositions of Hui Shi. Lie Zi and Xǔn Zi contain several paradoxes or bizarre statements that are identical or almost identical to those in Zhuang Zi. We shall list them and then discuss them individually, with special attention to P15, P16, and P21.

     P1. An egg has feathers.

     P2. A fowl has three legs.

     P3. Ying [the capital of the State of Qu] contains the whole world.

P4. A dog can be a sheep.

P5. Horses have eggs.

P6. Frogs have tails.

P7. Fire is not hot.

P8. Mountains issue from mouths.

P9. Wheels do not touch the ground.

P10. Eyes do not see.

P11. The zhi [universals] do not reach, but what reaches is endless.

P12. Tortoises are longer than snakes.

P13. Carpenters' squares are not square; compasses cannot make circles.

P14. Gimlets do not fit into their handles.

P15. The shadow of a flying bird has never moved.

P16. At times a flying arrow is neither in motion or at rest.

P17. A puppy is not a dog.

P18. A brown horse and a dark ox make three.

P19. A white dog is black.

P20. An orphan colt has never had a mother.

P21. If a stick one foot long is cut in half every day, it will still have something left after ten thousand generations.

P1. Feathers are potentially in certain kinds of eggs. Hence one can say: "An egg has feathers."

P2 and P18 have to do with Gong-sun Long's theory of universals. In addition to a fowl's two real legs, we have the universal of "fowl leg." Two and one make three. This is what is meant by "A fowl has three legs." Similarly, in P18, in addition to a brown horse and a dark ox, we have the universal of "a brown horse and a dark ox." Again two plus one equals three.

P3. No convincing explanation exists of its meaning. Feng You-lan suggests (without any explanation) that it has the same meaning as Hui Shi's third and ninth propositions.[14] Joseph Needham says that perhaps it means that as compared with illimitable space, Ying and all China are equally small.[15]

P4. This is another unclear and ambiguous statement. It would make sense if we interpret it as meaning that a dog can be considered as a sheep in certain circumstances (both dogs and sheep are quadrupeds.) It could also be interpreted as suggesting that because of the possibility of transmutation, a dog can become a sheep. But this is far-fetched. P3 and P4 are included in the list here for the sake of completeness.

P5. The dialecticians hardly had the idea of the mammalian ovum. This proposition probably implies that the processes of generation are basically the same in all animals.

P6. Frogs evolve from tadpoles. Hence tadpoles could be considered potential frogs. Tadpoles have tails, therefore (potential) frogs have tails.

P7.   The sensation of heat is in the mind that perceives it, not in the fire. A fire may have a high temperature, but it is not "hot."

P8.   This refers to the fact that mountains may issue from volcanic mouths in the earth.

P9.   Geometrically speaking, a perfect wheel touches the perfectly flat ground at one point. But since a geometric point has no size, a wheel does not really touch the ground. This proposition could also mean that when a cart is moving fast, at moments its wheels do not touch the ground.

P10.   Eyes do not "see" because seeing involves the whole brain (mind), not just the eyes.

P11.   Universals, being non-physical, do not reach our perception. What reach our perception are material things, and they are infinite in number.

P12.   This seems to be a case of equivocation. The tortoise may be longer than the snake if we are talking about longevity. Because the sentence is about the tortoise and the snake in general, the interpretation that it means that some tortoises are longer than some snakes is an indefensible one.

P13.   Carpenters' squares and compasses, being concrete particular objects, cannot draw perfect squares or circles. This proposition again calls to our attention that our perception does not reach universals.

P14.   This is similar to P13. It means that no perfect fit exists between gimlets and handles.

P15 and P16 may be discussed together. We could say that only concrete particular arrows and birds can move or rest, the universals of "flying arrow" and "flying bird" do not move or rest. A more interesting explanation of the two paradoxes is as follows: An object which is at two places during one instant of time is in motion, whereas an object which remains at one place in two instants is at rest. Consequently, an object which is at one place during one instant is neither in motion nor at rest. Therefore, since the shadow of a flying bird is at one place during one instant, it never moves. Likewise, since a flying arrow is at one point during one instant, it is neither in motion nor at rest. P15 and P16 are strikingly similar to Zeno's three paradoxes which we will discuss in conjunction with P21.

P17. A puppy can grow into an adult dog. This is just a matter of definition. This statement can also be considered a variation of the statement that a white horse is not a horse.

P19. People say that a dog is white because its fur is white. But a dog with white fur may have black eyes. Therefore when we are talking about dogs' eyes, white dogs may be black. Thus, a verbal catch is in this statement.

P20. After a colt becomes an orphan colt, it does not have a mother. This statement may be advice to use our terms carefully and clearly. "Every colt has a mother" is a true statement. But a distinction must be made between a colt and an orphan colt.

P21. The idea here is that of infinite divisibility of length or distance. The geometric series $1/2 + 1/2^2 + 1/2^3 + \ldots 1/2^n = 1 - (1/2)^n$ is a convergent one. The question arises as to what is the sum of this series when $\underline{n}$ approaches infinity. Because infinity (∞) is not a number, we cannot really say that the sum of this series is 1. In other words, we can only write it down as:

$$\sum_{k=1}^{\infty} (1/2)^k = \lim_{n \to \infty} \left[\sum_{k=1}^{n} (1/2)^k \right]$$

Mathematically, one foot can be divided into half and half again, <u>ad infinitum</u>. Physically, however, a foot of rod cannot be divided into half and half again indefinitely. Even if we have the technology to divide small pieces of material, sooner or later we will reach the atomic level. When we split the atom, we have mass-energy transformation ($E = MC^2$); so no mass would be left to be further divided.

The ancient philosopher Zeno of Elea (336-264 B.C.) formulated four famous paradoxes of motion, three of them similar to P15, P16, and P21.[16] They are:

Z1. You cannot get to the end of a racecourse. You cannot traverse an infinite number of points in a finite time. . . .

Z2. Achilles will never overtake the tortoise. He must first reach the place where the tortoise started, and by that time the tortoise will have got some way ahead. . . . He is always coming nearer but never catches up to it.

Z3. The arrow in flight is at rest. For if everything is at rest when it occupies a space equal to itself, and what is in flight always occupies a space equal to itself, it cannot move.

We will not go deeply into the technical complexities of the paradoxes. For a technically detailed discussion of Zeno's paradoxes, one may read Adolf Grünbaum's _Modern Science and Zeno's Paradoxes_.[17] Aristotle's non-technical analysis of Zeno's first paradox is helpful enough for our purpose of comparing P15, P16, and P21 with Zeno's. Aristotle says that length as well as time is continuous and infinite in divisibility:

> Hence Zeno's argument makes a false assumption in asserting that it is impossible for a thing to pass over or severally to come in contact with infinite things in a finite time. For there are two senses in which length and time and generally anything continuous are called "infinite": they are called so either in respect of divisibility or in respect of their extremities. So while a thing in a finite time cannot come in contact with things quantitatively infinite, it can come in contact with things infinite in respect of divisibility: for in this sense the time itself is also infinite; and so we find that the time occupied by the passage over the infinite is not a finite but an infinite time, and the contact with the infinities is made by means of moments not finite but infinite in number.[18]

d. Concluding Remarks.

We have seen that many of the dialecticians' paradoxes deal with logical reasoning rather than factual knowledge. The propositions about the relativity and divisibility of space and time as well as the proper definition of terms may have been devised to call our attention to the difference between logical reasoning and perceptual knowledge. In a sense, the dialecticians did "prove the impossible as possible, and affirm what others deny." However, most Chinese did not appreciate the mental exercise such as P15 and P16, when they could plainly see that arrows (or birds) do fly in the air. Since the Chinese value common sense more than intellectual acumen, and since common sense is based on perceptual knowledge, the dialecticians' paradoxes and bizarre propositions were condemned as frivolous and unprofitable, and their school died out after their own time. The dialecticians touched upon interesting questions of logic but failed to develop a systematic logic comparable to the one that evolved in Western philosophy. Three factors are responsible for the passing of the School of Names. The first was that the Chinese were more interested in morality and common sense than the science of logic. The second was the socio-political conditions of the time (the Warring States period) in which the dialecticians lived. Social upheaval and political confusion are not conducive to logical studies. The third was the intense competition of the other schools of thought which emphasized human problems and often offered concrete proposals for solving them.

The dialecticians were concerned with the proper relationship between "names" and "actualities"--a concern related to the social and political problems of the people. Because they had special talent in the technical use of language and argumentation, they concentrated their effort in this area and became what may be called "technical philosophers." They were like many of the professional American philosophers today who "talk" philosophy, but the subjects of their talk seem so remote from people's everyday life that their activities are regarded as "idle debate" by many people. Si-ma Tan's opinion of the dialecticians sounds fair:

> The School of Names made minute examination of trifling points in complicated and elaborate statements, which make it impossible for others to refute their ideas. They specialized in the definition of names, but lost sight of human feelings. Therefore I say: "They led men to a sparing use of words which makes it easy to lose the truth." Yet to force names to express actualities, and to study logical order so that there will be no error, is a task that must be investigated.[19]

Chapter 7

1. <u>Zhuang Zi</u>, ch. 33.

2. <u>Ibid</u>., ch. 17. We will discuss the meaning of "separating whiteness and hardness" in section b.

3. "On the Essential Ideas of the Six Schools" in <u>Historical Records</u>, ch. 130.

4. <u>Lü Shi Qun Qiu</u>, XVIII, 4.

5. <u>Ibid</u>., XVIII, 5. Gong-sun Long's argument is a clever one but does not justify Zhao's action. Here Gong-sun Long commits the fallacy of <u>tu quoque</u> (you're another). This fallacy is commited when one tries to reply to an opponent's charge by making the same or similar charge against him.

6. <u>Zhuang Zi</u>, ch. 33.

7. <u>Ibid</u>., ch. 17.

8. <u>Ibid</u>.

9. Cf. <u>A History of Chinese Philosophy</u>, vol. I, p. 199.

10. <u>Ibid</u>., p. 200.

11. Cf. <u>Zhuang Zi</u>, ch. 2.

12. <u>Gong-sun Long Zi</u>, ch. 2.

13. "Discourse on Hardness and Whiteness" in <u>Gong-sun Long Zi</u>.

14. A History of Chinese Philosophy, p. 216.

15. Science and Civilization in China, vol. II, p. 197.

16. The Buddhist dialectician Nagarjuna in the second-century India propounded paradoxes similar to those of the Chinese dialecticians and Zeno, purporting to prove the impossibility of motion.

17. A shorter version can be found in "Modern Science and Zeno's Paradoxes of Motion" in The Philosophy of Time, edited by R. M. Gale.

18. Aristotle, Physics, bk. VI, 239. For a mathematical account of the paradoxes, cf. Thomas Heath, Mathematics in Aristotle.

19. Historical Records, ch. 120.

Chapter 8

The Varieties of Chinese Buddhism

a. The Basic Concepts of Buddhism.

"Buddhism" means the philosophy of the Buddha, or the Enlightened One. "Buddha" is an honorific title. The real name of the founder of Buddhism is Siddhartha Gautama. Gautama is his surname. Because his family belonged to the clan of Sakya, he is sometimes called Sakyamuni, the sage of the Sakyas. He is also called Tathagata (thus come, naturalness, just is) which signifies his pure state of being. He was born about 563 B.C. in northern India. His father was an over-protective feudal lord who shielded his son from unpleasant realities such as poverty, sickness, and death. Young Siddhartha seemed to have everything: wealth, health, good looks, status, a beautiful and virtuous wife, and a son. Yet, inevitably, he was confronted with the misery and horror of old age, disease, and death. He asked himself questions about life but could not find any satisfactory answer. At the age of twenty-nine, he found the luxuries of the palace life intolerable and decided to become a wandering ascetic. While his wife and son were sleeping, he silently bade them farewell and left the palace. Outside of the city and at the edge of a forest, he cut off his long hair, discarded his princely robes, put on a beggar's clothe, and set out to seek the answer for the problems of old age, sickness, and death.

For six years, Gautama practiced extreme asceticism. His body was emaciated by fast. One day he fainted and almost died but was saved by a fellow ascetic. After this experience, Gautama realized that neither indulgence in pleasure and luxury nor mortification of body is the way of spiritual liberation. He then practiced the "middle way" until he gained enlightenment under the Bodhi tree. He became the "Buddha" and went about teaching the Four Noble Truths of salvation. If we take the Buddha's Four Noble Truths as epitomizing Buddhism, then the Four Noble Truths shows that Buddhism is basically a pragmatic psychotherapeutic philosophy rather than a theistic religion in the Judeo-Christian sense. The Four Noble Truths are as follows:

1. Life is dukkha (suffering).
2. The cause of suffering is tanha (selfish desire).
3. Suffering can be ended by the overcoming of selfish desire.
4. The way to overcome tanha is to practice the Eightfold Path: right knowledge, right intention, right speech, right action, right livelihood, right effort, right mindfulness, right meditation.

The First Noble Truth is largely responsible for the judgment that Buddhism is a pessimistic philosophy. Yet this judgment is passed without careful reading of the three other Noble Truths. So long as one holds that man's conditions can be improved, one cannot properly be charged with being pessimistic, even if one characterizes the conditions as dark. Indeed, insofar as suffering is inevitable in life, the First Noble Truth is realistic. The Second Noble Truth indicates the Buddha's interest in causal relationship. The Third Noble Truth follows logically from the Second and provides justification for the claim that early Buddhism is a form of psychotherapy. The Fourth Noble Truth (The Eightfold Truth) details the way of dispelling avidya (ignorance)[1] and gaining nirvana.

Nirvana means extinction, that is, the extinction

of the individual ego and selfish desires. According to the Buddhists, one may achieve nirvana by identifying his individual self with the Universal Mind or with what they call the Buddha-Nature. Different schools of Buddhism have slightly different interpretations of nirvana, which need not concern us here. The identification of the individual consciousness with the Buddha-Nature (ultimate reality) implies the emancipation of the individual from the wheel of birth and death (samsara). Thus, nirvana signifies absolute peace and perfect bliss and is the opposite of samsara, which is the world of endless suffering and anxiety. The samsara world is governed by the law of karma. Karma means causality, work, or action.[2] The Buddhists believe that every action must produce its results and that every disposition to act is the result of one's past action. By "action" they mean both physical and mental activities. The so-called "law of karma" is a kind of causal law which applies to both the physical and moral realms. As the Bible says, "Be not deceived; God is not mocked; for whatever a man soweth, that he shall also reap." (Galatians, 6: 7) Only through enlightenment, the destruction of the fundamental ignorance (avidya), can one overcome the operation of karma and step out of the endless cycles of samsara.

The right knowledge of the Eightfold path is concerned with the nature of the samsara world in general and man in particular. Everything is transient. The universe is in a flux of change, including the observer himself. Thus, the Buddhist doctrine of anatman (non-self)[3] says no eternal and permanent "soul" is a substance in man. In other words, only continuity of karma and skandhas (aggregates of consciousness, personality traits) exist, but no identity of soul from one time to another, or from one life to another. The doctrine of anatman is perhaps the most difficult aspect of Buddhism; it has an important consequence for the

Buddhist conception of rebirth. For the Buddhists, rebirth does not mean the journey of a soul from place to place. Instead, it is the transmission of the effects of our actions from one life to another, just like the image of an object being reflected in a mirror. The object does not enter into the mirror, but its effect is transmitted into a different medium. Candle flame is a favorite metaphor of the Buddhists; they often use it to illustrate the doctrine of anatman. Human life is like a flame. A candle flame is not an enduring entity but a process in which the stuff of the candle continuously becomes the light, heat, and smoke of the flame. When a candle is about to burn out, we may light a fresh candle from it. One flame goes out and another begins to burn. The burning process continues, but no entity has passed from one candle to another. Thus, Buddhism is a philosophy of becoming rather than of being.[4]

b. Introduction and Development of Buddhism in China.

Through trading with central Asia the Chinese heard of Buddhism as early as the second century B.C. However, not until 67 A.D. did we have an official record of the contact between the Chinese and the Indian Buddhists. Emperor Han Ming Di (reigned 58-76 A.D.) sent a Confucian scholar named Qin Jing to India with the purpose of bringing back Buddhist scriptures. Qin Jing returned with two Indian monks and many Buddhist scriptures. Commerce between the Chinese scholars and the Indian Buddhists increased, but on the whole Buddhism was either little known or misunderstood by the Chinese. Slowly but steadily, Indian and Chinese monks worked together to translate Buddhist scriptures into Chinese. By mid fifth-century, most of the Buddhist literature was translated into Chinese. The translation was a difficult task, as many Buddhist terms did not have Chinese counterparts. In this task, Kumarajiva's contribution was immense. Kumarajiva was born in the central Asian kingdom of Kushan (Yüe Zhi) to an Indian father. He was captured by the Chinese during an expedition about 382 A.D. and brought back to the city of Chang-an, where he was put in charge of the great translation project. Kumarajiva mastered both Sanskrit and Chinese, and with the help of the Chinese assistants translated 98 Buddhist scriptures into Chinese before his death in 413. Kumarajiva had many Chinese disciples; two of them, Seng-zhao and Dao-sheng, wrote long essays about nirvana and Buddha-Nature. Kumarajiva and his assistants often used Chinese philosophical (especially Daoist) terminology to explicate Buddhist concepts. For example, they used such Daoist terms as you (being), wu (non-being), you-wei (action), wu-wei (non-action) in their translations. This practice resulted in a creative synthesis of Buddhism and Chinese philosophy, leading to the emergence of many schools of Chinese Buddhism, including Chan (Zen) Buddhism. We must make a distinction between "Chinese Buddhism" and "Buddhism in China." "Chinese Buddhism" is the form of Buddhism which has evolved from the interaction of the original Buddhist ideas and Chinese philosophical tradition. "Buddhism in China" refers to the types of Buddhism which were introduced to China but remained unaffected by the indigenous Chinese philosophy. The school of Mere Ideation (Wei-shi Zong, subjective idealism) introduced by the famous Chinese monk Xüan-zang is an example of "Buddhism in China." "Buddhism in China" had a very small following and virtually died out in China.

Like any large system of beliefs, Buddhism was divided into major trends shortly after the death of Gautama: Mahayana (the greater vehicle) Buddhism and Hinayana (the lesser vehicle) Buddhism. "Maha" means great, "yana" means a raft or a vehicle, "hina" means little. Mahayana Buddhism is more inclusive; it accepts more readily the religious practices and philosophical ideas of the people it converted. It also emphasizes fellowship, charity, and social service. Thus, the name "greater vehicle" conveys the image of a big raft carrying a large number of people across the sea of suffering to the shore of enlightenment. Hinayana Buddhism, on the other hand, emphasizes individual self-effort, the attainment of prajna (wisdom), and the peace of mind. To avoid any impression of preferential treatment, many writers today use the name "Theravada" (the doctrine of the Elders) to refer to Hinayana Buddhism. Hinayana Buddhism is more demanding in that it insists that being a Buddhist is a full-time occupation. In order to enter nirvana, one must give up the world and become a monk or nun. The ideal of Hinayana Buddhism is the arhat (wandering ascetic); the ideal of Mahayana Buddhism is the Bodhisattva. A Bodhisattva is an enlightened one, "one whose essence (sattva) is perfected wisdom (bodhi)." Though a Bodhisattva has achieved enlightenment, he chooses to stay in this world to help others to attain salvation before entering nirvana himself. One Bodhisattva vowed not to enter nirvana before all the sentient beings are saved. Buddhists do not make any real distinction between humans and animals. Thus for the Mahayanists, karuna (compassion) is a cardinal virtue. Understandably, Bodhisattvas have become the popular gods of the Mahayanists. The Chinese Mahayanists changed the sex of the Indian Bodhisattva Avalokitesvara from male to female and worshipped "her" as the "Goddess of Mercy." The Goddess of Mercy (Guan-yin in Chinese, Kannon in Japanese) is still popular in China and Japan. The Buddha Amitabha was a Bodhisattva before he was worshipped as the great savior of the "Western Paradise (Pure Land)."

By and large, the Buddhism of China, Japan, Korea, and Vietnam is Mahayana; whereas the Buddhism of Sri Lanka (Ceylon), Burma, Laos, Kampuchea (Cambodia), and Thailand is Hinayana. Lamaism (Tibetan and Mongolian Buddhism) is generally considered a highly adulterated form of Buddhism that does not belong to either

212

Mahayana or Hinayana. In this chapter we shall discuss the major varieties of the early Chinese Buddhism, namely, the Pure Land School (Jing Tu Zong), the Middle Path School (Madhyamika, Kong Zong, or San-lun Zong), the Hua Yen School, the Tian Tai School, and Chan (Zen).

c. Early Chinese Buddhism.

1. The Pure Land School (Jing Tu Zong in Chinese, Jodo Shu in Japanese).

The Pure Land School is the least philosophical of Chinese Buddhist schools but the most popular one. Its popularity spread to Japan and it has become a major religious sect in Japan. The devotees of this school believe that the way to salvation is the simple act of faith in the saving power of Amitabha Buddha (ah-mi-to-fu in Chinese, Amida in Japanese), Lord of the Infinite Splendor of the Western Paradise (Pure Land). In Sanskrit, "Amita" means infinite, "abha" means splendor. Thus, "Amitabha Buddha" means Buddha of the Infinite Splendor. These Buddhists believe that faith is sufficient for salvation, even an unthinking act of faith such as chanting the name of Amitabha Buddha. Nirvana for them meant salvation in an afterlife in the Western Paradise. Such beliefs bear small resemblance to the original teachings of Gautama Buddha, but they satisfy the human need for hope and comfort. As Professor W. T. Chan has pointed out, many Chinese saw in the possibility of rebirth in the Western Paradise an extension of the age-old Daoist search for "everlasting life on Earth" and the Confucian ideal of sageliness or perfection of character, and they were therefore attracted to the Pure Land School.[5]

The Pure Land School was founded by Hui Yüan (c. 334-416), a Daoist monk, with the assistance of two Indian Buddhist monks named Buddhayasas and Buddhabhadra. Hui Yüan taught at the Lu-feng Monastery

213

in Hubei. Because the monastery was well-known for its ponds of white lotuses, this school was originally named "White Lotus Religion" (Bai Lian Jiao). It changed its name to "Pure Land School" to avoid confusion and suspicion when a rebellious society adopted the same name in the fourteenth century. Hui Yüan and his followers were mainly inspired by two sutras (scriptures): the Greater Sukhavati-Vyahasutra (Wu-liang Shuo Jing) and Smaller Sukhavati-Vyahasutra (also called Amitabha Sutra, Ah-mi-to Jing). The first sutra contains a vivid description of blissful life of the Pure Land, the second sutra is a summary of Amitabha's teaching on compassion.

The masters of this school taught that the present world is evil and we are guilty of violating nature. Yet, although men are weak, hope of salvation exists for those who have a trusting heart. The sutra promises help from infinitely superior beings--the Bodhisattvas and the Buddhas--in reaching the Pure Land of Bliss. Instead of relying on one's strength, man must invoke Amitabha's grace, which will enable one to the break the hold of karma. To receive this grace, one must practice the virtues of truthfulness, nonviolence, and compassion, and daily recite the holy name of Amitabha (Ah-mi-to-fu), or meditate fixedly on him, as long as posible, without distraction. This practice is called nian-fu (nembutsu in Japanese), in which a devotee recites "nan-wu-ah-mi-to-fu" (homage to Amitabha Buddha, "namu-Amida-butsu" in Japanese). St. Paul had the similar insight when he said: "For whosoever shall call upon the name of the Lord shall be saved."[6]

2. The Middle Path School (Madhyamika, Kong Zong, or San-lun Zong).

This school has its origin in the Madhyamika (middle path) philosophy, founded by the great Indian Buddhist philosopher Nagarjuna who lived between 150-

250 A.D. Two of Nagarjuna's treatises ("Middle Doctrine Treatise" and "Twelve Gates Treatise") and the "Shata Shastra" by Aryadeva and Vasubandhu were made the basic doctrine of this Chinese school of Buddhism. Hence it is sometimes called "The Three Treatises Sect" (San-lun Zong). Because of its considerable emphasis on the concept of emptiness (shunyata in Sanskrit, kong in Chinese), it is also called "The School of Emptiness" (Kong Zong). This school flourished in the Tang dynasty under the leadership of the monk Zi-zang (549-623 A.D.). The central concern of this school is the apparent antithesis between nirvana and samsara, between permanence and change, between the Absolute and the temporal. The Middle Path attempts to resolve this antithesis by saying that the so-called "Absolute" or "ultimate reality" is something which cannot be defined or described. To give a thing a definition is to say that it is something and not something else. If we were to define the Absolute, then immediately it would be limited by the very definition; this implies that we are not dealing with the Absolute anymore. Hence the Absolute is an indefinable emptiness or void.

The theory of the double truth occupies a central position in this school. According to Zi-zang, there are two kinds of truth (the common sense truth and the higher sense truth), and both kinds of truth have three different levels. Zi-zang explained his theory as follows:

(1) On the first level, to say that everything is you (being) is a common sense truth. But if we look at everything from a higher level, everything is empty. Therefore to say that all things are wu (non-being) is a higher sense truth. In other words, the common sense affirms being; the higher sense affirms non-being.

(2) On the second level, we understand that to say that everything is wu is one-sided, just as it is one-sided to say that all things are you. But

everything is both you (being) and wu (non-being). Take a tree. It is constantly changing into something else: the tree of this moment is different from the tree of the preceding moment. Therefore on the second level of double truth, to say either that everything is you or that everything is wu is a common sense truth. Saying that everything is neither you nor wu is a higher sense truth.

(3) On the third level, we realize that to say that everything is neither you nor wu is still making a distinction. But all distinctions are one-sided. Therefore, on this level, saying that everything is neither you nor wu is a common sense truth. A higher sense truth would be to say that everything is neither you nor wu, neither not-you nor not-wu; that the middle path is neither one-sided nor not-one-sided.

The Middle Path's method of philosophizing is a negative one. We are advised that reality is to be understood as the total absence of specific characteristics. To approach reality, we must follow the "middle path of eightfold negation," namely, no production or extinction, no permanence or annihilation, no unity or diversity, no coming or going. In the end, we must conclude that the highest truth cannot be put into any form of words. Thus, after the eighth century A.D. the Middle Path School became almost indistinguishable from the philosophy of silence of the Meditation School (Chan, Zen).

3. The Hua Yen (Flower Garland) School.

This school derived its name from its favorite scripture, the Avatamsaka-sutra (Hua Yen Jing, the scripture of the adornments of Buddha). In Japan, this school is called Kegon. This sutra is said to have been the first discourse of the Buddha only two weeks after his enlightenment. It is among the most philosophical and important scriptures in Chinese

216

Buddhism. The nominal founder of this school was Du-shun (557-640) but its great master was Fa-zang (643-712). Fa-zang's philosophy was initially a reaction to the monk Xüan-zang's subjective idealism, which stresses the unreality of the phenomenal world. Fa-zang also disagrees with Xüan-zang's doctrine of gradual enlightenment and maintains that everyone has the potentiality to be suddenly enlightened. Fa-zang proposes the philosophy of objective idealism which reconciles the important function of the mind with the objectivity of the world by saying that the mind is the basis of phenomenal manifestations and yet the objective world can exist without the mind.

Fa-zang is known for his use of the ten mirrors and an illuminated figure of Buddha to explain the doctrine of mutual interpenetration of the one and the all. Fa-zang's device is a variation of "Indira's net" of pearls which mirror each other. To explain that everything in the world of events is interconnected and interfused and that unity exists in the multiplicity of things, he arranged ten mirrors, one at each of the eight points of the compass, put a small lighted figure of Buddha in the center and put the other two mirrors above and below it, all the mirrors facing the center. Thus, the image of Buddha is reflected in each mirror; each mirror also reflects the image of every other mirror, multiplying and redoubling each other's images endlessly. In this way, Fa-zang shows that one is in all, and all is in one. He calls this doctrine shi shi wu ai, or "unobstructed interfusion of events."

Another doctrine of the Hua Yen School is shi li wu ai, or "unobstructed interfusion of appearance and reality." Shi means events or appearance; li ordinarily means reason, principle, or reality. In the Hua Yen School, li is often used to mean the ontologically absolute reality which is void or non-being. Here "void" does not mean "nothingness" in the sense that something once was and now is not. Instead,

217

it means the ontological ground from which events or things manifest themselves. Qeng Guan (c. 738-839) illustrates the doctrine of the interfusion of shi (appearance) and li (reality) by comparing shi and li to water and waves. He says that no wave is not water, and all water can make waves. Thus, reality and appearance are essentially one. In Aristotelian terms, we may say that although matter and form are conceptually distinguishable, they are nevertheless inseparable in reality. Qeng Guan continues that the mind of the common man is the same as Buddha-Nature. In the year 704, while attempting to explain the problem of the one and the many and the doctrine of shi li wu ai to Empress Wu of the Tang dynasty, Fa-zang pointed to a golden lion in the court and delivered his famous lecture "Essay on the Golden Lion," or Jin Shi Zi Zhang. He says that the gold symbolizes reality while the lion symbolizes appearance. Gold has no form of its own but is shaped to the form of a lion as its appearance. Similarly, reality is formless by itself but assumes any form that circumstances allow it. On the other hand, the lion is simply a form or appearance; it cannot exist without gold (reality). However, appearance reveals the existence of reality, for without the form of lion there is no expression of gold. When one sees the figure in the court as a lion, the lion is evident, the gold is neglected. When one sees only gold, the lion is obscured from sight. At times both the gold and the lion can be seen, at other times neither is seen. When one intuits the perfectly harmonious merging of the lion and the gold, one sees that the lion is the gold and the gold is the lion. The dichotomy of shi and li disappears and one understands the doctrine of shi li wu ai.

4. The Tian Tai (Tendai in Japanese) School (The Heavenly Terrace School)

This school was named for the mountain where its main monastery was located in eastern Zejiang province.

Its founder was Zhi-kai (sometimes called Zhi-yi, 538-597). He was a war orphan who turned to Buddhism as he grew up. His favorite scripture is <u>Saddharma-pundarika</u> (<u>Lotus</u> <u>Scripture</u> <u>of</u> <u>the</u> <u>Mysterious</u> <u>Law</u>, <u>Miao</u> <u>Fa</u> <u>Lian</u> <u>Hua</u> <u>Jing</u> or simply <u>Fa-Hua</u>), although he believed that all Buddhist scriptures and sects have their place in the Buddhist philosophy and could be harmonized. Zhi-kai shares the views of the Hua Yen School that appearance and reality are identical and that all is one and one is all. Zhi-kai stresses that Buddha-Nature is everywhere in the world and insists that everyone can be saved and become a Buddha. He completely rejects the theory of <u>icchantika</u> which says that some beings are devoid of Buddha-Nature. The difference between Buddhas and ordinary beings is that of enlightenment <u>vs</u> unenlightenment. Enlightenment is the destruction of fundamental ignorance. Because of their fundamental ignorance (which in turn was produced by impure <u>karma</u>), the unenlightened people do not know that they live in impurity; they are like dreamers who do not know they are dreaming. A rather literal meaning of this statement according to the Buddhists, is that the "higher consciousness" of the unenlightened people has not been awaked yet. Hence, they are to be treated with sympathy rather than blamed.

The Tian Tai masters developed a special meditation technique called <u>zhi-guan</u> (calmness and insight): <u>zhi</u> means to stop or to rest; thus it connotes putting the mind to rest (calmness). <u>Guan</u> means contemplation or intuitive way of seeing; thus it connotes the gaining of insight. According to Feng You-lan, the way of calmness (<u>zhi</u>) brings an end to the deluded thinking and hence is a negative cessation (resting in calmness), whereas <u>guan</u> is a positive contemplation and produces the insight that all objects of thought are illusory.[7] By <u>zhi</u> (cessation) one may come to the threshold of <u>nirvana</u>, but by <u>guan</u> (positive contemplation) one may choose not to enter <u>nirvana</u> but to return to the world to save all the sentient beings.

Hence, we have the possibility of Bodhisattvahood. The Tian Tai masters also interpret nirvana in terms of permanence, bliss, purity, and ego rather than in terms of the Hinayanist nihilistic doctrine of extinction and non-ego. According to W. T. Chan, the Tian Tai School thus represents a fundamental transformation of Buddhist thought.[8] Furthermore, Professor Chan points out, the Tian Tai masters, by emphasizing that Buddha-Nature is in everyone, paved the way for the Meditation School (Chan, Zen) which stresses the inward seeing of one's own Buddha-Nature.

d. Chan (Zen): The Meditation School and the Philosophy of Silence.

Because of its influence on China and Japan and its popularity in the west, we treat Chan (Zen) separately in this section. Its name comes from the Sanskrit dhyana, meaning meditation. D. T. Suzuki's works on Zen Buddhism in general contributed greatly to the popularity of Zen in the West, even though Suzuki's background was in the Rinzai (Lin Ji) sect of Zen. Because in the West this type of Buddhism is known as Zen, I shall use this name. Explaining Zen is odd, for Zen is not suppposed to be explained. To talk about Zen is like telling a joke. One hopes that listeners will get the point and laugh, but one does not want to "explain" a joke. If a disciple of a Zen master asked about the true meaning of Buddhism, he might be yelled at and beaten with a stick. He was supposed to think things out for himself. But let us begin with the work of Bodhidharma who brought the spirit of Zen Buddhism to China from India. Bodhidharma was the twenty-eighth patriarch of a Buddhist sect in India which emphasized that nirvana is within reach of every man and that every man must find it for himself. He came to Guangzhou (Canton, China) in 475 A.D. and became the first patriarch of Zen in China. He then moved north to the city of Loyang. There, according to the tradition, he spent nine years facing a wall in the

220

Shao Lin monastery to exemplify his teaching of the supreme value of deep meditation. Disregarding the study of scriptures and scorning rituals, Bodhidharma taught by precept and example that the best way to achieve the Buddhist goal of enlightenment was to concentrate on the Buddha-Nature within one's own mind.

> A special transmission outside the
> scriptures:
> No dependence upon words and letters;
> Pointing directly to the human mind;
> Seeing into one's nature and
> attaining Buddahood.[9]

According to Zen tradition, the spirit of Zen came from Gautama Buddha. The scriptures were for the common masses. Some more perceptive disciples of Gautama received from him esoteric insight that was transmitted independently of the written texts. Gautama's Flower Sermon exemplifies this transmission of insight. It is said that once while Gautama was standing on a mountain with his disciples around him, he chose not to resort to words. He simply held aloft a golden lotus. All the disciples were puzzled, except Mahakasyapa, who smiled quietly. Thereupon Gautama said that Mahakasyapa had gotten the point and appointed him his successor. The insight gained in the Flower Sermon was transmitted through twenty-seven patriarchs to Bodhidharma, who carried this secret of Zen to China. Before Bodhidharma died in 536 A.D., he passed on to his disciple Hui Ko (486-593) his robe and begging bowl as symbols of appointment to the high office of the second patriarch in China. With this appointment, the interaction between Daoism and Buddhism entered a new stage, for Hui Ko was a Daoist before becoming a Zen monk. When the fifth patriarch Hong-ren decided to retire, he asked his disciples to write a short poem which would best convey the teaching of Zen. The author of the poem judged by Hong-ren to be the best would be appointed the sixth patriarch. One of his bright disciples, Shen-xiu wrote:

> The body is like the bodhi-tree;
> The mind is like the mirror bright.
> Take heed to keep it always clean,
> And let no dust collect upon it.

Another student, Hui-neng, immediately responded with the following quatrain:

> Bodhi is not really a tree;
> The mind is not a mirror shining.
> As there is nothing from the first,
> Whereon can the dust fall?

Hong-ren judged that Hui-neng's quatrain captures the Zen insight and appointed him the sixth patriarch. There were, however, differences in opinion on Shen-xiu and Hui-neng. Shen-xiu's poem emphasizes the Universal Mind or Buddha-Nature while Hui-neng's emphasizes the fundamental Nothingness. Shen-Xiu later became the founder of the Northern School of Zen. As the above verses suggest, the Southern School held that enlightenment comes suddenly, like leaping over a precipice; the Northern School took enlightenment as a long gradual process and thus counselled regular meditation. Later developments in China showed that most practitioners followed the Southern School.

The essential teaching of Zen is that to live authentically we must see things as they are, without any imposition of rational, logical categories on them, although Zen practitioners would not like to put it this way. Enlightenment is nothing but the intuitive understanding of the way things really are. This understanding, call it "the truth," "the first principle," "the Buddha-Nature," or whatever, cannot be expressed in words. Therefore, Zen does not express itself in intellectual discussions, but in interpersonal situations between the master and the disciple in which words may or may not play a part. An aspirant of Zen usually consults his master twice a day in private audience known as sanzen (chan-chan in Chinese) or consultation concerning meditation. An aspirant also devotes long hours daily to "seated meditation" (zazen in Japanese, zuo-chan in Chinese). An intriguing heuristic device used in the training of Zen students is koan (gong-an in Chinese) which originally meant a public document or theme but came to mean a paradox or deliberately illogical statement. About 1700 koans exist in the Zen literature which are said to be suitable for encouraging the experience of satori (enlightenment, wu in Chinese). While many koans are puzzling, some are entertaining anecdotes or recountings of historical events. Koans are designed not so much to induce correct answers as to break down the structure of our rigid logical habit, clearing the way for sudden enlightenment. "What is the sound of one hand clapping?" and "What is your original face, before you were born?" are two koans that have become well-known. Here are more examples:

A monk asked a master: "What is myself?"
The master: "Myself."
The monk: "How could yourself be myself?"
The master: "That is yourself."[10]

Zen is like a man up on a tree who hangs on a branch by his teeth with his hands and feet in the air. A man at the foot of the tree asks him: "What is the point of Bodhidharma's coming from the West?" If he does not answer he would seem to evade the question. If he answers he would fall to his death. In such a predicament what response should be given?[11]

Riko (Li Ku), a high government officer of the Tang dynasty, asked Nansen (Nan-chuan): "A long time ago a man kept a goose in a bottle. It grew larger and larger until it could not get out of the bottle any more; he did not want to break the bottle, nor did he wish to hurt the goose; how would you get it out?" The master called out: "O Officer!"--to which Riko at once responded "yes!" "There, it is out!"[12]

Doko, a Buddhist philosopher and a student of the Vijnaptimatra (absolute idealism) came to a Zen master and asked:
"With what frame of mind should one discipline oneself in the truth?"
Said the Zen master, "There is no mind to be framed, nor is there any truth in which to be disciplined."
"If there is no mind to be framed and no truth in which to be disciplined, why do you have a daily gathering of monks who are studying Zen and disciplining themselves in the truth?"
The master replied: "I have not an inch of space to spare, and where could I have a gathering of monks? I have no tongue, and how would it be possible for me to advise others to come to me?"
The philosopher then exclaimed: "How can you tell me a lie like that to my face?"
"When I have no tongue to advise

224

others, is it possible for me to tell a lie?"

Said Doko dispairingly, "I cannot follow your reasoning."

"Neither do I understand myself," concluded the Zen master.[13]

A Zen monk once went into a temple and spat on the statue of the Buddha. When he was criticized, he said: "Please show me a place where there is no Buddha."[14]

Zen masters sometimes order their disciples to tear their scriptures to shreds or to chop up the wooden statue of the Buddha. The purpose of the exercise is not to encourage disrespect but to correct the disciples' attitude toward the statue of the Buddha and the scriptures. The value of the statue and the scriptures is in the wisdom they direct our attention to. They are no more than a finger pointing to the moon. Some people attend to the finger instead of the moon. Hence the exercise. Huston Smith relates the following anecdote:

A Western professor, wishing to show that he had grasped Zen's determination to pass beyond forms, expressed surprise when the abbot of the temple he was visiting bowed reverently to images of the Buddha they were passing. "I thought you were beyond such things," he said. "I am," he continued. "Why, I would just as soon spit on these images." "Very well," replied the abbot, "you spit, I bow."[15]

We can take this anecdote as a koan.

Although a "correct" construal of a <u>koan</u> does not exist, insofar as <u>koans</u> are designed to make a point, they may be studied and discussed. Take the "goose in the bottle" <u>koan</u>, for example. The goose has come out of the bottle so easily because it was never in the bottle. So the problem was the officer's own making. By calling the officer and getting a response from him, the <u>Zen</u> master dissolved the problem. <u>Zen</u> does not offer a solution to the problems of life; it dissolves them. <u>Zen</u> shows us in many ways that we mislead ourselves into thinking that serious problems exist in life when none exist. Enlightenment in many cases is the realization that no solutions exist for the problems of life because no such problems exist in the first place. In <u>Zen's</u> view, many of what we may regard as profound religious and metaphysical questions bearing on the deepest human concerns should not have been asked in the first place. "What is myself?" is one such question; "What is the meaning of life?" is another. The mere asking of such questions leads us hopelessly astray. The influential twentieth-century Western philosopher Ludwig Wittgenstein arrived at the same conclusion when he said:

> We feel that even if all possible scientific questions be answered, the problems of life have still not been touched at all. Of course there is then no question left, and just this is the answer. The solution of the problem of life is seen in the vanishing of this problem.[16]

A <u>Zen</u> enlightenment experience is often an "AHA" experience. When a person searches his house from the basement to the attic for his pen and finally realizes that he has had the pen behind his ear, he often laughs aloud. Not to utter something aloud in such cases is difficult. Similarly, a person in <u>Zen</u> enlightenment may laugh out loud at the comic foolishness of his ignorance and in the enjoyment of his new-found insight. This insight is not so much a discovery of something new as a recovery of what we lost through our ignorance.

Zen is the art of living, not of thinking. A wise man lives his life in simplicity, naturalness, and spontaneity. "In carrying water and chopping firewood therein lies the wonderful Dao."[17] The meaning of life manifests itself in the living of it, not in any collection of words. If one cannot find the meaning of life in such simple things as carrying water and chopping wood, it is to be found nowhere. The obsession with meaning is itself the disease for which it pretends to be the cure. (This is a paraphrase of Wittgenstein's statement that the traditional philosophy is itself the disease for which it pretends to be the cure. Wittgenstein's idea of philosophy is that it is "a battle against the bewitchment of our intelligence by means of language."[18]) For Zen, reality simply is. Those who inquire into the questions of whether it is good or evil, or what meaning it has, spin an abstract conceptual web with no hope of extricating themselves. The king in Alice in Wonderland sounds like a Zen man when he says: "If there is no meaning in it, that saves a world of trouble, you know, as we needn't try to find any." Archibald MacLeish puts it this way in his poem: "A poem should not mean/ But be."[19]

e. The Philosophical Significance of Meditation.

Mencius talked about cultivating the great qi (vital energy) and Zhuang Zi mentions meditative states such as "sitting in forgetfulness" and "breathing through the heels." However, the Buddhists emphasize meditation more than any other school and require daily meditation as part of their discipline. Their highly elaborate and sophisticated analysis of the states of consciousness attests to the value they put on

227

meditation. In the perspective of the Buddhist philosophy, the human problem is this: We are deceived by the cosmic spectacle. We see through a glass darkly, we live in the illusion of maya (the Sanskrit word "maya" means illusion or unreality; it is related metaphorically and etymologically to "mirage") in which we are perplexed, and we must see through the trick of maya in order to attain enlightenment and salvation. Meditation is the key to this process because introspective reflection is the central concern of the Buddhist philosophy; one must understand the true nature of self and attain inner peace and integrity of mind before one can apprehend outer reality in its wholeness. The purpose of meditation is not simply to understand truths but to incorporate them, so that truths may be actualized in oneself. In this light, meditation is the Buddist's communication and identification with the fundamental reality of the universe. One meditative technique for the Buddhists is to gaze into a mirror to see one's own face. When one is spiritually advanced, one would see that one's face in the mirror disappears and one's karma becomes visible. The saying: "When face disappears, karma appears," is subject to many interpretations, but in this context it means the gaining of insight which enables one to pierce through the phenomenal illusions and see real acts, the usually invisible forces that shape a man's fate, a process similar to an x-ray's piercing through the flesh to the skeleton. Knowing the causal factors which lead to one's present state helps make one's experience in life intelligible, and with wasteful tensions and doubts released, one is better able to lead a free and independent life. Thus, the Buddhists maintain that the attainment of higher consciousness in meditation will bring about intuitive knowledge of higher truth, and thereby release. Being able to see the karma, and not one's own face, means one transcends one's ego and sees things under the aspect of cosmic causation.

All great religious founders, prophets, saints, and seers had a period of retreat from the mundane world to engage in prolonged and intensified meditation. Its effects are the liberation from ordinary concepts and percepts, and the gaining of insights into the nature of reality. Jesus and Mohammed had their stay in the desert; Buddha had his long period of meditation under the Bodhi tree. As the seeing of <u>karma</u>, the liberated souls are able to read the invisible holy writ. Perhaps mystics are right in saying that within each man's mind there is a contact point with what is experienced as God, as fundamental reality (T. S. Eliot's still point of the turning world), a glimpse of which yields inner freedom from all practical desire, and "in the completion of the partial ecstasy the resolution of the partial horror."[20]

The Buddhist emphasis on meditation reflects both the recognition of the limitation of human reason and the conviction that higher truths can be reached by transcending reason. The Buddhists do not simply say that meditation calms the mind and that when the mind is quiet, it can reflect the world of phenomena better, like a body of calm water. They assume that intellect is only a small part of the power of human mind. A person can imprison himself in his own intellectualizations and thinks he will escape if he improves on this intellectual system. With the awakening of higher consciousness and enhanced awareness, one realizes that one had been the captive of one's own intellect. Meditation is the Buddhist's way of reaching beyond the confines of reason. The insights thus gained transcend reason; yet despite its supra-rational character, enough people have reported on the results of meditation for us to say that its results have an appropriate kind of objectivity and trustworthiness.

Much of Western philosophy today is based on

Descartes's philosophy in which "I think therefore I am" is the beginning point of epistemological construction. For the Cartesians, the existence of the substantial ego is apodeictically certain. If we recall the doctrine of anatman, the most fundamental axiom of Cartesianism is the fundamental illusion of Buddhism. For the Buddhists, the ego is only a persona which masks the true nature of the individual; the power to think, which most people take pride in, is to be transcended. Meditation is not basically a problem-solving activity. It is more affective than cognitive. Although initially some intimate mingling of sensation, cognition, and affection occurs in meditation, it is different from both perceiving and thinking. The mind becomes restful and serene and is filled with a feeling of love toward all beings; it becomes aware that a sea of beauty and life surrounds and sustains all beings. Meditation attains not knowledge but prajna (wisdom) and karuna (love or compassion). It usually results in an experience of joy and peace that passes understanding. Freud called it "oceanic feeling."

> In which the affection gently leads
> us on--
> Until, the breath of this corporeal
> frame
> And even the motion of our human
> blood
> Almost suspended, we are laid asleep
> In body, and become a living soul:
> While with an eye made quiet by the
> power
> Of harmony and the deep power of joy,
> We see into the life of things.[21]

Notes

Chapter 8

1. The Chinese Buddhist translation of _avidya_ is _wu-ming_ (non-enlightenment).

2. The Chinese translation of _karma_ is _ye_, or _ye-li_ (force of action).

3. _Anatman_, the negation of _atman_, is a Sanskrit word; the Pali word for it, also commonly used is _anatta_.

4. The doctrine of _anatman_ is graphically explained by the monk Nagasena in his dialogue with the king Milinda. Cf. H. C. Warren (tr.), _Buddhism in Translation_, pp. 129 ff.

5. Cf. W. T. Chan, "Transformation of Buddhism in China," in _Philosophy East and West_, vol. VII, 1958.

6. _Romans_, 10: 13.

7. Cf. Feng You-lan, _A History of Chinese Philosophy_, vol. II, pp. 380-383.

8. Cf. W. T. Chan, "Transformation of Buddhism in China", _Philosophy East and West_, vol. VII, 1958.

9. Attributed to Bodhidharma but probably of later formulation.

10. D. T. Suzuki, _The Field of Zen_, p. 61.

11. Sohaku Ogata, _Zen for the West_, p. 97.

12. D. T. Suzuki, _An Introduction to Zen_, p. 70.

13. Ibid., p. 57.

14. Yang Yi, Record of the Transmission of the Light, ch. 27.

15. Huston Smith, The Religions of Man, p. 327.

16. Tractatus Logico-Philosophicus, 6.52.

17. Record of the Transmission of Light, ch. 8. "Carrying water and chopping wood" has become a familiar Zen expression.

18. Philosophical Investigations, section 109.

19. "Ars Poetica," third stanza.

20. T. S. Eliot, Four Quartets.

21. William Wordsworth, "Lines," 1798.

Chapter 9

Neo-Confucianism: The Grand Harmony

a.   The Rise of Neo-Confucianism and the Early Masters.

The Buddhist influence in China reached its zenith in the middle of the Tang dynasty. Classical Confucianism had lost its vitality by this time and could not meet the people's interest in metaphysical problems which was stimulated by the introduction of the Mahayana Buddhist metaphysics and the revival of Daoism. Many Confucianists felt the need to defend Confucianism against both Buddhism and Daoism. They criticized Buddhism on the grounds that it was a foreign religion and that it neglected an individual's familial and social obligations. Daoism, too, was condemned for its anti-political and quietistic orientation. The Confucianists maintained that human society is the primary metaphysical reality and that knowledge and values must be related to the activities of the individuals in the society. If the great wonderful Dao consists in carrying water and chopping firewood, they said, does not the wonderful Dao also consist in serving one's family and the state? Moreover, the Confucianists began to construct a metaphysics, with considerable appropriations from Buddhism and Daoism, which would provide a foundation for the Confucian ethic and a philosophically more satisfying understanding of the universe. As has happened so often in the history of ideas, the Confucianists were affected by the very ideas they were criticizing. Given the synthetic tendency of Chinese philosophers, the new philosophy which resulted from the Confucianists' interaction with Buddhism and Daoism would understandably incorporate features of Buddhism and Daoism along with the strong moral and social concerns of Confucianism. To distinguish this type of Confucianism from the early classical Confucianism of

233

Confucius, Mencius, and Xùn Xi, we call it Neo-Confucianism.

The Tang dynasty Confucianists Han Yù (768-824) and Li Ao (d. 844) are generally considered the forerunners of Neo-Confucianism. Han Yù and Li Ao were great essayists and are well-known for the excellence of their literary style. Philosophically they did not have anything new to say, but they concentrated their attention on the problems of human nature and attacked Buddhism and Daoism. They pointed out the importance of the Great Learning, the Doctrine of the Mean, and the Book of Changes, which became the source of ideas for the Neo-Confucianists. They argued that the Buddhists and the Daoists do not have the monopoly on the Dao, and they identified Mencius as the man through whom the Dao was transmitted to the later ages. According to them, a scholar could best develop sagehood not merely within himself but in relation to others and the universe.

Zhou Dun-yi (also called Zhou Lian-zi, 1017-1073) determined the direction of Neo-Confucianism. His Tai-ji-tushuo (An Explanation of the Diagram of the Supreme Ultimate) and Tong-shu (Penetrating the Book of Changes) impart metaphysics into Confucian ethics. Zhou said that sagehood is based on ren (human-heartedness) and yi (righteousness) which are derived from the essence of qian (yang), the creative power of Dao. Zhou Dun-yi was well versed in Daoism and the Book of Changes. The notions of yin and yang as two opposing aspects of reality were familiar to him. As the Daoists had argued that Dao is the source of being and non-being, or yang and yin, Zhou Dun-yi maintained that Tai Ji (the supreme ultimate) is prior to yin and yang and is the foundation of these two productive powers. Through the interaction of yin and yang, the five agents of water, fire, wood, metal, and earth are produced. Then, through further interaction, all the rest of the universe is produced. Because the five

234

agents are conceived of as material principles rather than as concrete things, they can be considered the common basis for all things. In the beginning, because of the abundance of energy within Tai Ji, it began to move and thus produced the yang. In Zhou's words,

> The supreme ultimate through movement generates yang. When its activity reaches its limit, it becomes tranquil. Through tranquility the supreme ultimate generates yin. When tranquility has reached its limit, there is a return to movement. Thus movement and tranquility, in alteration, become each the source of the other. The distinction between the yin and yang is determined and the two forms (that is, the yin and yang) stand revealed. By the transformations of the yang and the union therewith of the yin, the five qi (ether, agents) of water, fire, wood, metal, and earth are produced. These five qi become diffused in harmonious order, and the four seasons proceed in their course. ... Thus, yin and yang produced all things, and these in their turn produce and reproduce, so that transformation and change continue without end.[1]

This passage provides the basic outline of the cosmology of Zhu Xi, one of the greatest Neo-Confucianists. Notice that Zhou Dun-yi's explanation of how the yin and yang are produced from the supreme ultimate makes use of the Daoist idea that "reversal is the movement of the Dao."

Zhou Dun-yi also traces human intelligence and

235

moral principles to the supreme ultimate. He believes that man alone receives the material forces in their highest excellence, and hence he is most intelligent. Moreover, man's five moral principles of ren (human-heartedness), yi (righteousness), li (propriety), zhi (wisdom), and xin (faithfulness) correspond to the five agents of nature and are aroused by them. Thus the principle of the sage, or perfect man, is the same as the principle of the supreme ultimate, and therefore a sage forms a harmony with the universe. To become a sage and be in harmony with the universe, a person must be true to the moral principles.

Another early Neo-Confucianist, Shao Yong (or Shao Yao-fu, 1011-1077) attempted to write his philosophy of human life on the basis of the cosmology of the Book of Changes (Appendix V). He regarded persons as the products of the creative activity of the supreme ultimate (or Dao), working through the yin and yang. But unlike other creatures, man has an almost unlimited capability for mental, moral, and spiritual perfectibility. For Shao Yong, a sage is one who can use his power of perception and discrimination to comprehend the Absolute, penetrate the innermost secret of life, and reach an empirical understanding of Destiny. The ideal sageliness may correspond to that of the Book of Changes: "They plumbed Principle to its depths and completely penetrated the nature, thereby reaching to an understanding of Destiny."[2]

Shao Yong believed that all changes are governed by principles that can be represented in mathematical formulae. He constructed a system of numerical progression from one to sixty-four, corresponding to the generation of the 64 hexagrams in the Book of Changes. He also constructed a diagram which shows all the 64 hexagrams and claimed it represents the evolution of things in the universe. Man is the most intelligent of the products of natural evolution, but like all other things he is governed by numbers (that is, hexagrams).

With the first line of the hexagram Fu, the world comes into being; and with the hexagram Kun the whole world would cease to be. Thereupon another world begins with the first line of the recurring hexagram Fu, and the whole process of creation starts over. Shao Yong calculated that each created world has a duration of 129,600 years. According to Shao Yong's chronology of our existing world, the world was created in 67,017 B.C. and will end in 62,583 A.D. His "Table of Cosmic Chronology"[3] reveals his belief in the Buddhist theory of four world-periods, namely, formation, existence, destruction, and non-existence. Shao Yong believed that the history of the world repeats itself after each creation. This periodic creation and destruction of the world can be represented by his circular diagram of the evolution of the world. Thus, there is nothing new under the sun. The idea that everything involves its own negation is an old one.[4] It also sounds like Hegelian dialectic. Shao Yong's dialectic differs from Hegel's. For Hegel, when a thing is negated, a new thing is thereby produced. Negation of negation generates a higher level entity. Thus, synthesis, which is the negation of antithesis, is not on the same level as the original thesis. This is Hegel's idea of Aufhebung (uplifting). In Shao Yong's dialectic, when a thing is negated, the ensuing thing simply repeats the old: no Aufhebung. As Feng You-lan is fond of pointing out, Shao Yong's philosophy is characteristic of an agrarian people such as the Chinese.[5] Shao Yong's cosmology exerted a considerable influence on the later Neo-Confucianists and thus is worthy of mention here.

Another early Neo-Confucianist who developed a cosmological theory based on the Appendices of the Book of Changes was Zhang Zai (1020-1077 A.D.). Zhang Zai emphasized the idea of qi, which in the Neo-Confucian context often means material cause of a thing or the physical matter that makes up individual things. Qi in its entirety is called "The Great Harmony." In Zheng Meng (Correct Discipline for Beginners), Zhang Zai's major book, he says:

> The Great Harmony is known as the Dao. Because in it are interacting qualities of floating and sinking, rising and falling, movement and quiescence, therefore there appear in it the beginnings of the emanating forces which agitate one another, overcome or are overcome by one another, and contract or expand, one with regard to the other.[6]

When influenced by the yang qualities, qi floats and rises; when influenced by the yin qualities, qi sinks and falls. Since qi is under the constant influence of yin and yang qualities, it is constantly condensing or dispersing. Condensation of qi results in the formation of concrete things, while dispersion or rarefaction of qi results in the dissolution of things. Zhang Zai sought to combat the Daoist concept of wu (non-being, emptiness) and the Buddhist concept of shunyata (void, the emptiness of all Being) by saying that wu or shunyata is not really an absolute vacuum; it is simply the qi in its rarefied state which is invisible.

> The great void, that is, the great harmony, [the Dao] cannot but consist of qi; this qi cannot but condense to form all things; and these things cannot but become dispersed so as to form once more the great void. The perpetration of these movements in a cycle is inevitable.[7]

Zhang Zai is particularly admired for his "Western

Inscription," a section of his major work Zheng Meng separately inscribed on the western wall of Zhang Zai's study. In the "Western Inscription" Zhang Zai emphasizes the importance of the practice of ren in relation to parents and "all men without discrimination." Here he echoes not only Mo Zi's universal love but also the Buddhist ideal of Bodhisattvahood. Zhang Zai says:

> . . . I, therefore, am the substance that lies within the confines of Heaven and Earth, and my nature is that of the two commanders (Heaven and Earth). All people are my blood-brothers and all creatures are my companions. . . . In life I follow and serve the universal parents, and when death comes, I rest.[8]

This passage distinguishes the Confucian attitude toward life from that of the Buddhists or Daoists. The Confucian sage realizes that "life entails no gain nor death any loss."[9] He neither tries to escape from the world, as do the Buddhists, nor does he try to prolong his life by extraordinary means, as do the Daoist magicians. He simply lives his normal life, doing his best to fulfill his duty as a member of society and as a member of the universe. He "rests" when death comes. No fear, no anxiety is raised by death, and no sense of tragic end when death comes.

Zhang Zai's nephews, the Cheng brothers, Cheng Hao (1032-1085) and Cheng Yi (1033-1108), were two other influential Neo-Confucianists. Cheng Yi, the younger brother, started the realistic school of Neo-Confucianism which was completed by Zhu Xi (1130-1200) and is often referred to as the Cheng-Zhu School. Cheng Hao, the elder brother, initiated the idealistic wing of Neo-Confucianism which was completed by Wang Yang-ming (1473-1529). The realistic Neo-Confucianism and the idealistic Neo-Confucianism will be discussed in the next two sections.

Cheng Hao's ideas center around the notions of "Heavenly Principle" (Dao-li) and "Spiritual Cultivation." "Heavenly Principle" for Cheng Hao is natural form or pattern immanent in all things. "Spiritual Cultivation" consists in getting to understand ren. One who truly understands ren understands the unity of heaven, earth, and man. Oneness with all things is the main characteristic of ren. Cheng Hao believed that man is endowed at birth with qi which could be both good and bad. Evil is deviating from the golden mean--going too far or doing too little. Spontaneous acts are considered to be good (as following from the Heavenly Principle). Acts motivated by selfish calculation are judged evil. To avoid the disruption of harmony with the universe by our selfish desires, we need only to return to a renewed union of spirit with the Heavenly Principle in the universe.

In Chinese medicine the term for paralysis is "not-ren." Cheng Hao says:

> The doctor describes the paralysis of
> a man's arms or legs as not-ren; this
> is a very good description of the
> disease. The man of ren takes Heaven
> and Earth as being one with himself.
> To him nothing is not himself.
> Having recognized them as himself,
> what cannot he do for them? If no
> such relationship exists with the
> self, it follows that no condition
> exists between the self and others.
> If the hand or foot are not-ren (that
> is, paralyzed), it means that the qi
> is not circulating freely and the
> parts of the body are not connected

with each other.[10]

Like his brother Cheng Hao, Cheng Yi also talks a great deal about "Heavenly Principle," "human nature," and "spiritual cultivation." Cheng Yi's idea of "Heavenly Principle" came directly from the Appendices of the Book of Changes. For him, Heavenly Principles (Li)[11] exist eternally and independently from concrete things. Following the Book of Changes, Cheng Yi distinguishes between what is "within shapes" and what is "above shapes"; what is "within shapes" are concrete particular things, what is "above shapes" are abstract principles. Cheng Yi believes that the abstract principles (Li) govern the concrete particular things and exist antecedently to them.

Cheng Yi's discussions on ethics and spiritual cultivation are similar to those of Cheng Hao. He stresses not only the development of inner composure through complete impartiality, but also an exhaustive study of the principles in things over a long time and over a wide range of subjects. He emphasizes sincerity or integrity, and maintains that knowledge of good entails the ability to do good.

b. Zhu Xi and the Realistic School.

Zhu Xi was born in the province of Fujian in 1130 A.D. and died in 1200 at the age of 70. He was attracted to Buddhism for a while but then turned his attention to the study of Confucianism, perhaps because of his reading of Cheng's works. Zhu Xi lectured at the Bai Lu Dong (White Deer Grotto), in the foothills of the Lu-shan mountain range near Jianxi. His lectures attracted many students and brought fame to the old Confucian College there and to himself. He was a prolific writer who gave Confucianism a new philosophical foundation and set a new direction in Neo-Confucian interpretation which dominated the intellectual life of China for eight centuries until

241

the introduction of Western philosophy in China in recent years. Carsun Chang, the twentieth-century Neo-Confucianist aptly calls Zhu Xi "The Great Synthesizer." Zhu Xi's commentaries on the Four Great Books (Great Learning, Doctrine of the Mean, Analects, Mencius) became the standard texts in China, and for almost seven hundred years knowledge of Zhu Xi's commentaries on the Four Great Books was a conditio sine qua non for success in the state's civil service examinations.

      (1) On Li (Principle or Form) and the Supreme Ultimate.

In section a we have seen that Zhang Zai explains the appearance and disappearance of concrete things in terms of the condensation and dispersion of qi. The condensation of qi results in the formation and appearance of particular things. But Zhang Zai's theory fails to explain why different categories of particular things exist. Men, animals, flowers, and trees are all condensations of qi. But the question remains as to why men are different from animals if they are both condensations of qi. Here Zhu Xi's concept of Li provides an answer to the question. According to Zhu Xi, the universe as we see it came into being as a result of the condensation of qi and the working of Li (principle, form). Different categories of things come into being because the condensation of qi is effected in different ways in accordance with different Li. Thus, a man is a man because he is the result of the condensation of qi effected in accordance with the Li of man; a tree is a tree because it is the condensation of qi taking place in accordance with the Li of the tree. A man is a concrete instance of the Li of man, and a tree is a concrete instance of the Li of tree.

The Li are eternal. The Li of things exist before the creation of concrete things and after the destruction of these things. When a student asked: "Before heaven and earth had yet come into existence, were all the things of later times already there?" Zhu Xi said: "Only the Li were there."[12] In a letter to his friend Zhu Xi writes: Li exist, even if no things exist. In that case only such-and-such Li, but no such-and-such things."[13] Zhu Xi's metaphysics is like Plato's. In Platonic terms, we may say that all things in the world are the embodiment of some principle (Li) in some material. But even before the human invention of atom bombs, for example, the Li of atom bombs is already present. What we call the invention of atom bombs, therefore, is the discovery by some people of the Li of atom bombs and production of atom bombs in accordance with their Li. Thus, so-called "invention" is the discovery of the Li of things. Similarly, artistic creations, such as Beethoven's composition of his Fifth Symphony, are a discovery of Li. According to Zhu Xi , we may say that Beethoven discovered the Li of the musical score of his Fifth Symphony. But it existed before Beethoven wrote the symphony. Zhu Xi's theory that in our nature (xing) there are the Li of all things is similar to Plato's theory of a previous knowledge. Plato says: "We acquire knowledge before birth of all the essences."[14] But not all people can recall their previous knowledge. Only those who have "learned to see the beautiful in due course and succession . . . can suddenly perceive a nature of wondrous beauty."[15] Scientific invention or artistic creation is a form of sudden enlightenment, an intuition of the Li of things.

Li is also the ultimate standard of things. When Li is used in this sense, Zhu Xi often uses the word Ji (end, highest ideal) to refer to it. The word Ji originally meant the ridge pole at the peak of the roof of a building. However, Neo-Confucianists use it to mean the ideal type of things. Zhu Xi says: "Everything has an ultimate Ji, which is the ultimate Li. That which unites and embraces the Li of heaven,

243

earth, and all things is the Supreme Ultimate (Tai Ji)."[16] Thus Tai Ji is the Li of all Li, the Li of the universe as a whole. Tai Ji has no bodily form. "The Supreme Ultimate is what is highest of all, beyond which nothing can be. It is the most high, most mystical, and most abstruse, surpassing everything."[17]

Zhu Xi believes that the Supreme Ultimate is not only the Li of the universe as a whole, but it is also immanent in each and every individual thing. Every individual thing has in it the Li of its particular category, and at the same time the Supreme Ultimate in its entirety is inherent in it too. Here Zhu Xi has the problem of explaining the unity of the Supreme Ultimate. Is it one or many? How is the Li of the universe as a whole related to each and every individual thing? He says:

> But one Supreme Ultimate exists, which is received by the individuals of all things. This one Supreme Ultimate is received by each individual in its entirety and undivided. It is like the moon shining in the heavens, of which, though it is reflected in rivers and lakes and thus is everywhere visible, we would not therefore say that it is divided.[18]

The reflection of the moon in rivers and lakes is a metaphor of frequent use in Buddhism, and Zhu Xi's use of the metaphor shows his indebtedness to Buddhist metaphysics.

Our concrete physical world with its myriad individual things is a combination of matter (qi) and principle (Li, form):

> The Li is the Dao that pertains to

"what is above shapes," and is the
source from which all things are
produced. The qi is the material (or
instrument) that pertains to "what is
within shapes," and is the means
whereby things are produced. Hence
men or things at the moment of their
production, must receive this Li in
order that they may have a nature of
their own. They must receive this qi
in order that they may have their
bodily form.[19]

An individual thing is a condensation of qi "in-formed"
by Li. Whenever a condensation of qi occurs, Li is
necessarily present. Zhu Xi maintains that at no time
did no qi exist, and since Li is eternal, the priority
of Li over qi is a logical one, not a temporal one.
All creation was an evolutionary process from simple to
complex life, through a continuous succession of birth,
decay, death, and re-creation. In view of the role
played by Li and qi in the production of things, Joseph
Needham's translation of Li as "principle of
organization" and "qi as "matter-energy" in Science and
Civilization in China are quite apt.

(2) On Mind and Nature (xing).

Human nature (xing) is the principle (Li) of
humanity that is contained within the matter (qi) to
form an individual human being. The Li for all humans
is the same; it is the qi that makes them different.

Those who receive a qi (physical
endowment) that is clear, are the
sages in whom the nature is like a
pearl lying in clear cold water. But
those who receive a qi that is
turbid, are the foolish and
degenerate in whom the nature is like

a pearl lying in muddy water.[20]

For Zhu Xi, nature (xing) is different from mind. The original human nature is the same as the nature of heaven and earth, and is therefore good. Pure Li cannot be evil, Zhu Xi asserts. The mental facility in man belongs to mind, not nature. The nature (xing) is nothing but Li, but the mind is a combination of Li and qi. Nature is more abstract than mind. Li lacks volition and has no creative power. Mind is the result of the interaction of Li and qi. Thus, mind can have activities such as thinking and feeling, but nature cannot. Hence, while we may say that some person has an evil mind, to speak of him as having an evil nature is senseless. The good mind reflects the clear physical endowment, whereas the inferior mind betrays the turbidity of qi.

We read in Chapter 2 that Mencius maintains that four constant virtues exist in human nature which manifest themselves as the "four beginnings" (human-heartedness, righteousness, propriety, and wisdom). Here Zhu Xi tries to provide a metaphysical justification for Mencius's psychological theory. He says that the four constant virtues pertain to Li and belong to the nature, while the four beginnings are the operation of the mind. We can know our nature only through our mind. Because we have the feeling of commiseration, the sense of duty, the desire to be courteous, and the ability to distinguish between right and wrong, we know that the four virtues of human-heartedness, righteousness, propriety, and wisdom are within our nature. In a criticism of Buddhism, Zhu Xi says: "The Buddhists regard the nature as unreal (or empty). We of the Confucian tradition regard nature as real." The idealistic school of Neo-Confucianism holds that the mind is the nature. Zhu Xi distinguishes the two. This is a difference between the realistic school and the idealistic school.

246

(3) On Ge-wu (investigation of things) and Spiritual Cultivation.

Another difference between the two schools is that the realistic school emphasizes "the extension of knowledge through the investigation of things," whereas the idealistic school emphasizes the introspection of the mind. According to Zhi Xi, the Supreme Ultimate, the totality of the Li of all things, is within each of us. But because of our physical endowment, the Li of all things are not properly manifested. The Supreme Ultimate that is within us is like a pearl in muddy water. Spiritual cultivation is the method of making this pearl shiny. This method consists in making an exhaustive investigation of the Li (principles) of things in order to preserve the rational mind. Effort must be concentrated on expanding the mind, until "complete understanding . . . of all multitude of things . . . will open before me . . . and every exercise of the mind will be marked by complete enlightenment."[21] Zhu Xi's "investigation of things" (ge-wu) is not only a search for pure knowledge, but also the means to an end, namely, clarification of the mind and self-cultivation. Later the proponents of the idealistic school question the value of the investigation of things in the clarification of the mind. Zhu Xi insists that the purpose of the investigation of things is to extend our knowledge of the eternal Li, and we must know Li through ge-wu (the investigation of things). To investigate Li directly is like clutching at emptiness in which nothing exists to catch hold. Li are abstract, and things are concrete. We should investigate the abstract through the concrete. Zhu Xi puts it this way: "We should seek for 'what is above shapes' through 'what is within shapes.'"[22] The more we know Li, the more we know our nature (xing). Zhu Xi carefully notes that in trying to understand our nature, we should use both induction and deduction. Objective observations may inductively support a general principle from which further

247

observational data can be deduced.

The psychological prerequisite for the exhaustive investigation of things is cheng (sincerity) which, for Zhu Xi, includes seriousness (jing). The attainment of virtuous character and the pursuit of knowledge are inextricably bound up with each other. Sincerity entails that we may say a thing is when it is and is not when it is not. If we are sincere and earnest, the other four virtues of human-heartedness (ren), righteousness (yi), propriety (li), and wisdom (zhi) will be expressed. Be sincere and practice love: this is the way to attain the Truth (Dao). Thus, Zhu Xi completes his comprehensive system of philosophy which incorporates the six major concepts advocated by earlier philosophers, namely, the Supreme Ultimate (Tai Ji), principle (Li), material force (qi), nature (xing), the investigation of things (ge-wu), and love (ren).

c. The Idealistic School: Lu Chiu-yüan and Wang Yang-ming.

Lu Chiu-yüan (1139-1193) held several government posts in the Southern Song dynasty but was more interested in teaching than in the work of a magistrate. He lectured at the school on the Elephant Mountain (Xiang-shan), hence he is also known as Lu Xiang-shan. One day when Lu was thinking about the nature of space and time, he reportedly experienced a sudden enlightenment and said: "The universe is my mind; my mind is the universe."[23] The statement implies that the mind is identical with the Li of the universe and that "the investigation of things" means clarification of the mind.

In 1175 Lu Xiang-shan met Zhu Xi who was his senior contemporary. They discussed the differences between their philosophies but could not reach an agreement. Six years later, they met again at Nan-kang. By request, Lu delivered a lecture to Zhu Xi's students at White Deer Grotto. This was followed by long correspondence between Lu and Zhu. Although their relationship was friendly, the fundamental difference between Zhu's dualistic view of reality and Lu's monistic view was not resolved or synthesized. For Lu, mind is the same as principle (Li). The world is nothing but the manifestation of the mind. Zhu Xi, however, says only that nature (xing) is Li. The mind, for Zhu Xi, is the concrete embodiment of Li in qi. Hence, the mind is not identical with the abstract Li. The mind has two dimensions: the human mind and the moral mind. The moral mind always follows Li, whereas the human mind is liable to mistakes because it works through the agency of qi. This is Zhu's thesis of the contrast between the Principle of Nature (Tian Li, or Principle of Heaven) and human desire (ren-yü).

Lu considers Zhu's distinction between nature and mind a merely verbal one. He says: "Scholars of today devote most of their time to the explanation of words. For instance, such words as feeling, nature, mind, and ability all mean one and the same thing. It is accidental that a single entity is denoted by different terms."[24] The difference between Lu's and Zhu's philosophies is reflected in their way of life. Zhu stresses theoretical contemplation ("following the path of study and enquiry"), whereas Lu emphasizes practical action ("honoring the moral nature").

Wang Yang-ming (1472-1528, also called Wang Shou-ren) develops Lu's sketchy theory into a comprehensive system of idealism. Wang was born in the province of Zejiang on the eastern seacoast. He had an inquisitive mind and was earnest in his search for truth. One story about him relates that on his wedding day, Wang became so absorbed in an argument with a Daoist priest about the question of immortality that he forgot to go home until the next morning. He was interested in Zen Buddhism and also studied diligently Daoism and Zhu

Xi's doctrines of Li and the investigation of things, but he was never satisfied with any of them. Wang started his official career at the age of twenty-eight, serving as a middle level magistrate in the Ming dynasty. Unfortunately, Wang was bitterly frustrated in his political career. He was beaten forty times in the presence of the Ming emperor and exiled to the Guizhou frontier for protesting the imprisonment of a fellow scholar official. From 1516 to 1519 he successfully conducted a military campaign to suppress several rebellions. But the emperor took the credits away from him and claimed that the emperor himself had pacified the rebellions.

While living in virtual isolation in Guizhou, Wang was driven to search within his own mind. One night in 1508, he experienced sudden enlightenment and understood the meaning of ge-wu (investigation of things) and the doctrine of the extension of the innate knowledge of the good (zhi liang-zhi). Later, his fame spread, and many scholars came to study under him, including Wang's official superiors. He wrote down his major ideas and doctrines in the Inquiry on Great Learning shortly before his death. Although Wang's official career was not a success, he had an intellectually stimulating and spiritually rewarding life. He said his doctrines were achieved from "a hundred deaths and a thousand sufferings."[25]

On the Identity of Mind and Li.

For Wang, a Li is not something different from or outside of the mind. The mind is the totality of our experience. The mind is the legislator of the universe and is that by which all the Li are legislated. "Mind is Li. How can affairs and Li be outside the mind? . . . The substance of the mind is the nature and the nature is Li. Therefore, since the mind of filial love exists, the Li of filial piety exists. If no such mind existed, no such a Li would exist."[26] If principles were outside the mind, Wang says, then the principle of filial piety (the desire to be filial), for example, would cease to be as soon as one's parents pass away. But this is not the case. Hence the principle of filial piety is nothing but the exercise of the mind. The same is true for other principles, and even things and affairs, for they must be perceived and exercised by the mind in order to have any reality. Wang insists that Heaven, Earth, and all things are actually present within our minds. His theory of reality is akin to George Berkeley's doctrine that to be is to be perceived (esse est percipi), a consubstantiationism of internal and external reality. This idealistic construal of reality is something with which Zhu Xi would surely disagree. This is also a construal which even Wang's contemporaries found difficult to accept. When he was asked what the mind had to do with blossoming trees on the high mountains, he answered that their colors show up when one looks at them and left it at that. (This is the Chinese version of the question: "If a tree falls down in the forest where there is no one around to perceive it, how can we know that a tree falls?")

On Intuitive Knowledge.

According to Wang Yang-ming, every person possesses an intuitive knowledge which is the manifestation of his original mind, and through which he immediately knows the difference between right and wrong. This intuitive knowledge of man is like the sun: it is often obscured by clouds (of selfish desire) but has the power of penetrating the obscuring dark clouds. It is perfect and needs no strengthening.

> The learning of the great man consists entirely in getting rid of the obscuration of selfish desires in order by his own efforts to make manifest his clear character, so as

to restore the condition of forming
one body with Heaven, Earth, and the
myriad things, a condition that is
originally so, that is all. Outside
of the original substance something
can not be added.[27]

Wang uses Mencius's example of our seeing a small
child who is about to fall into a well to illustrate
his notion of intuitive knowledge. When we see the
child about to fall in the well, we immediately <u>know</u>
the child is in danger and we should help him. This
knowledge is the manifestation of our original nature;
Wang calls it "intuitive knowledge." All we need do is
follow its dictates straightforwardly. If, however, we
stop to find excuses for not following the dictates, we
will be adding something to, or taking something out
of, the intuitive knowledge. This is rationalization
which is due to selfishness. Morality is a matter of
keeping the mind clean. The intuitive knowledge is
like a clean mirror which gives a faithful reflection
of our original mind. We must always clear it of dirt
and obscuration.

On the Unity of Knowledge and Action: Wang's
Pragmatic Intuitionism.

Wang Yang-ming is most concerned with the
separation of "theory and practice," "words and deeds,"
"thought and action" in earlier Chinese thought. The
Confucianists have always stressed the correspondence
and equal importance of knowledge and action, but Wang
identifies them as one. He insists that "knowledge is
the beginning of action and action the completion of
knowledge."[28] True knowledge of moral principles
entails moral action. The mind holds within itself
sufficient, innate moral knowledge, which would express
itself in moral action if the mind could be rid of its
muddy confusion, unless it is hindered by insuperable
external conditions. The quieting and clarification of

the mind may take some time but will eventually lead to the union of knowledge and action. The basis for the unification of the mind and action is Wang's emphasis on will or choice rather than reason or knowledge. Intellectual or discursive knowledge of the kind characteristic of the sciences can be separated from choice or morality. But practical knowledge of the value of things has no significance apart from the activity of choosing and acting. Moreover, a person's choices are revealed in the action taken, and this shows the combination of knowledge and action.

Wang's interpretations of "extension of knowledge" and "investigation of things (ge-wu)" in the Great Learning follow his doctrine of the unity of mind and action. For Wang, the extension of knowledge means the extension of our intuitive knowledge. Self-realization is nothing more than the following of one's intuitive knowledge and putting it into practice. Cheng Yi and Zhu Xi interpret the term ge-wu in the Great Learning as meaning "the investigation of things," and hold that the investigation of things (acquisition of facts from the external world) is needed to complete our knowledge of Li. Wang Yang-ming rejects Cheng Yi's and Zhu Xi's interpretation of ge-wu, and maintains that it means "rectification of affairs." Wang insists that ge means "to rectify" and wu means "human affairs." He does not believe that investigation of external things is an essential part of learning or cultivating ren (love). He reported that once when he was young, he followed Zhu Xi's doctrine of the investigation of things and sat in front of bamboos to investigate the principles of bamboos, only to get ill after seven days without knowing what the principles are! Wang felt that Zhu Xi's insistence that every blade of grass and every tree possesses principle and therefore should be investigated, diverts people from the basic principles of things and the fundamentals of life. Because Wang's concern is primarily a moral one, he says that ge-wu means to do good and remove evil (rectification of

253

affairs).

> The activity of the mind is called yi
> (will, thought), and the objects
> toward which yi are directed are
> called wu (things, affairs). For
> instance, when the object of one's yi
> is the serving of one's parents, then
> this serving of one's parents is the
> wu.[29]

The wu may be right or wrong, but the inner light of
our mind (intuitive knowledge) will enable us to know
whether it is right or wrong. When we intuit a thing
to be right, we must sincerely do it, and when we
intuit a thing to be wrong, we must sincerely stop
doing it. In this way, we rectify our affairs and at
the same time extend our intuitive knowledge.

Criticisms of Buddhism.

Although Wang talks much about the "attentiveness
of the mind," "the original nature of the mind" (Zen
Buddhist terminology), he presents several criticisms
of Buddhism. The most important criticism is his
judgment that the Buddhists are afraid of the troubles
involved in human realtionships and seek to escape from
the pains and worries of life and death. Wang says
that the Buddhists, in seeking detachment from the
world, show that they are really attached to the world.
The Confucianists do not claim to be detached from the
world but have no attachment to the transitory
phenomena. The Confucianists respond spontaneously to
human relationships and thus suffer no fear or worries.
Wang says:

> The relationship between father and
> son exists; we [the Confucianists]
> respond to it with love. The
> relationship between sovereign and

254

subjects exists; we respond to it with righteousness. And the relationship between husband and wife exists; we respond to it with mutual respect. We have no atachment to phenomena.[30]

The Buddhists, however, flout marriage as the foundation of society by their formation of an unnatural society of celibate monks and nuns. The reality of human society cannot be denied. Yet, the Buddhists attempt to abnegate it and seek oblivion in nirvana. "Extending one's intuitive knowledge" means actualizing moral deeds. It does not mean "to stupefy oneself with shadows and echos and suspend oneself in empty unreality (as the Buddhists do in their meditation on 'emptiness')."[31] Everyone must drive out passion and obey natural law, not to gain a Buddhist tranquility, but to establish the mind on firm principles. We should seek not tranquility but pure action without passion. Pure action unmoved by passion is the highest good.

An Appraisal of Wang Yang-ming.

The idealism of Wang Yang-ming has its philosophical difficulties. However, when Zhu Xi's realistic metaphysics degenerated into pedantic hair-splitting of trivial details after Zhu Xi's death, Wang Yang-ming's pragmatic philosophy of action replaced the realistic school and dominated China during a large part of the Ming dynasty. The basic value of Wang's philosophy is ren (love), and his final goal is the unification of Heaven, Earth, and the myriad things ("forming one body with all things"). So far as the basic value and purpose of his philosophy is concerned, Wang is a typical Confucianist. His teachings are refreshingly new and challenging. Wang maintains that if his mind judges something to be wrong, he would surely not consider it right, even if Confucius had

255

taken it to be right. His teaching technique is similar to that of the Zen Buddhists. For this, Wang has been criticized by many Confucianists. Wang's emphasis on independent judgment and the doctrine of the unity of knowledge and action have inspired many Chinese and Japanese. Wang's philosophy held great appeal for the Meiji Restoration in Japan in 1868 ("Oyomei" is the Japanese pronunciation of his name). Modern Chinese thinkers such as Sun Yat-sen and Xiong Shi-li believed that Wang's dynamic and idealistic philosophy has much to offer in a troubled China.

d.   Dai Zhen and Empirical Realism.

Neo-Confucian philosophy through Wang Yang-ming had emphasized the principles (Li) of things over their material constitution (qi) and elevated the "original mind" over the actual experiences. In the seventeenth and eighteenth centuries arose an opposition to both Zhu Xi's realism and Wang Yang-ming's idealism. Scholars paid more attention to the feelings and actual experiences of people and emphasized empirical verification in their methodology. Dai Zhen (1724-1777) is generally regarded as the greatest of the empirical Neo-Confucianists of the Qing dynasty. Dai Zhen (also known as Dai Dong-yüan) was a native of Huizhou in Anhui province. His early training included the usual study of the Classics and the works of the Neo-Confucianists of the Song and Ming dynasties. Dai was a man of broad interests who studied mathematics, Chinese dialects, philology, law, and history. Although Dai was attracted to materialism, his major concern is still with human nature and morality.

Dai Zhen's view of reality is basically materialistic. He believes that the Li (Principle or Dao) can only be found in the activities of material things, involving the interaction of yin and yang in the five agents. Li is nothing but the internal structure or system in things, and the goal of learning

256

is to discover the Li of things without any preconceived prejudices. Empirical observation of concrete individual things is necessary for our mind's understanding of Li. The way to discover general laws (governing the phenomena) is to first observe occurrences, then collect data and analyze them.

For Dai, human nature consists of human blood, breath, and mental faculty: what the realistic school of Neo-Confucianists would call "the physical nature." This physical nature does not necessarily contain the Li of things. But because of the presence of the mental facility, human nature can understand Li. Thus we are all potentially capable of comprehending moral values and acting morally. The sage differs from ordinary people in that he has a much higher capability to understand, comprehend, and cooperate with the Li of things.

Evil in the world does not arise from the physical nature of man but from defects in his knowledge, desires, or feelings, notably selfishness and delusion. The best way to dispel delusion is to study, and the best way to disperse selfishness is to strengthen altruism. We should become aware of other people's needs and desires. People's basic desires such as food and sex must find civilized expressions instead of being suppressed. These desires cause evil only when they go to excess. Like a modern psychologist, Dai Zhen urges that people channel their desires toward productive activities.

> When the mind attains the Heavenly virtue, maintaining the proper restraint and correctness, the desires will not degenerate into license. . . . Yü controlled the floods by guiding the water through channels. The Confucian gentleman controls his desires by guiding them

257

into the path of righteousness.[32]

Dai Zhen considers the orderly fulfillment of human desires and expression of human feeling as having the greatest ethical significance. "The highest morality consists of nothing more than insuring that the desires of all men reach fulfillment, and their feelings reach expression."[33]

Dai Zhen's idea of ge-wu comes close to Zhu Xi's. Dai Zhen does not reject the concepts and principles of earlier Neo-Confucianists. Instead, he reinterprets them in such a way that the concrete and particular become primary. Dai felt that the Neo-Confucianists have gone too far in their attempt to provide metaphysical suppport for the classical Confucian ethic. For Dai, some of the Neo-Confucianists have allowed the metaphysics of morality to supplant morality per se. His empiricism is his attempt to re-emphasize the primacy of persons and the moral virtues in the Confucian tradition.

Chapter 9

1. <u>Collected Works of Zhou Dun-yi</u>, ch. 1. Cf. Wing-tsit Chan, <u>A Source Book in Chinese Philosophy</u>, p. 463.

2. <u>Yi Jing</u> (<u>Book of Changes</u>), Appendix V.

3. Cf. Feng You-lan, <u>A History of Chinese Philosophy</u>, vol. II, p. 473.

4. We find this recurrent idea in Lao Zi's <u>Dao De Jing</u> and the <u>Book of Changes</u>.

5. Feng You-lan, <u>op. cit.</u>, introduction.

6. Ch. 2, <u>Correct Discipline for Beginners</u>.

7. <u>Ibid.</u>

8. Feng You-lan, <u>A History of Chinese Philosophy</u>, vol. II, p. 493.

9. <u>Ibid.</u>

10. <u>Literary Remains of the Two Chengs</u>, ch. 2a.

11. Cheng Yi's idea of <u>Li</u> (principle) is the same as <u>Dao</u> explicated in the <u>Book of Changes</u>.

12. <u>Collected Literary Writings of Zhu Xi</u>, ch. 1.

13. <u>Ibid.</u>, ch. 46.

14. Plato, <u>Phaedo</u>, 75.

15. Plato, Symposium, 211.

16. Zhu Xi, Recorded Sayings, ch. 94.

17. Zhu Xi, Complete Works of the Master Zhu, ch. 49.

18. Zhu Xi, Recorded Sayings, ch. 94.

19. Zhu Xi, Collected Literary Writings, ch. 58.

20. Zhu Xi, Recorded Sayings, ch. 4.

21. Cf. Feng You-lan, op. cit., vol. II, p. 604.

22. Zhu Xi, Complete Works of Master Zhu, ch. 46.

23. Collected Works of Lu Xiang-shan, ch. 36.

24. Ibid., ch. 35.

25. Complete Works of Wang Yang-ming, p. 15.

26. Wang Yang-ming, Record of Instructions, ch. 11, part 2.

27. Wing-tsit Chan, A Source Book of Chinese Philosophy, p. 600.

28. Wang Yang-ming, Records of Instructions, ch. 5. Cf. Wing-tsit Chan, A Source Book in Chinese Philosophy, pp. 667-670.

29. Ibid., ch. 1.

30. Ibid., ch. 3.

31. Quoted by Feng You-lan in A History of Chinese Philosophy, vol. II, p. 602.

32. Quoted by Frederick G. Henke, The Philosophy of

Wang Yang-ming (Chicago: Open Court Publishing Co.), p. 342.

33.   Ibid., p. 117.

Chapter 10

Contemporary Chinese Philosophy

a. Introductory Remarks.

Dai Zhen's empiricist philosophy provoked a revived interest in metaphysics, particularly Zhu Xi's rationalistic philosophy of principle. However, because of the political and social upheaval in China during the nineteenth and twentieth centuries, the revival of the Song dynasty Neo-Confucianism never developed into a mature philosophy. The Opium War of 1840-1842 and the subsequent series of humiliating military and diplomatic defeats forced the Chinese intellectuals to focus their attention on matters directly related to national survival rather than philosophic speculation. After the Sino-Japanese War of 1894, a movement for strengthening and saving the nation sprang up among the Chinese people. This culminated in the works of Kang You-wei (1858-1927) and Sun Yat-sen (1866-1925). Kang and Sun lived in Guangdong province where the Western influence was strongest, and both men were heavily influenced by Western ideas in their thinking. They became convinced that China's weakness was due primarily to political decadence, and only secondarily to military inferiority. Kang was a learned Confucian scholar and a courageous statesman. He was the leader of the ill-fated Hundred Days Reform in the late Manchu dynasty. Although Kang re-interpreted Confucian classics, he was true to the Confucian teaching of putting philosophy into practice in government and society. His radically revolutionary ideas on world government are expressed in his book Da Tong Shu (Book of Great Unity). Sun Yat-sen, a medical doctor turned revolutionary, became the leader of the Nationalist Party and the founder of the Republic of China. His most important book is San Min Zhu-yi (Three Principles of the People) in which he

263

discusses his ideas on economics and politics.

In terms of influence on the lives of the Chinese people, Mao Ze-dong (1893-1976) must be given the first place. This place is due not so much to his originality of thought or scholarly production as to his political eminence. Mao's thought is heavily influenced by Marx and Lenin but is basically in tune with the attitudes and principles of traditional Chinese philosophy. Mao's most significant work is the lecture he delivered in 1937 entitled "On Practice," where he explains the relationship between theory and practice, maintaining that theory originates in practice and returns to practice for its justification and fulfillment.

Xiong Shi-li (1885-1968) and Feng You-lan (1895-   ) can be considered professional philosophers. Their writings are well-organized and their ideas are more carefully worked out in terms of analysis and argument. However, their names are probably unknown to Westerners except for a few professional philosophers. Xiong tried to revive Wang Yang-ming's idealistic philosophy and incorporate it into his Buddhist "consciousness-only" (Wei-shi) philosophy. His most important work is Xin Wei-shi Lun (New Doctrine of Consciousness-only). Xiong's analysis of causation shows the depth of his thought. Feng You-lan is generally regarded as the most outstanding and competent of contemporary Chinese philosophers. Feng is basically a realistic Neo-Confucianist who tries to construct a new system of rational philosophy by synthesizing Neo-Confucianism, Daoism, and Western rationalism. His most significant work is Xin Li-xüe (The New Rational Philosophy). His monumental A History of Chinese Philosophy (translated into English by Derk Bodde) contains his insights and interpretations on Chinese philosophy and has become a standard textbook.

b.   Kang You-wei and Sun Yat-sen.

Kang was born in the Nan-hai district of Guangdong province to a family of Confucian scholars. In 1895 he obtained the degree of "presented scholar" in Beijing and founded Jiang-xüe Hui (Society for the Advancement of Learning) and Bao-guo Hui (National Protection Society) there. In 1898 he succeeded in convincing the young emperor Guang-xü of the necessity and urgency of his reform program. Kang was in power from June 11 to September 16, 1898, rapidly issuing many reform orders. Kang's reform program involved the abolition of the eight-legged style of essay and the introduction of tests on current affairs in the civil service examination. The reform was opposed by the Empress Dowager Ci Xi. Kang attempted a coup d'état to arrest the Empress Dowager. The coup failed. Kang fled to Hong Kong, and thence to Japan, America, and Europe. After the founding of the Republic of China in 1912, Kang advocated Confucianism as the state religion in China and even took part in the 1917 abortive attempt to restore the deposed Manchu emperor Xüan-tong. Kang failed again and died in disgrace. But Kang was a brilliant scholar and did much to stimulate the thinking of the Chinese people and teach them a critical attitude toward Confucian classics.

Kang attempted to break down the prestige of the popular Han School interpretation of Confucian classics and to open up new possibilities of thought. He maintained that the so-called Confucian classics of the Old Script School which was defended by Liu Xin, one of the most respected scholars of the Han period, were forgeries, while the books of the New Script School, headed by Dong Zhong-shu, were the authentic texts. In his writings, Kang presents Confucius as a great reformer rather than a conservative. According to Kang, Confucius was a man of social vision who laid down all the principles and institutions needed to change the old customs and traditions. More significant than his attempts to re-interpret and reconstruct Confucianism is Kang's conception of a new world government. This he called Da Tong (the Great Unity), a term taken from the "Li Yün" chapter of the Book of Rites (Li Ji). The Da Tong passage in the "Li Yün" chapter is an inspiring passage generally attributed to Confucius. This passage has been studied by every Chinese school student and is worth quoting in full:

> When the great Dao was pursued, a public and common morality ruled over the world; men of talents, virtue, and ability were selected; sincerity was emphasized and harmony was cultivated. Therefore, men did not love their parents only, nor did they treat as children only their sons. A competent provision was secured for the aged till their death, employment was given to the able-bodied, and the means of growing up was provided for the young. Kindness and compassion were showed to widows, orphans, childless men, and those who were disabled by disease, so that they were all sufficiently supported. Men had their proper work, and women had their homes. They developed the wealth of natural resources, disliking that it should be discarded under the ground, but not wishing to keep it for their own use. They labored with their strength, disliking that it should not be exerted, but exerting it not for their own benefit. In this way, all cunning designs became useless, and theft and banditry did not show themselves, so that the outer doors

remained open, and were not shut.
This was called <u>Da Tong</u>.[1]

This passage provides Kang with inspiration for a
concrete picture of the ideal world, which he depicts
in his famous book <u>Da Tong Shu</u> (<u>Book</u> <u>of</u> <u>Great</u> <u>Unity</u>).[2]
In his depiction of the ideal world, Kang drew
inspiration from Christian, Buddhist, and probably
communist sources. The book was written in 1884. But
because it contains many radical ideas, it was
published posthumously in 1935.

Kang conceived of human history not as cyclical
but as evolutionary. He claimed that Confucius taught
the theory of Three Ages, that history progresses from
the Age of Chaos to that of Small Peace (Approaching
Peace) and finally to that of Great Unity (Great
Peace). Kang continued that the growing communication
between East and West, and the political and social
reforms in Europe and America, show that the world is
evolving from the Age of Chaos toward the Age of Small
Peace. The last stage of human progress, the Age of
Great Unity, will follow. However, the establishment of
a world government based on the concepts of unity,
equality, and brotherhood must precede the arrival of
the Age of Great Unity. When the Age of Great Unity
finally arrives (Kang expected this to happen within
three hundred years), national states will be
abolished, class distinctions will disappear, racial
distinctions will be eliminated (through migration and
intermarriage), men and women will be equal in all
respects and family will vanish, different traditions
and cultures will be synthesized into a harmonious
whole, and everyone will enjoy true peace and
happiness. Derk Bodde remarks on <u>Da Tong Shu</u> that

> . . . the whole book is remarkable as
> a mixture of Chinese and Western
> utopian thinking. It combines
> idealism, radicalism, and keen

prophetic insight, with a curiously
naive confidence in the technological
progress as the key to human
happiness, which in this respect
makes it quite un-Chinese and typical
of Western nineteenth-century
optimism.[3]

A brief description of Kang's ideal society will convey
Kang's radicalism. People of the world commonwealth
live in communes (no private ownership), using a
universal language, calendar, and system of weights and
measures. Children are taken care of in public
nurseries, while old folks are cared for in nursing
homes. Men and women wear unisex clothes. Marriage
contracts are valid for one year but are renewable.
Euthanasia is used for patients suffering from
incurable illness. After death, all persons are to be
cremated and their ashes used for fertilizer. All
people are to be vegetarians, and all animal species
are to be preserved as much as possible. Though this
sounds like Aldous Huxley's Brave New World,
surprisingly this was envisioned by a Confucian scholar
in the late nineteenth century.

Kang's theory of historical progress and his
interpretation of the central Confucian concept of ren
(love) are the philosophical foundation of his
political theory of utopia. Ren is love, mercy,
compassion. Kang agrees with Cheng Hao and Wang Yang-
ming that "the man of love takes Heaven, earth, and all
things as one with himself." He tries to support his
thesis with ideas drawn from Western science and says
that ren is also the power of attraction (like
gravitational attraction) that unites all people as
one. It is like "ether" or electricity. It is the
"element of elements," the force of origination
permeating everywhere. It enables an individual to be
an individual, an organization an organization, and it
makes possible communication between two individuals.

In short, it is universal love. We recall that in the traditional Confucian theory of love, one proceeds from respect and love of one's parents to loving all people, and finally to being kind to all creatures. Kang's ideal of D̲a̲ T̲o̲n̲g̲ (Great Unity) is the logical culmination of this extension of love.

After Kang's "Hundred Days Reform" failed, those Chinese who wished to see a modern independent China concluded that the Manchu regime must be overthrown. They joined the standard of another rebel and revolutionary, Sun Yat-sen.

Sun Yat-sen was born to a peasant family in a village near Guangzhou (Canton) in 1866. He began his schooling at seven, and at fourteen left his home to visit his elder brother in Hawaii. Sun returned home in 1883. In 1887 he enrolled in the Alice Memorial Hospital medical school in Hong Kong. He decided to become a revolutionary there and then, because, he said, the number of lives a physician could save is rather limited whereas a great statesman could save the lives of an entire country. Sun's social and political philosophy is inspired by his reading of Kang You-wei's D̲a̲ T̲o̲n̲g̲ S̲h̲u̲ (B̲o̲o̲k̲ o̲f̲ G̲r̲e̲a̲t̲ U̲n̲i̲t̲y̲) and influenced by his knowledge of Western political theories.

Sun accepts Wang Yang-ming's doctrine of the unity of knowledge and action. But, at the same time, Sun maintains that people could do without first knowing. "To do is easy, to know is difficult," Sun quotes Wang Yang-ming with apparent approval. Knowledge comes from action. The acquisition of knowledge is like the construction of a bridge. Sometimes a temporary foundation must first be constructed in order to build the superstructure of a bridge. The superstructure can then be used to improve the foundation which supports the superstructure. Applying the doctrine that "to do is easy, to know is difficult," to the political scene, Sun argues that revolution must first be d̲o̲n̲e̲, then the

269

people could talk about knowing or learning to do better. The important thing about getting things done is to go ahead with our ideas and not wait to be told what to do or how to do things. Otherwise, things would never get off the ground. Revolutionaries must attempt the revolution before success is assured. Taking this attitude is risky. But revolutionaries must take the risk without regret.

The social and political doctrines of Sun are embodied in several lectures he gave in 1924 in Canton which were collected and edited under the title San Min Zhu Yi (The Three Principles of the People). Sun argues that the new Republic of China must seek to realize national sovereignty, implement democratic processes, and improve the standard of living of the people. The three principles are, therefore, nationalism, democracy, and socialism (min-sheng, people's livelihood).

The Principle of Nationalism.

This principle was first directed against the Manchu government and then, after the fall of the Manchus, against foreign imperialism. China could develop as a nation only by shaking off the imperialistic yoke, especially foreign economic imperialism. To achieve this goal, the Chinese people must unite and restore the traditional national spirit and morality. Chinese national spirit and morality are the strongest protector of China's sovereignty. Sun adopted Confucianism as the moral basis of his political philosophy. He therefore adopted as the ethical norm of his revolutionary movement the eight cardinal Confucian virtues: loyalty, filial piety, humanity, love, faithfulness, righteousness, harmony, and peace.

The Principle of Democracy.

Sun points out first that, contrary to the general belief, all men are not created equal. Equality should mean equality in opportunity rather than achievement, for intelligent and able people should be allowed to fulfill their potentiality. However, everyone should have the same political rights, such as the right to vote or to be protected by the law. The operation of the government should be in the hands of the able and the wise. The best government is that which ensures popular control through electoral processes and yet gives a strong executive wide powers to manage all the nation's business. Hence, the goal of the principle of democracy is to achieve a centralized government on a popular basis. Here Sun develops his theories of the five powers (neng) and four rights (chüan). The government should have the five powers: executive, legislative, judiciary, examination, and censorship. The people should have four rights: the right to elect and recall public officials, the right to initiate legislation when their representatives failed to introduce it, and the right of referendum with regard to all important legislation. This way, Sun hopes, the powers of the government and rights of the people would be separated and balanced, so that the government run by able and wise officials can be efficient and yet responsible to the people.

The Principle of Socialism (Min-Sheng, People's Livlihood).

This principle embraces a variety of social and economic theories, but its meaning is vague. Sun defined the term min-sheng as "people's livelihood," "society's existence," "the nation's economy," and "the life of the masses." He tried to give the term a meaning which would satisfy all of his followers, and consequently this principle has been given different interpretations. The principle can best be described

271

as a moderate socialism. To carry out this principle, Sun made two concrete proposals: land reform and the regulation of capital. Sun wanted the peasants (tillers) to own their lands. But he said that the transfer of land ownership should be achieved by peaceful, gradual means rather than by radical methods such as nationalization of all land and its redistribution among the peasants. To increase the wealth of the nation, people must be given incentives. Large industries which "affect the welfare of the people as a whole" should be owned and controlled by the government. However, enough opportunities should be left for private enterprise and individual initiative. Foreign capital is to be welcomed so long as foreign investment does not affect China adversely as a sovereign nation.

Sun's position on communism is not clear. He seemed to think that communism may be a distant goal for China. But he was more interested in finding ways to increase wealth for China than ways of redistributing China's wealth. Having seen the increasing conflicts between capital and labor in his lifetime, Sun rejected capitalism. Yet, he could not agree with the Marxist doctrine that the motivation of social progress is class struggle. On the contrary, he believed that a human being by nature has a "sense of humanity" or "the consciousness of kind" and knows how to avoid conflicts in social relations and achieve progress through compromise and cooperation.

c. Mao Ze-dong and Chinese Communism.

Mao Ze-dong (1893-1976) was born to a peasant family in Hunan province in south-central China. His father was a shrewd farmer who succeeded in bringing prosperity to the family, partly by speculating in the rice market. Mao was a born rebel. He disliked Confucian classics, and his relationship with his father and teachers was a bad one. He despised

272

authorities and established conventions. Like many Chinese of his time, he was greatly disturbed by the possibility that China might be carved up by the Western Powers or conquered by Japan. He admired Sun Yat-sen and hoped to join his organization. In 1918 he went to Beijing University to work as an assistant librarian. He audited the lectures of many prominent professors although he was not a registered student. His work at the Beijing University library gave him an excellent opportunity to read a variety of revolutionary pamphlets, newspapers, and books of various ideologies. His supervisor, the chief librarian, Li Da-cao, was an avowed Marxist. Under Li Da-cao's guidance, Mao became Marxist-oriented. Mao then realized that the solution of China's problems requires more than the adoption of Western technology. The solution, he said, lies in the transformation of the Chinese society. Mao joined the Chinese communist party in 1921. Mao early on urged reliance upon the Chinese peasantry rather than the Chinese proletariat to carry out the revolution. In his "Report on an Investigation of the Peasant Movement in Hunan," published in early 1927, Mao says:

> In a very short time, in China's central, southern, and northern provinces, several hundred million peasants will rise like a tornado or tempest, a force so extraordinarily swift and violent that no power, however great, will be able to suppress it. They will break all trammels that now bind them and rush forward along the road of liberation. They will send all imperialists, warlords, corrupt officials, local bullies, and bad gentry to their graves. All revolutionary parties and all revolutionary comrades will stand before them to be tested, and

273

to be accepted or rejected as they
decide.[4]

Mao's report was ignored by the Moscow-trained Chinese
party leaders who regarded Mao's ideas unorthodox and
heretical. However, after 1930, developments in the
conflict between the communists and the nationalists
(Jiang Kai-shek's nationalist party) vindicated Mao's
view. From then Mao steadily rose to the position of
undisputed leader of the Chinese communist party.

The most philosophical of Mao's works is On
Practice, which was written in 1937 when he was living
in the caves of Yenan. In On Practice, Mao synthesizes
the Marxist dialectical materialism with the theory of
the unity of knowledge and action. His thesis is that
practice and knowledge reinforce each other in a
dialectically upward progression.

> To discover truth through practice,
> and through practice to verify and
> develop truth. To start from
> perceptual knowledge and actively
> develop it into rational knowledge,
> and then, starting from rational
> knowledge, actively direct revolu-
> tionary practice so as to remold the
> subjective and the objective world.
> Practice, knowledge, more practice,
> more knowledge; the cyclical
> repetition of this pattern to
> infinity, and with each cycle, the
> elevation of the content of practice
> and knowledge to a higher level.
> Such is the whole of the dialectical
> materialistic theory of knowing and
> doing.[5]

For Mao, philosophy acquires its value only in the
discovery and solution of practical problems.

Idealism, subjectivism, and abstract theories of all kinds are to be rejected in toto. All knowledge has its beginnings in practice, in the activity of changing the world. The so-called "rational knowledge" is based on perceptual knowledge, but rational knowledge remains incomplete until it is applied in the practice of changing the world. In a passage reminiscent of Karl Marx, Mao says:

> What Marxist philosophy regards as the most important problem does not lie in understanding the laws of the objective world, thereby becoming capable of explaining it, but in actively changing the world by applying the knowledge of its objective laws.[6]

Theory and practice are not two different things. They are the dialectical opposites of one process--living and acting in the world.

On Contradiction was written by Mao in 1937 for internal use within the Chinese Communist Party. This essay became an important statement on Chinese communist ideology after Mao delivered the speech "On the Correct Handling of Contradictions among the People" in February 1957. Mao maintains that conflict is inherent in human relations and must therefore govern politics. Mao distinguishes two types of contradictions: antagonistic and non-antagonistic contradictions. The antagonistic contradictions exist between hostile classes and hostile social systems, such as those between landlords and tenants, capitalism and socialism. These contradictions exist "between the enemy and ourselves" and are the substance of the inexorable process of history. The non-antagonistic contradictions exist within the socialist society, such as the contradiction between the interests of the nation as a whole and those of the individuals, between democracy and centralism, between the leaders and the led, between men and women, between the government and the people. This second type of contradiction is like the complementary dualism of the yin-yang naturalists. Since a distinction exists between the two types of contradiction, a difference must exist in the mode of resolution for each one of them. The first type of contradiction can be resolved only by violent force. The mode of resolution for the second type of contradiction is nonviolent; these can be resolved through the process of "discussion, criticism, and education." Mao states that it is of paramount importance for us to understand correctly the law of contradiction in things, so that, on the basis of such analysis, we may find out the methods of solving contradictions.

According to Mao, contradictions are universal, existing in all processes of the development of things, and running through all processes from beginning to end. He stresses not only the orderly resolution of contradictions but also confrontation and conflict. This is a departure from the traditional Chinese ideology of Confucianism, in which harmony and social order were the highest values. Mao challenges the Chinese to get rid of the fear of disorder and struggle. Mao agrees with Marx that history proceeded out of conflict, but Mao goes further and idealizes conflict. Mao believes that struggle for its own sake has merit.

Mao's On New Democracy (published 1940) is both a theoretical discussion of the value of the Chinese cultural heritage and a persuasive propaganda document. Mao believes that a splendid culture was created by the ancient Chinese. But it contained the institutions and "all the rotten things" of the reactionary feudal ruling class, as well as the fine popular culture which was more or less democratic and revolutionary in character.

276

As China's present new politics and new economy have developed out of her old politics and old economy, and China's culture has also developed out of her old culture, we must respect our own history and should not cut ourselves adrift from it. However, this respect for history means only giving history a definite place among the sciences, respecting its dialectical development, but not eulogizing the ancient while disparaging the modern, or praising any noxious feudal element.[7]

In On New Democracy, Mao divides the existing governments in the world into three groups: (1) "republics under bourgeoisie dictatorship" such as most of the Western countries, (2) "republics under the dictatorship of the proletariat" such as the Soviet Union, and (3) "republics under the joint dictatorship of several revolutionary classes." China, he says, belongs to the third category, where the power of the government should be vested in the proletariat, the peasantry, the intelligentsia, and other sections of the petty bourgeoisie. Mao envisages a system of government known as "Democratic Centralism" in which all power is centralized, but it is democratic, because it is jointly ruled by the various "revolutionary classes" and based on elections in which all citizens participate through suffrage that is "real, popular, and equal." Mao's revolution would be divided into two stages--the democratic and the socialist:

> The first stage of the Chinese revolution [itself subdivided into many minor stages] belongs, so far as its social character is concerned, to a new type of bourgeois-democratic

277

revolution, and is not yet a proletarian-socialist revolution; but it has long become part of the proletarian-socialist world revolution and its great ally. The first step in, or the first stage of, this revolution is certainly not, and cannot be, the establishment of a capitalistic society under the dictatorship of the Chinese bourgeoisie; on the contrary, the first stage is to end with the establishment of a new-democratic society under the joint dictatorship of all Chinese revolutionary classes headed by the Chinese proletariat. Then, the revolution will develop into the second stage so that a socialist society can be established in China.[8]

To bring about the first stage of revolution, Mao believes it necessary and desirable for the communists to collaborate with all those who are willing to work with them. This makes On New Democracy good propaganda material because it justifies the united front of all revolutionary classes and reaffirms the communist party's long-term mission. In economic terms, the Chinese economy under the New Democracy would be a "new-democratic" economy, which is the same as conceived in Sun Yat-sen's "principle of people's livelihood." Three types of enterprise--private, cooperative, and state--would exist concurrently, with the first strictly controlled and the third dominant. Mao skillfully relates his political and economic doctrines to Sun Yat-sen's Three People's Principles and claims for the New Democracy a direct descent from Sun Yat-sen.

Mao fanatically believed in the power of the human

will. In his younger days, Mao once thought that to make China strong and independent, all that need be done is for China to possess Western technology-- railroads, telegraphs, steamships, airplanes, and "machines of all kinds." As he matured, he realized this was a mistake. He then expounded the thesis that technology can be compensated for by sheer determination and hard work of the people, even though this belief is not consistent with the orthodox Marxist "scientific socialism." For Mao, the dialectic of history is more the contradiction between the spirit of revolutionary progress and the tendency toward selfishness and complacency than the clash of class interests. Mao's belief in the power of human will or spirit has pragmatic values. China was, and still is, a populous poor country with limited technology. Chinese economy is labor-intensive rather than technology-intensive. Since the Chinese are quite capable of hard work, Mao's emphasis on willpower and human effort contributed greatly to the increase of China's productivity. This feature of Mao's thought also found its expresson in the Maoist doctrine of guerrilla warfare, according to which the dedicated and courageous guerrilla warriors armed with primitive weapons would ultimately triumph over armies equipped with modern sophisticated weapons.

On the morning of October 1, 1949, Mao announced, on top of the Tiananmen (Gate of Heavenly Peace) Tower in Beijing, the establishment of the People's Republic of China. He was then on the peak of his power and prestige. He declared: "We will work bravely and industriously to create our own civilization and happiness and will at the same time promote world peace and freedom. Our nation will never again be insulted. We have stood up." The turmoil and destructions of the "Great Proletarian Cultural Revolution" (or simply "Cultural Revolution" which lasted from 1966-1976) have been widely reported. Mao was responsible for this disaster. The exigency of defending himself

279

politically, and the genuine ideological differences between Mao and many of his colleagues, caused Mao to launch the cultural revolution. Today the consensus on Mao is that despite the serious errors he made in his later years, his earlier achievements of unifying China (except Taiwan) and making her a truly independent country should be recognized. The Chinese communist party has adopted the principle of separating Mao's thought from Mao's leadership qualities.

d. Xiong Shi-li's Subjective Realism.

Xiong Shi-li (1885-1968) was a native of the Hubei province. His intellectual development started with the study of science and politics, then shifted to Buddhism and Hinduism, and finally to the Book of Changes and the Lu-wang idealistic Neo-Confucianism. He became a professor of philosophy at Beijing University in 1925. He was a creative thinker, whose philosophy is a synthesis of Lu-wang idealistic Neo-Confucianism, Buddhist philosophy of consciousness, the Book of Changes, and Henri Bergson's vitalism. He named his own philosophy New Consciousness-Only Doctrine. When the communists took over China in 1949, Xiong decided to remain silent but refused to bow to the communist ideology. Though no one accepts his whole philosophical system, his influence upon those Chinese philosophers who attempted to reconstruct Chinese philosophy has become increasingly noticeable. Xiong's major work is Xin Wei-shi Lun (New Doctrine of Consciousness-Only, 1944), whose theses may be recapitulated as follows:

(1) The so-called "reality" is perpetual transformation, manifesting itself in a running current of countless phenomena which is not illusory (as Buddhists would say). By an inter-dependent, alternating "closing" (bi) and "opening" (he), the universe differentiates the One into many. But reality and manifestation, or the one and the many, are the

same. "Closing" is the congealing operation that produces apparently concrete objects of matter ever under the directing activity of "opening," or mind. "Opening" or mind is part of the "original mind," which is mind, will, and consciousness. Thus, the seemingly contradictory tensions of "opening" and "closing" result in an orderly and constant transformation.[9]

(2) Reality is a process. It is never completely passive but always producing and reproducing a harmonious synthesis of Heaven, Earth, and Men. This has been recognized by all Confucianist men of ren from Confucius to Wang Yang-ming.

(3) Xiong agrees with the Buddhist idealists that matter is a product of mind but disagrees with them with respect to the theory of causation.

(4) Body is a part of nature; mind interprets and understands nature. The mind of ren inspires and infuses all subjective moral idealism.

To understand Xiong's philosophy of process and reality, we must discuss the Wei-shi theory of causation. Xiong rejects the Buddhist theory of causation by "perfumed seeds." Xiong's criticisms of the Buddhist theory of causation and his own theory of causation will be discussed later in this section. According to Kuei-ji's[10] interpretation, there are four types of causes: (1) cause proper (yin yüan), (2) preceding moment (deng wu-jian yüan), (3) object (suo-yüan yüan), (4) predominating condition (zeng-shang yüan). A proper cause must have the following characteristics: (i) it must have the energy to produce an effect; (ii) it must produce an effect distinct from its own being; (iii) it must produce its effect by its own force without mediation. A preceding moment is a supplementary cause which has the following characteristics: (i) it must precede the next moment, and its substance as well as its function must be similar to that of the next moment; (ii) it must be continuous with the next moment without interruption-- it must lead toward the next moment; (iii) it must inevitably be followed by the next moment. Xiong holds that human minds can conceive of causal relationship only through an understanding of deng wu-jian yüan (the preceding moment). Suo-yüan yüan, or object, is another supplementary cause. It must have the following characteristics: (i) it must be correlated with a subject as its object; (ii) it must determine and also be determined by its correlated subject; (iii) it must be the objective portion of the consciousness which is strictly correlated with the subjective portion of the consciousness. Object as cause is a necessary condition of the formation of our phenomenal knowledge. The zeng-shang yüan, or the predominating condition, must have the following characteristics: (i) it must exert a predominating function over its effect; (ii) it must either be a sufficient or a necessary condition of its effect; (iii) it must remove the conditions that obstruct the production of its effect, and it must create new conditions that lead toward its realization. Some predominating conditions may be direct while others may be remote and indirect. For example, the gravitational balance among the planets of the solar system may be taken as an indirect predominating cause of life on earth. If we admit all the four types of causes, then everything in the universe is causally connected with everything else.

The Wei-shi cosmology is inextricably connected with the Wei-shi theory of the eight types of consciousness. In the Wei-shi cosmology, the phenomenal universe as experienced in daily life is not the real world but a product of elaborate mental constructions. The content of the sensible world can be analyzed into the subjective portion and the objective portion of the first five consciousnesses. The five organs of eyes, ears, nose, mouth, and body correspond to the five kinds of sense objects, namely, colors, sounds, smells, tastes, and touches. The five consciousnesses of sight, hearing, smell, taste, and touch are the products of the interaction between the sense organs and the sense objects. The relationship between the five sense organs and the five sense objects is of reciprocal determination. The five consciousnesses have the function of discrimination. But, if we had only the five consciousnesses, we would not have a unified and integrated world. Hence the Wei-shi school postulates the sixth or the sense-center consciousness (manovijnana), which synthesizes the experiences of the first five consciousnesses. All these six consciousnesses direct their attention to the objects of the phenomenal universe and have the tendency to erroneously presume these objects to be real, substantial, ontological entities. The origin of this error is traced back to the function of the seventh or the thought-center consciousness (manas). This consciousness is the ego-consciousness which clings to the self as a substantial, ontological entity. Because of its stubborn clingings we are entangled within the cycle of life and death and suffer from its deep-rooted sorrows. The objects of the ego-consciousness, however, are not substantial, but are the projections of the eighth or the alaya consciousness. The alaya consciousness is like a storehouse which contains both the pure and impure seeds. Therefore both the subjective portions and the objective portions of the first seven consciousnessses are nothing but the transformation of the alaya consciousness. They are manifestations that can be traced back to the function of the seeds contained in the alaya consciousness as their causes. The seeds are the only real causes in a metaphysical sense. What are the seeds? They are individual existents, each different from the others. However, they are not like the atoms of Democritus. The seeds maintain their identity through a dynamic continuity, much like a human being maintains his identity even though his body and mental states change every moment. Different seeds

283

create different manifestations. They never violate the rules. Hence the universe as we experience it is an orderly cosmos. The relationship between seeds and manifestations is that the seeds create the manifestations. The seeds are always hidden. However, a reciprocal relationship between the seeds and the manifestations also exists. The seeds create the manifestations, yet the manifestations have the power to "perfume" the seeds, which in turn become causes of further manifestations. The "perfumed" seeds are to be distinguished from the original seeds. The subjective portion and the objective portion of the same consciousness are created by different seeds. Even the mind and its functions are to be traced back to different seeds. The evil seeds existed since time immemorial. They form a torrent. Only when the function of the impure seeds contained in the <u>alaya</u> consciousness is completely stopped can the pure seeds manifest their functions. Then the eighth consciousness will no longer be called <u>alaya</u> consciousness. Such a state of consciousness is called <u>tathata</u> (suchness, thusness).

By combining the Wei-shi theory of causation and the theory of the four causes, the concept of cause proper (<u>yin yüan</u>) applies only to the seeds, while the other three types of causes are secondary "causal occasions" for the transformation of things. Xiong thinks that the Wei-shi theory is dualistic. It is a dualism between the world of manifestations and the world of seeds; it is also a dualism between the impure and the pure seeds; finally, it is a dualism between the pure seeds and <u>tathata</u>. Xiong criticizes this dualism for unduly separating the world of seeds from the world of manifestations. Moreover, since the pure seeds and the impure seeds are both ontologically fundamental, the dualism between the two is a final one not to be transcended in any way. By saying that the cessation of the function of the impure seeds brings about the function of the pure seeds, the Wei-shi school implies that <u>tathata</u> is the function of the seeds. Xiong, however, asserts that <u>tathata</u> can in no way be identified with the function of the pure seeds, and therefore it should have no position in the Wei-shi philosophy.

Xiong accepts the basic Buddhist tenets that no real world can exist apart from the transformation of consciousness and that nothing is substantial or eternal in the phenomenal universe. He benefits from Buddhism by taking the Buddhist concept of instantaneous transformation and applying it to the doctrine of production and reproduction in the <u>Book of Changes</u>. Xiong maintains that the ultimate metaphysical principle must be one (rather than many), or else the unity of the universe could not be explained. This ultimate metaphysical principle is the principle of creativity alluded to in the <u>Book of Changes</u>. The principle of creativity operates in accordance with the principle of unity of opposites (opening and closing). Creativity without creating forms would be no creativity at all; forms suggest order and stability. Hence, in its process of creation the principle of creativity has a tendency to work against itself and to manifest itself as a world of form and order as if it were constant and stable, even if in reality everything is constantly changing. Therefore the manifestations are the manifestations of the principle of creativity. For Xiong, only the principle of creativity is the cause proper, the true metaphysical cause. Seeds in the <u>alaya</u> consciousness, "perfumed" or not, are not the metaphysical causes. To say that the manifestations are the manifestations of the principle is, in Neo-Confucian terms, to identify <u>Li</u> (principle) with <u>qi</u> (material force). Since the principle of creativity by its nature creates incessantly, the preceding moment as a supplementary form of cause holds. Every moment rises and perishes. It always leaves room for and leads toward the next moment. Only in this way is novelty and new creation conceivable. Hence the succession of moments acquires an added significance in Xiong's philosophy.

Although Xiong subordinates the external world, he thinks that the objects in the phenomenal universe are not to be taken as entirely illusory. Xiong is willing to admit objects as supplementary cause. As causal occasions the objects and the subjects mutually condition each other. The phenomenal world is real in the sense that a constant conjunction exists between the objective portion and the subjective portion of the consciousness. The phenomenal world is unreal in the sense that it is not a substantial ontological entity. Predominating condition as a supplementary cause is also admissable for Xiong. According to him, all the sciences study the predominating conditions from a phenomenal point of view. Only philosophy is capable of revealing the metaphysical principle of creativity. Therefore science and philosophy cannot contradict each other, for science studies the functional aspect, whereas philosophy studies the ontological aspect of the same reality. Professor W. T. Chan concludes:

> . . . Xiong has definitely made an advance in Neo-Confucianism, particularly in the identification of the principle (Li) and material force (qi). The objection of Zhu Xi's bifurcation of them and Wang Yang-ming's idea that material force is only an aspect of the mind is now overcome. It is true that he has not clarified the relationship between the mind and principle, but he has given idealistic Neo-Confucianism a more solid metaphysical basis and a more dynamic character.[11]

e.   Feng You-lan's Philosophic Synthesis.

Feng You-lan (1895-   ) was born in the central province of Henan. He graduated from Beijing University and went to Columbia University where he earned a Ph.D. degree in 1923. Feng is probably the most competent, most discussed, and most criticized Chinese philosopher in the last fifty years. Feng espouses the Marxist ideology and generally interprets Chinese history and civilization in terms of Marxist economics. However, he asserts that China's new culture developed from the traditional Chinese culture and that the Chinese must respect and study China's history. Feng has been a controversial scholar in the People's Republic of China and has survived several political crises. Despite severe criticisms against him, Feng has won the respect and confidence of the Chinese political and academic leaders. He has been appointed professor and director of the history of Chinese philosophy seminar in Beijing University, member of the academic committee of the Academy of Science, and a member of National Political Consultative Council. He has lectured in the United States, Great Britain, and Europe. In the summer of 1982, at age 87, he went to Honolulu, Hawaii to attend a conference on the philosophy of Zhu Xi.

At age 27, Feng showed himself to be a perceptive critic of the classical Chinese philosophers in his article "Why China Has no Science,"[12] where he discusses Confucianism, Daoism, and Mohism with respect to their differences on the relative value of nature and art. He observes in the article that had China followed Mo Zi's emphasis on utility or Xún Zi's interest in controlling nature, she might have produced science in the modern sense. But Confucianism and Daoism won the mind of the Chinese with their stress on the cultivation of the inner man rather than the development of external things. He also points out that in Chinese history, whenever the Confucianists interacted with Daoists, Confucianism benefited from it and was raised to a higher level. His History of Chinese Philosophy shows his solid scholarship and won him an international reputation. He presented his comprehensive philosophical system in Xin Li Xüe (The New Rational Philosophy), published in 1939. His position as the leading Chinese philosopher was then firmly established. In the New Rational Philosophy, Feng synthesizes the realistic Neo-Confucianism and Western realism and logic. The book consists of the elucidation of the four main metaphysical concepts, namely, Li (principle), qi (material force), Dao-ti (the substance of Dao), and Da Qüan (the Great Whole). Let us consider them separately.

1. Li (Principle).

Feng's concept of Li is derived from the realistic Neo-Confucianist proposition that "As there are things, there must be their specific principles."[13] For a thing to exist, it must follow the Li by which it is what it is.

> If a certain class of things is, then there is that by which that class of things is (what it is). . . . In other words, that which all mountains have in common is that by which mountains are mountains (though they are different in size and shape). That which all rivers have in common is that by which rivers are rivers. This is what the New Rational Philosophy designates as the Li of mountains and the Li of rivers.[14]

Feng explains that the Li of a thing is logically prior to the be-ing of a thing. A thing needs to follow principle but principle does not need to be actualized in a thing. We can infer from the non-subsistence of a certain Li that no such thing exists, but we cannot infer from the non-existence of a thing the non-subsistence of the Li. Therefore more Li exist than actualized classes of things. The summation of the principles is called Tai Ji (the Supreme Ultimate). The world of Li, as in Plato's world of ideas, is "empty, silent, without a sign, and yet with all forms there."[15]

2. Qi (material force).

Feng's concept of qi is quite abstract. Qi is the primary undifferentiated material out of which all individual things are formed. If a thing is to exist, the material force must be by which it can exist.

> A Li cannot actualize itself. . . .
> Since things must have that by which
> they can exist before they do exist,
> we, therefore, maintain that if Li
> is, then qi must be, by which we mean
> that if actualization of a Li occurs,
> the qi which actaulizes the Li must
> exist.[16]

In itself, qi is only a potentiality of existence, a material of actualization. Like Li, it is only a formal logical concept.

3. Dao-ti (the substance of Dao).

The concept of Dao-ti deals with the becoming or evolution of Dao. The universe is the manifestation of the "great functioning" of incessant change and renewal. "Existence viewed as a whole is the continuous process of actualization of the Tai Ji (the Supreme Ultimate) by means of the primodial qi. This may be called the evolution of the Dao."[17] The evolution of Dao may be described as the "pure activity of qi."

4.   Da Quan (the Great Whole).

In Feng's metaphysics, the sum total of things is the Great Whole. The Great Whole is only the general name for all and not an assertion about the actual world. We may also call it Dao or Heaven. It is comparable to the "Absolute" in Hegel's philosophy. It is the

> . . . goal of life which is to be fulfilled through the investigation of things, the fulfillment of one's nature, and serving Heaven. When this is done, one will reach the highest sphere of life, that of 'forming one body with all things,' which is the sphere of great ren (humanity).[18]

In 1943, Feng published Xin Yüan-ren (A New Treatise on the Nature of Man) where he offers a theory of four different spheres of living, similar to Søren Kierkegaard's theory of the three stages of life.[19] The function of philosophy, Feng says, is not the increase of empirical knowledge, but the elevation of the mind. Philosophy can help us achieve the higher spheres of living. The four spheres of living are as follows:

1. The innocent sphere: In this lowest sphere a person does not know what he is doing. He simply does what his instinct or the custom of his society dictates. He is not self-conscious of what he does, nor does he understand what he does. Hence his actions have little significance, if any, for significance of an act comes from one's understanding and self-consciousness.

2.   The utilitarian sphere: In this second

sphere, a man is aware of himself and does everything for self-benefit. Even when a man's action benefits others, the motive behind the act is still utilitarian self-benefit. Here, a man's actions have significance, namely, utility for himself. A man of utility is not necessarily immoral. But for a group of people to live together harmoniously and productively in a society, they need to transcend the utilitarian sphere to the moral sphere.

3. The moral sphere: When a man understands that he is a member of a society and that his well-being depends on the well-being of the other members of the society, he is able to act for the benefit of the society as a whole. Being able to act in this way, he becomes a moral man, and his actions have moral significance. As the Confucianists would say, a moral man acts for the sake of righteousness (yi), and not for the sake of personal profit (li).

4. The transcendent sphere: Finally, a man may come to understand that he is not only a member of his society but also a member of the universe (the Great Whole). He transcends his own society and becomes a "citizen of Heaven." Because he acts for the benefit of the whole universe, his actions have not only moral values but also super-moral values. To live in the transcendent sphere is to become a sage which, according to the tradition of Chinese philosophy, is the highest perfection of man as man. In identifying himself with the universe, a sage transcends his intellect. The function of Chinese philosophy is to help man achieve this goal.

In his work Xin Zhi-yen (A New Treatise on the Methodology of Metaphysics, 1946), Feng maintains two methods of studying metaphysics: the positive and the negative. The positive method is to say something about the object of metaphysics; the negative method is to show that certain aspects of the so-called "reality" are not susceptible to positive description or analysis. Western philosophy is dominated by the positive method, whereas in Chinese philosophy the negative method is dominant. Lao Zi and Zhuang Zi exemplify this negative method, for in these two books one does not read about what Dao is, but what it is not. When one knows what it is not, one does understand in some way what it is. Feng believes that the combination of Daoism and Buddhism in China reinforced the negative method.

The positive and the negative methods do not contradict but complement each other. Ideally, a metaphysical system should start with the positive method and end with the negative one. The positive method yields clear thinking which is essential for philosophy. But if a philosophical system does not include the negative method, it fails to touch the highest plane of philosophy. Philosophy is systematic reflective thinking on life and the universe. Because of its reflective nature, it ultimately has to think on "something" that logically cannot be the object of thought. For example, the "Great Whole" cannot logically be the object of thought, because it is the totality of all that is. "The Absolute," "the unknowable," "the first principles" are other examples. Yet one needs to think about them in order to realize that they are beyond one's thought. Thus philosophy, in its development, will inevitably become "the knowledge that is not knowledge."[20] Identification with the "Great Whole" is not an intellectual activity, but a super-rational state of mind. Feng believes that Western philosophy on the whole neglects the negative method, and he hopes Chinese philosophy with its negative method will contribute significantly to the future philosophy of the world.

Notes

Chapter 10

1. Li Ji, book IV, section 9.

2. Translated by Laurence G. Thompson, under the title
   The One-World Philosophy of Kang Yu-wei (London:
   Allen and Unwin, 1958).

3. Feng You-lan, A History of Chinese Philosophy,
   vol. II, p. 690.

4. W. T. De Bary and others (eds.), Sources of Chinese
   Tradition, p. 867.

5. Selected Works of Mao Ze-dong, vol. I, p. 297.

6. Ann Freemantle, Mao Tse-tung: An Anthology of His
   Writings, p. 184.

7. Selected Works of Mao Ze-dong, vol. III, p. 155.

8. W. T. De Bary and others (eds.), op. cit., pp. 885-
   886.

9. The concepts of "closing" (bi) and "opening" (he)
   are taken from the Book of Changes.

10. Kuei-ji was a student of Xüan-zang, the founder of
    the Wei-shi school. The following account of the
    Wei-shi theory of causation is sketched from Liu
    Shu-hsien, "Hsiung Shih-li's Theory of Causation,"
    Philosophy East and West, vol. 19, no. 4, 1969.

11. W. T. Chan, A Sourcebook in Chinese Philosophy,
    p. 764.

12. *International Journal of Ethics*, vol. 32, no. 3, 1922.

13. *The Spirit of Chinese Philosophy*, (tr. by E. R. Hughes), p. 205.

14. *Ibid.*

15. *Ibid.*, p. 206.

16. *Ibid.*, p. 208.

17. *Ibid.*, p. 209.

18. W. T. Chan, *op. cit.*, p. 752.

19. Kierkegaard's three stages of life are: esthetic, moral, and religious. Feng's four stages of living are: innocent, utilitarian, moral, and transcendent.

20. Or "knowledge of no knowledge," "*Dao*-experience." Cf. section 3c.

Bibliography

The following books are all written in English (or Chinese with English translation on facing pages), and are selected on the basis of their broad intellectual appeal. For an annotated comprehensive bibliography of Chinese philosophy, see Charles Wei-hsun Fu and Wing-tsit Chan, Guide to Chinese Philosophy, Boston, G. K. Hall & Co., 1978.

Le Blanc, C. and Dorothy Borei (eds.), Essays on Chinese Civilization, Princeton, Princeton University Press, 1981.

Chan, Wing-tsit, A Sourcebook in Chinese Philosophy, Princeton, Princeton University Press, 1963.

_____, Religious Trends in Modern China, New York, Columbia University Press, 1953.

_____, "Chinese Theory and Practice, with Special Reference to Humanism," in Moore (ed.), Philosophy and Culture, pp.80-95.

_____, "The Evolution of the Chinese Concept Jen," Philosophy East and West, 4, (1955), pp. 295-319.

_____, "Neo-Confucianism and Chinese Scientific Thought," Philosophy East and West, 6, (1957), pp.309-332.

Chang, Carsun, The Development of Neo-Confucian Thought, New York, Bookman Associates, 1957.

Creel, H.G., Chinese Thought: From Confucius to Mao Tse-tung, Chicago, The University of Chicago Press, 1953.

_____, What is Taoism? And Other Studies in Chinese Cultural History, Chicago, The University of Chicago Press, 1970.

Cua, A. S., The Unity of Knowledge and Action: A Study in Wang Yang-ming's Moral Psychology, Honolulu, University of Hawaii Press, 1982.

De Bary, William Theodore, Neo-Confucian Orthodoxy and the Learning of the Mind and Heart, New York, Columbia University Press, 1981.

De Bary, William, Wing-tsit Chan, and Burton Watson (eds.), Sources of Chinese Tradition, New York, Columbia University Press, 1960.

Dubs, H. H. (tr.), The Works of Hsüntze, London, Probsthain, 1928.

Forke, A., "The Chinese Sophists," Journal of the China Branch of the Royal Asiatic Society, vol. 34, 1901-1902.

Fu, Charles Wei-shun and Wing-tsit Chan, Guide to Chinese Philosophy, Boston, G.K. Hall & Co., 1978.

Fung, Yu-lan (tr. Derk Bodde), A History of Chinese Philosophy, Princeton, Princeton University Press, 1953.

_____, A Short History of Chinese Philosophy, New York, The Free Press, 1966.

Hsu, Francis L. K., Chinese and Americans (3rd ed.), Honolulu, University of Hawaii Press, 1981.

Hughes, E. R., Chinese Philosophy in Classical Times, New York, Dutton, 1942.

Legge, James (ed. and tr.), The Chinese Classics, 5 vols., Oxford, Oxford University Press, 1893.

Lin, Yütang, The Wisdom of China and India, New York, Random House, 1942.

_____, The Wisdom of Confucius, New York, The Modern Library, 1938.

McNaughton, William (ed.), The Confucian Vision, Ann Arbor, University of Michigan Press, 1974.

Mei, Y. P., Motse: The Neglected Rival of Confucius, London, Probsthain, 1934.

_____, "The Kung-sun Lung Tzu," Harvard Journal of Asiatic Studies, vol. 16, 1953, pp. 404-437.

_____, "Some Observations on the Problem of Knowledge among the Ancient Chinese Logicians," Tsing Hua Journal of Chinese Studies, vol. 1, 1956, pp. 114-121.

_____, The Ethical and Political Works of Motse, London, Probsthain, 1929.

Moore, Charles (ed.), The Chinese Mind, Honolulu, East-West Center Press, 1967.

_____, Philosophy and Culture, Honolulu, East-West Center Press, 1961.

Needham, Joseph, "Human Laws and Laws of Nature in China and the West," Journal of the History of Ideas, vol. 12, 1959.

_____, Science and Civilization in China, 7 vols., Cambridge, Cambridge University Press, 1954- , as of 1985, complete through vol. 5 and vol. 6, part 2.

Waley, Arthur, *The Analects of Confucius*, London, George Allen and Unwin, 1938.

_____, *The Way and Its Power: A Study of the Tao Te Ching and Its Place in Chinese Thought*, New York, Random House, 1966.

Watson, Burton (tr.), *Basic Writings of Mo Tzu, Hsun Tzu, and Han Fei Tzu*, New York, Columbia University Press, 1967.

_____, *The Complete Works of Chuang Tzu*, New York, Columbia University Press, 1968.

Weber, Max, *The Religion of China: Confucianism and Taoism*, New York, The Free Press, 1959.

Welch, Holmes, *Taoism: The Parting of the Way*, Boston, Beacon Press, 1966.

Wilhelm, Hellmut, *Heaven, Earth, and Man in the Book of Changes*, Seattle, University of Washington Press, 1977.

Wright, A. F., *Studies in Chinese Thought*, Chicago, The University of Chicago Press, 1953.

Wu, John C. H., "Chinese Legal Philosophy: A Brief Historical Survey," *Chinese Culture*, I, no. 4 (1958), pp. 7-48.

Wu, Kuang-ming, *Chuang Tzu: World Philosopher at Play*, New York, Crossword Publishing Co., 1982.

Chronology of Chinese Philosophers

Dynasties	Philosophers

Xia (c. 2205-1766 B.C.)

        legendary culture heroes

Shang (c. 1766-1122 B.C.)

Zhou (c. 1122-211 B.C.)   Confucius (551-479 B.C.)
Mo Zi (fl. 479-438 B.C.)
Lao Zi (6th or 4th
        century B.C.)
Zhuang Zi (fl. 399-295
        B.C.)
Xǔn Zi (fl. 298-238
        B.C.)
Mencius (371-289 B.C.)
Hui Shi (380-305 B.C.)
Gong-sun Long (b.380
        B.C.)
Zou Yen (305-240 B.C.)
Han Fei Zi (d. 233
        B.C.)
Shang Yang (d. 338
        B.C.)
Shen Bu-hai (d. 337
        B.C.)

Qin (221-207 B.C.)

Han (202 B.C.-220 A.D.)   Dong Zhong Shu
(c. 179-104 B.C.)
Yang Xiong (53 B.C.-18
        A.D.)

	Wang Zhong (b. 27 A.D.)
	Si-ma Qian (145-86 B.C.)
	Huai-nan Zi (d. 122 B.C.)
Three Kingdoms (220-280)	Wang Bi (226-249)
Jin (265-240)	Guo Xiang (d. 312)
	Seng-zhao (384-414)
	Dao-an (d. 385)
Southern and Northern Dynasties (420-589)	Dao-sheng (d. 434)
	Hui Yüan (d. 416)
	Zhi-kai (538-597)
	Zi-zang (549-623)
Sui (590-618)	
Tang (618-906)	Xüan-zang (596-664)
	Fa-zang (643-712)
	Hong-ren (605-675)
	Hui-neng (638-713)
	Shen-xiu (d. 706)
Five Dynasties (907-960)	
Song (960-1279)	Zhou Dun-yi (1017-73)
	Shao Yong (1011-77)
	Zhang Zai (1020-77)
	Chen Hao (1032-85)
	Chen Yi (1033-1108)
	Zhu Xi (1130-1200)
	Lu Chiu-yüan (1139-93)
Yüan (Mongol, 1280-1367)	
Ming (1368-1643)	Wang Shou-ren (Yang-ming) (1472-1529)

Qing (Manchu, 1644-1911)	Wang Fu-zhi (1619-93)
	Huang Zhong-xi (1610-95)
	Yen Yüan (1635-1704)
	Dai Zhen (1723-77)
	Kang You-wei (1858-1927)
	Tan Si-tong (1865-1898)
Republic of China (1912-)	Sun Yat-sen (1866-1925)
People's Republic of China (1949-)	Zhang Dong-sun (1886-1962)
	Xiong Shi-li (1885-1968)
	Mao Ze-dong (1893-1976)
	Feng You-lan (1895-)

Glossary

Wade-Giles	Pin-yin	Chinese characters	Explanation
Ai	Ai	愛	love
ch'an	chan	禪	meditation
che hsüeh	zhe xüe	哲学	philosophy
chen chü	zhen chü	真句	true sentence
chen jen	zhen ren	真人	true man, perfect man
chen li	zhen li	真理	truth, true principle
ch'i	qi	氣	energy, life force
chien ai	jian ai	兼愛	universal love
chih	zhi	知	knowledge
chih	zhi	智	wisdom
chih-kuan	zhi-guan	止觀	calmness and insight
Ching	Jing	経	scripture, treatise

303

Wade-Giles	Pin-yin	Chinese characters	Explanation
chü-tzu	chü-zi	鉅子	supreme leader, head
chün-tzu	chün-zi	君子	superior man, gentleman
chung	zhong	忠	loyalty, conscientiousness
fa	fa	法	law
feng shui	feng shui	風水	wind and water (geomancy)
hsia (or yu-hsia)	xia (or yu-xia)	俠(遊俠)	knights-errant
hsiang chih	xiang zhi	相制	mutual control
hsiang hua	xiang hua	相化	mutual change, mutual masking
hsiang seng	xiang seng	相生	mutual production
hsiang sheng	xiang sheng	相勝	mutual conquest

Wade-Giles	Pin-Yin	Chinese characters	Explanation
hsiao	xiao	孝	filial piety
hsiao ku	xiao gu	小故	minor cause
hsien	xian	仙	immortal man
hsin	xin	信	faithfulness, trust-worthiness
hsin	xin	心	mind, heart
hsüan hsüeh	xüan xüe	玄学	abstruse learning (Neo-Daoism)
Hua Yen Tsung	Hua Yen Zong	華嚴宗	The Hua Yen School of Buddhism
jen	ren	仁	human-heartedness love
jen-cheng	ren-zheng	仁政	benevolent government
jen-yü	ren-yü	人欲	human desire

Wade-Giles	Pin-Yin	Chinese Characters	Explanation
Ju Chia	Ru Jia	儒家	The school of Literati (Confucianism)
ko-wu	ge-wu	格物	investigation of things
ko-yi	ge-yi	格義	investigation of meaning
k'ung	kong	空	emptiness
K'ung Tsung	Kong Zong	空宗	The school of emptiness
li	li	礼	propriety, proper conduct
li	li	利	profit
Li	Li	理	principle, form
liang-chih	liang-zhi	良知	innate knowledge
ming	ming	名	name
ming	ming	命	fate, destiny

Wade-Giles	Pin-Yin	Chinese characters	Explanation
pa kua	ba gua	八卦	eight trigrams
seng hsü	seng xü	生序	cosmogonic order
Shang-ti	Shang-di	上帝	God
shang-t'ung	shang-tong	尚同	agreement with the superior
she	she	色	phenomena
shih	shi	實	substance, reality
shih	shi	势	power, position
shih-li-wu-ai	shi-li-wu-ai	事理無礙	harmonious interfusion of reality and appearance
shih-shih-wu-ai	shi-shi-wu-ai	事事無礙	harmonious interfusion of events
shu	shu	恕	altruism
shu	shu	術	technique, strategy

Wade-Giles	Pin-Yin	Chinese characters	Explanation
Ta Ch'üan	Da Qüan	大全	the Great Whole
ta ku	da gu	大故	major cause
T'ai Chi	Tai Ji	太極	the supreme ultimate
T'ai Chi Ch'üan	Tai Ji Qüan	太極拳	the supreme ultimate exercise
Tao	Dao	道	the way
Te	De	德	virtue
Ti	Di	帝	God, emperor
T'ien	Tian	天	Heaven
T'ien Li	Tian Li	天理	Heavenly principle
T'ien-t'ai Tsung	Tian-tai Zong	天台宗	The Tian-tai School of Buddhism
t'i-jen	ti-ren	体認	personal under-standing
t'i-yen	ti-yen	体驗	immediate experience
tzu-jan	zi-ran	自然	naturalness

Wade-Giles	Pin-Yin	Chinese characters	Explanation
wang	wang	王	king
wang	wang	忘	forget-fulness
wang-tao	wang-dao	王道	the way of the true king
Wei-shih Tsung	Wei-shi Zong	唯識宗	the school of mere ideation
wu	wu	無	non-being
wu	wu	悟	under-standing, insight
wu-hsin	wu-xin	無心	no-mind
Wu Hsing	Wu Xing	五行	the five agents
wu-ming	wu-ming	無明	ignorance, avidya
wu-wei	wu-wei	無為	non-action
wu-yü	wu-yü	無欲	no desire
yeh	ye	業	karma, deed
yi	yi	義	righteousness

Wade-Giles	Pin-Yin	Chinese characters	Explanation
Yi Ching	Yi Jing	易経	The Book of Changes
yin-yang	yin-yang	陰陽	the negative and positive forces in the universe
yu	you	有	being
yu-wei	you-wei	有為	action (exertion)